ESSAYS IN POSTFOUNDATIONALIST THEOLOGY

Essays in Postfoundationalist Theology

J. WENTZEL VAN HUYSSTEEN

WILLIAM B. EERDMANS PUBLISHING COMPANY
GRAND RAPIDS, MICHIGAN / CAMBRIDGE, U.K.

© 1997 Wm. B. Eerdmans Publishing Co.
255 Jefferson Ave. S.E., Grand Rapids, Michigan 49503 /
P.O. Box 163, Cambridge CB3 9PU U.K.

Printed in the United States of America

02 01 00 99 98 97   7 6 5 4 3 2 1

Library of Congress Cataloging-in-Publication Data

Van Huyssteen, Wentzel.
    Essays in postfoundationalist theology / J. Wentzel van Huyssteen.
        p.   cm.
    Includes bibliographical references and index.
    ISBN 0-8028-4309-3 (pbk. : alk. paper)
    1. Philosophical theology. 2. Postmodernism —
Religious aspects — Christianity. I. Title.
BT40.V33 1997
230'.01 — dc21   97-10576
                                                        CIP

I dedicate this book to

ANNIE VAN HUYSSTEEN
wonderful friend
perfect mother

Contents

Acknowledgments

"Rational Judgment and Responsible Choice: Some Reflections in Theology and Interdisciplinarity" was first read, in much more abbreviated form, at the Highlands Institute for American Religious Thought, Highlands, North Carolina, in June 1995.

"Critical Realism and God: Can There Be Faith after Foundationalism?" was published in *Intellektueel in Konteks: Opstelle vir Hennie Rossouw,* copyright Human Sciences Research Council, South Africa 1993 (Pretoria: HSRC Press 1993). Reprinted with permission.

"Truth and Commitment in Theology and Science: An Appraisal of Wolfhart Pannenberg's Perspective" was previously published in *Hervormde Teologiese Studies* 45, no. 1 (1989): 99-116. Reprinted with permission.

"Is the Postmodernist Always a Postfoundationalist? Nancey Murphy's Lakatosian Model for Theology" was previously published in *Theology Today* 50, no. 3 (1993): 373-86. Reprinted with permission.

"The Realist Challenge in Postmodern Theology: Religious Experience in Jerome Stone's Neo-Naturalism" was first published in *The American Journal for Theology and Philosophy* 15, no. 3 (1994): 293-305, with the title "Is There a Realist Challenge in Postmodern Theology? Religious Experience and Explanatory Commitment in Jerome Stone's Neo-Naturalism." Reprinted with permission.

"Systematic Theology and Philosophy of Science: The Need for Methodological and Theoretical Clarity in Theology" was originally published in *The Journal of Theology for Southern Africa* 34 (1981): 3-16. Reprinted with permission.

"The Realism of the Text: A Perspective on Biblical Authority" originally appeared as part of the C. B. Powell Lectures in Print. Copyright University of South Africa 1987. (*Miscellanea Congregalia* 28, UNISA 1987). This abbreviated version of the original text is published with the permission of UNISA Publishers, Pretoria, South Africa.

"Experience and Explanation: The Justification of Cognitive Claims in Theology" first appeared in *ZYGON: Journal of Religion and Science* 23, no. 3 (1988): 247-62. Reprinted with permission.

"Narrative Theology: An Adequate Paradigm for Theological Reflection?" was published in *Hervormde Teologiese Studies* 45, no. 4 (1989): 767-77. Reprinted with permission.

"Evolution, Knowledge, and Faith: Gerd Theissen and the Credibility of Theology" was originally published in *Hervormde Teologiese Studies* 44, no. 1 (1988): 6-22. It also appeared in *Modern Theology* 5, no. 2 (1989): 145-60. Reprinted with permission.

"Theology and Science: The Quest for a New Apologetics" was previously published in *The Princeton Seminary Bulletin* XIV/2 (1993): 113-33. Reprinted with permission.

"The Shaping of Rationality in Science and Religion" was first read as a paper for the Royal Institute for Philosophy at the University of Warrick, Coventry, United Kingdom (March 1995). It was recently published by *Hervormde Teologiese Studies* 52, no. 1 (1996). Reprinted with permission.

"The Postmodern Challenge in Theology and Science" was presented, in various earlier draft forms, as lectures at the Annual Meeting of the *Swiss Theological Society* in Emmetten, Switzerland (September 1995), and also at the Biannual Meeting of the *European Society for the Study of Science and Theology* in Krakow, Poland (March 1996).

Introduction

THIS COLLECTION OF *ESSAYS IN POSTFOUNDATIONAL THEOLOGY* IN many ways represents an overview of a complex intellectual and spiritual journey. It reflects my struggle with issues that reveal the inevitable contextuality (in the most concrete sense of the word) of the kind of intellectual challenge that I believe faces philosophical theology in the West today. These essays in philosophical theology were produced in the context of my own journey, which was also geographical: my family and I, after several increasingly frequent and extensive visits to the United States of America during the eighties, finally made the difficult and challenging move literally halfway around the world from the University of Port Elizabeth in South Africa to Princeton Theological Seminary in Princeton, New Jersey, in January 1992. Evolving out of my commitment to and involvement with Christian theology's precarious interdisciplinary status as it faces the diversity and inevitable pluralism of contemporary postmodern thought in our times, these essays also reflect my deep conviction that only a truly accessible and philosophically credible notion of interdisciplinarity will be able to pave the way for a plausible public theology that wishes to play an important intellectual role in our fragmented culture today.

Those of us who work in philosophical theology find ourselves at a crossroad, faced with a rather bewildering set of questions: how, and why, do some of us hang on to some form of religious faith in the midst of the confusion of this fragmented postmodern age? How can we speak of the certainty of faith, of passionate commitments and deep convictions, in a postmodern cultural context that seems to celebrate cultural and religious pluralism with such abandon? Can Christian theology, as a disciplined reflection on religious experience, ever really claim to join this postmodern conversation, and if it does, will it be able to maintain its identity in the conversation without retreating to an esoteric world of private, insular knowledge claims? Another way of asking this question would be to focus quite specifically on theology's presumed location in the contemporary interdisciplinary discussion: how does theological reflection relate to other modes of intellectual inquiry, and especially to natural scientific knowledge, which very often is accepted unchallenged as the ultimate paradigm of human rationality in our times?

At the heart of this contemporary form of the problem of inter-disciplinarity obviously lies the deeper problem of identifying the similarities and differences between the epistemic and nonepistemic values that shape the rationality of theological reflection and those that shape other modes of reflection, especially the sciences. This is the epistemological reason for my argument in all of these essays (either directly or indirectly) that contemporary philosophy of science, with its enduring focus on the problem of rationality, has earned a place as perhaps the most important link in the ongoing interdisciplinary debate about the nature and status of theological knowledge. The challenge of postmodern pluralism, of course, makes it hardly possible to speak any more in such a broad and generic sense about "rationality," "knowledge," "religion," "science," "theology," or even "God." Postmodernism, as we will see, has proved to be as protean and multivalent as it is challenging. Not only in philosophy of science, but also in theology, alternative interpretations and constructive appropriations of postmodern themes have now become viable options.

This positive appropriation of some constructive forms of postmodern criticism is the central idea that binds together this collection of diverse essays in philosophical theology. This appropriation finds its main focus in what I am calling *postfoundationalist theology*. Postmodernism is, as I see it, first of all a very pointed rejection of all forms of epistemological foundationalism, as well as of its ubiquitous, accompanying metanarratives that so readily claim to legitimize all our knowledge, judgments, decisions, and actions. *Foundationalism*, as is generally defined today, is the thesis that all our beliefs can be justified by appealing to some item of knowledge that is self-evident or indubitable. Foun-

nonfoundationalism ——→ lies fidelism ——→ foundationalism in disguise

dationalism in this epistemological sense therefore always implies the holding of a position inflexibly and infallibly, because in the process of justifying our knowledge-claims, we are able to invoke ultimate foundations on which we construct the evidential support systems of our various convictional beliefs. These "foundations" for our knowledge are accepted as "given," and therefore are treated as a privileged class of aristocratic beliefs that serve as ultimate terminating points in the argumentative chains of justification for our views.

In both theology and philosophy of science, foundationalism is often rejected in favor of *nonfoundationalism*. Philosophically, nonfoundationalism (or antifoundationalism) is certainly one of the most important roots or resources of postmodernism. Nonfoundationalists deny that we have any of those alleged strong foundations for our belief-systems and argue instead that all of our beliefs together form part of a groundless web of interrelated beliefs. In a strong reaction against modernist and generic notions of rationality, nonfoundationalism also highlights the crucial epistemic importance of community, arguing that every community and context has its own rationality, and that any and all social activities may in fact function as a test case for human rationality. In its most extreme form nonfoundationalism implies a total relativism of rationalities and, in a move that will prove to be fatal for the interdisciplinary status of theology, claims internal rules for different modes of reflection. This extreme form of conceptual pluralism leads to a relativism so complete that any attempt at a cross-disciplinary conversation faces the threat of complete incommensurability.

At the heart of this epistemological brand of nonfoundationalism we often find *fideism:* an uncritical, almost blind commitment to a basic set of beliefs. In this sense fideism can in some cases ironically turn out to be a foundationalism-in-disguise. A certain form of fideism and foundationalism certainly go hand in hand in theology when the boundaries between the *trust,* or the personal faith we have in God, and *the set of beliefs in which we hold this trust,* become blurred or hazy. In theology the basic fideist move therefore occurs when a specific set of beliefs, in which we hold our faith commitment to God, is first isolated in a very definite protective strategy and then confused with faith in God itself. What is believed and trusted here is not so much God, but *our own* various sets of beliefs *about* God, *about* the nature of God, *about* God's action in the world, and *about* what *we* see as God's will for us and for our world.

Over against the alleged objectivism of foundationalism and the extreme relativism of most forms of nonfoundationalism, a *postfoundationalist theology* wants to make two moves. First, it fully acknowledges contextuality, the epistemically crucial role of interpreted experience, and the way that tradition shapes the epistemic and nonepistemic values that inform our reflection about God and what some of us believe to be God's presence in this world. At the same time, however, a postfoundationalist notion of rationality in theological reflection claims to point creatively beyond the confines of the local community, group, or culture towards a plausible form of interdisciplinary conversation. Postfoundationalism in theology is therefore revealed as a viable third epistemological option beyond the extremes of foundationalism and nonfoundationalism. The essays in this volume are therefore all held together by this one overriding concern: while we always come to our cross-disciplinary conversations with strong beliefs and even prejudices, epistemological postfoundationalism enables us to acknowledge these strong commitments, to identify the shared resources of human rationality in different modes of reflection, and then to reach beyond the walls of our own epistemic communities in cross-contextual, cross-cultural, and cross-disciplinary conversation.

In a postfoundationalist Christian theology the focus will therefore always be first of all on a relentless questioning of our uncritically held crypto-foundationalist assumptions. This should allow a free and critical exploration of the experiential and interpretative roots of all our beliefs, with the recognition that we relate to our world primarily through interpreted experience, even (maybe especially) in matters of faith, religious commitment, and theological reflection. The Christian theologian is thus freed to speak and reflect from within a personal faith commitment, and in cross-disciplinary conversation to discover patterns that might be consonant with the Christian paradigm. The persuasiveness of these patterns should be taken up in critical theological reflection, where their problem-solving ability should be evaluated and judged in an open, postfoundationalist conversation, which will allow for the creative fusion of hermeneutics and epistemology. In this conversation the shaping role of experience, of tradition, and of the classic Biblical text should be carefully evaluated, as we ask whether or not these shaping criteria themselves can help us determine why and how we hold on to our beliefs about God. This is the definitive move in postfoundationalist theological reflection, whereby we overcome the kind of fideism in which our own experiences and explanations are never challenged or contested and the kind of nonfoundationalism in which the need for transcommunal or intersubjective conversation is not taken seriously.

*   *   *

I am grateful for the privilege to bring together these interrelated, yet very diverse, reflections on the interdisciplinary status of theological reflection as a collection of essays in philosophical theology. Each in its own way represents a facet of my own struggle as a philosophical theologian to somehow find a way to participate plausibly and intelligibly in cross-cultural and cross-disciplinary conversation. Because these essays are all held together by a philosophical concern for a public theology, I have decided not to group them chronologically, but rather more thematically, according to three important dimensions of the contemporary interdisciplinary challenge to theology.

In Part One: Theology and Epistemology, I explore the dynamics involved when a philosophical theologian enters the interdisciplinary conversation with strong personal convictions. The postmodern challenge to critique our foundationalist assumptions compels us to accept that there are no more universal or neutral standards of rationality against which we can measure our beliefs or traditions. Our ability to make responsible judgments and share them within and between various epistemic communities does mean, however, that we can communicate transcontextually through conversation, deliberation, and evaluation (Chapter One). This ties in closely with an awareness of the fact that theology's quest for meaning and intelligibility is ultimately dependent on broader rational resources than just the purely cognitive. For a postfoundationalist theology this means that at the very least the realist assumptions and faith commitments of experienced Christian faith are relevant epistemic issues that deserve to be taken seriously in cross-disciplinary discussion (Chapter Two). In a postfoundationalist theology a strict demarcation between theological rationality and the rationality of other modes of critical reflection is inevitably blurred. What this might mean for issues of justification and objectivity in theology, and how this relates to faith, commitment, and theological notions of revelation, is explored by way of a critical analysis of Wolfhart Pannenberg's provocative revisioning of the academic status of theological reflection (Chapter Three). Indeed, only a few theologians have taken seriously the interdisciplinary complexity of the challenge of contemporary philosophy of science to theological epistemology. Another example is found in Nancey Murphy's appropriation of Imre Lakatos's philosophy of science as a model for nonfoundationalist theology (Chapter Four). All of these essays reveal the high degree of personal commitment in religious and theological theorizing. This not only points to the relational character of our being in the world, but also epistemologically implies the mediated and interpreted character of all relgous experience. The richness, as well as the limitations, that Jerome A. Stone's naturalist philosophy brings to his minimalist vision for divine transcendence is critically brought to bear on the experiential epistemology of postfoundationalist theology (Chapter Five).

Part Two: Theology and Methodology focuses on the need for Christian theology to break out of an insularity that is concerned only with its own community and with the church and to relate publicly and plausibly to our contemporary intellectual world. As examples of related, but very different, attempts at providing a public theology with such an accepted scientific status, the contributions of German theologians Gerhard Sauter and Wolfhart Pannenberg are critically discussed (Chapter Six). Can the fact that the Bible (as Christianity's classical text) has always played a crucial and pivotal role in the Christian tradition be made accessible to interdisciplinary deliberation, or should we resign ourselves to accept this text as an esoteric and remote criterion active only on the "inside" of an equally esoteric and inaccessible tradition of faith? If the undeniable fact that this text has always functioned as the Christian faith's primary explanatory construct can be revisioned as a quest for the epistemological status of the Biblical text in theological reflection, it may be possible to fuse hermeneutics and epistemology so that the problem of the authority of this text is drawn into an interdisciplinary dialogue with contemporary philosophy of science (Chapter Seven). This is closely related to the issue of the status of cognitive claims in theology and the question of how the role of metaphor may serve to make "weak" claims for reference in theological language more accessible (Chapter Eight). The epistemological problem of assessing criteria for theology's truth claims, and the hermeneutical problem for distinguishing between good or bad receptions of Christianity's classic text, leads finally to my critical analysis of some of the claims of contemporary narrative theology. Here it will become clear that the liberating move beyond foundationalism could also imply, for theology at least, the very effective (but risky) bracketing of truth claims (Chapter Nine).

Part Three: Theology and Science turns to some of the important issues in the current theology and science dialogue as concrete examples of interdisciplinarity in postfoundationalist theology. I begin with Gerd Theissen's timely warning that theology should always and at all costs avoid the intellectual coma of positivism and his broadening of the boundaries of traditional theology by drawing the challenge of contemporary theories of evolution into an interdisciplinary discussion with theology. We will ask whether theological statements should be reformulated in such a way that they could be shown to be expressions of contemporary religious experience (Chapter Ten). The current theology and science dialogue presents itself as an opportunity for contemporary apologetics for the Christian faith. My proposal towards this discussion has been that theology and science both share the rich resources of human rationality and that these two modes of reflection — although often very different in many important ways — are linked together in a common quest for intelligibility (Chapter Eleven). The emerging contours of a postfoundationalist notion of rationality in theology and science, and what the ramifications of an ensuing fallibilist epistemology might be for notions of rationality, objectivity, truth, and progress, are discussed against the background of the pressing question of whether or not we have good reasons for still regarding the natural sciences as our best available example of rationality at work (Chapter Twelve). The cultural and political dominance of the rationality of the natural sciences, however, is today seriously challenged and rejected by postmodern philosophy of science, which sharply critiques metanarratival notions of truth and progress and appeals to respect for local contexts of inquiry and to the social embeddedness of all scientific inquiry. In response to this jettisoning of metanarratives in different forms of skeptical or affirmative postmodernism, much of contemporary theology has similarly rejected, in diverse ways, modernist notions of rationality. However, if we can no longer assume that our trusted Christian metanarratives can be relied on to provide ultimate religious meaning and truth, how can we ever make them accessible for interdisciplinary conversation and provide even a tentative basis for a cross-disciplinary conversation between theology and the sciences? These issues are highlighted in Chapter Thirteen.

*   *   *

I am deeply grateful to the William B. Eerdmans Publishing Company for their sustained support for this project and for their giving me the opportunity to share with friends, students, and colleagues how I have tried to integrate what it has meant for me — philosophically and theologically — to take the huge step of moving from one continent to another. I am especially indebted to Mr. William B. Eerdmans Jr. for his unfailing personal support and encouragement. A very special word of thanks also goes to my research assistant, LeRon Shults, for the wonderful enthusiasm and energy he has put into this project. His unique editing abilities have made it easier — almost comfortable, in fact! — to live in my second first language, and he has contributed tremendously to making this a much more readable book. My endless gratitude also goes to Denise M. Schwalb, faculty secretary at Princeton Theological Seminary, who was courageous enough to take on this manuscript as a special project, and delivered it on time with her typical dedication and integrity.

The overwhelming scope of my gratitude to my wife Hester, and to our children, is truly beyond expression. The full story of all the ramifications of uprooting our family by moving from Port Elizabeth to Princeton will most probably never be told. I am incredibly grateful especially to Hester for her love and enduring support. Without her brave commitment and total care, my work over the last years — some of it reflected in this volume — could never have been done.

Finally, I dedicate this book to my mother, Annie van Huyssteen. Her faith, her care, and her devotion have been a radiant presence in our lives, and through the depths of her own suffering she has taught me to discover unexpected transcendence and joy in everyday life.

J. WENTZEL VAN HUYSSTEEN
Princeton Theological Seminary
Summer 1996

Part One

Theology and Epistemology

Chapter One

Is Rational Judgment Always a Responsible Choice? Some Reflections on Theology and Interdisciplinarity

=====

"When a question is raised about the authority or dispensability of the idea of God or of an ultimate point of reference, . . . functional criteria alone will not serve to establish it in such a way as to enable it to fulfill those functions and to provide an object of loyalty and a critical perspective. . . . Theology must somehow reconstitute itself as genuine inquiry."

Wayne Proudfoot[1]

THOSE OF US WHO WORK IN PHILOSOPHICAL THEOLOGY, AND WHO believe that this mode of reflection does have some legitimate interdisciplinary status, are faced with a complex, if not bewildering, set of questions: What, from an epistemological point of view, is the status of an ultimate religious commitment and thus of one's preferred religion? Are there "real" or "true" religious experiences as opposed to "false" ones? How, and why, do some of us hang on to some form of

---

1. Wayne Proudfoot, "*Regulae fidei* and Regulative Idea: Two Contemporary Theological Strategies," in Sheila Greeve Davaney, ed., *Theology at the End of Modernity: Essays in Honor of Gordon Kaufman* (Philadelphia: Trinity Press International, 1991), 113.

faith in a postmodern age, and what happens to the problem of religious certainty in a postmodern context that celebrates pluralism? Can theology, as a reflection on religious experience, indeed claim to be a credible partner in the postmodern conversation; and if so, what will the effect of this conversation be on theology's claim to some form of knowledge? And last but not least, how does all of this relate to the shaping of other modes of inquiry, especially scientific knowledge, which often still seems to go unchallenged as the ultimate paradigm of human rationality?

Those of us who are concerned with these difficult questions, and especially with establishing theology as a genuine mode of inquiry, should realize that the most important point to this challenge will be reconstruction of theological reflection as a mode of cognition with a legitimate interdisciplinary location. At the heart of this reconstruction of theology's interdisciplinary location, we find the quest for the epistemic and nonepistemic values that shape the rationality of religious/theological, and of scientific, reflection. I also believe that in this interdisciplinary quest for the values that shape the rationality of theological and scientific reflection, at least two points have already been clearly established through a positive and constructive appropriation of the postmodern critique of foundationalist epistemology. First, when postmodernism is seen constructively as an ongoing and relentless critical return to the questions raised by modernity, and not just as a radical opposition to modern thought, it shows itself best in the ongoing interrogation of our foundationalist assumptions, and thus as part of the to-and-fro movement between the modern and the postmodern elements of our various modes of intellectual inquiry (what we could broadly call the experience of knowing). Second, based on this imperative always to return to our epistemological assumptions with critical and responsible judgment, it seems to be highly implausible and certainly premature to claim that all arguments about epistemology belong to the "preliminaries," which as such — along with modernity — are now passé, and thus jettisoning them will free us finally to "do" theology in terms of its own internal "logic." The epistemological task of reflecting on the epistemic and nonepistemic values that shape the rationality of theology and of science is therefore never done. This also seems to be the main reason why Calvin Schrag has claimed that postmodernism has not been able to deal with the issue of rationality in an adequate sense at all.[2]

Also in theological reflection, then, a postmodern critique of foundationalist assumptions will therefore be an inextricable part of a postfoundationalist model of rationality, and will definitely shape the way in which theology is located within the context of interdisciplinary reflection. My attempt to argue for this quite specific epistemic location has already revealed remarkable overlaps between the respective quests of theology and science for intelligibility.[3] I have also shown that the rationality of theology and science share important cognitive, evaluative, and pragmatic resources, involve the crucial epistemic skill of responsible, critical judgment, and exhibit an ongoing process of progressive problem solving. Locating theology within the context of interdisciplinary reflection also seems more possible (and plausible) when one opts for relating the rationality of science to the rationality of theological reflection, and not just generically to "religion." Obviously the interdisciplinary discussion between theology and the sciences is possible only because all religions, and certainly the Christian religion, presuppose views of the universe, of the nature of reality, of some form of "ultimate reality," of human beings, and of the nature of morality. Stanton Jones has rightly called this the cognitive dimension of religion, and as such it indeed is the dimension of religion most relevant to the sciences.[4] Obviously this does not mean that religion is only, or even primarily, a cognitive phenomenon, but it is the dimension of religion that presents itself to us forcibly in theological reflection, and as such remains the dimension of religion most relevant for interdisciplinary reflection.

Significant epistemological overlaps between scientific and theological rationality (as I have identified them in the quest for intelligibility and optimal understanding, responsible judgment skills, and progressive problem solving) have also revealed a significant breakdown of the

---

2. Calvin Schrag, "Rationality between Modernity and Postmodernity," in Stephen K. White, ed., *LifeWorld and Politics: Between Modernity and Postmodernity* (Notre Dame: University of Notre Dame Press, 1992), 155.

3. J. Wentzel van Huyssteen, *The Shaping of Rationality in Theology and Science* (forthcoming).

4. Stanton Jones, "A Constructive Relationship for Religion with the Science and Profession of Psychology: Perhaps the boldest model yet," *American Psychologist* 49, no. 3 (1994): 187.

traditional positivist demarcation between scientific and nonscientific rationality. Scientific knowing thus differs from other forms of human knowing, and therefore from theological knowing, only in degree and emphasis: theology and the various sciences all grapple with what we perceive as different but very real aspects of our experience.[5] This not only opens up broader notions of rationality and an awareness of the various values that shape different forms of human knowing, but also highlights the crucial importance of experiential and pragmatic factors in rational judgment, where we now find ourselves without any of the rules of the classical model of rationality.[6]

On this view a postfoundationalist model of rationality not only focuses on the experience of knowing, and thus on the experiential dimension of rationality itself, but — for both theology and science — very specifically implies an accountability to human experience.[7] Despite many important differences, I see this epistemic goal of experiential accountability functioning similarly between empirical adequacy for science and experiential adequacy for theological understanding, respectively. This will closely relate, as will soon become clear, to the differences between epistemological focus and experiential scope in theology and science. We all know today that the failure of foundationalism also was the failure of all forms of objectivist justification as handed down by the classic model of rationality. But the extremes of both an objectivist foundationalism and a relativist or subjectivist nonfoundationalism reflect the inability of our intellectual culture to unite personal experience and personal conviction with some form of rational justification.[8] I have, however, recently argued for the retrieval of the experiential dimension of personal, responsible judgment as a truly postfoundationalist move to unite personal conviction with some form of plausible, rational evaluation or justification through communally shared expertise.[9] Because of the shared resources of rationality between our various modes of human knowing, this fallibilist alternative to the

5. See Jones.

6. See Harold Brown, *Rationality* (London/New York: Routledge, 1990), 37.

7. See Jones.

8. See Michael G. Harvey, *Personal Conviction and Rational Justification* (unpublished paper for a Ph.D. seminar on "Theology and Rationality" at Princeton Theological Seminary, April 1994).

9. Van Huyssteen, *Shaping of Rationality*.

opposites of foundationalist and nonfoundationalist models of rationality now indeed again appears as a viable option for both theological and scientific reflection. And through the crucial epistemic role of judgment in the interpretation of our experience, the difficult question of whether our personal convictions, opinions, and beliefs can be transformed into "genuine" knowledge may finally be answered positively.

Faith and Interpreted Experience

Experiential accountability in theology and science now reveals another unexpected epistemological overlap between theological and scientific modes of inquiry: we relate to our world epistemically only through the mediation of interpreted experience, and in this sense it may be said that theology and the various sciences offer alternative interpretations of our experience.[10] "Alternative," however, in the sense not of competing or conflicting interpretations of experience, but of complementary interpretations of the manifold dimensions of our experience. In this sense it could also be said that the epistemic communities of theology and of science make cognitive claims about the "same" world. And if these are the languages of our different experiences of the world — even if they are about different domains of the same world — we should not remain content with a nonfoundationalist pluralism of unrelated languages. The fact that we relate to our world epistemically only through the mediation of interpreted experience now facilitates a postfoundationalist reading of Ian Barbour's statement: "If we seek a coherent interpretation of all experience, we cannot avoid the search for a unified world view".[11] For the Christian theologian the possibility of locating theology within an interdisciplinary context is one huge step towards achieving this coherent interpretation of our experience, and is finally made possible by revealing and retrieving the shared resources of rationality of our different and often diverse modes of human knowing.

10. See Holmes Rolston, *Science and Religion: A Critical Survey* (New York: Random House, 1987), 1-8.

11. Ian G. Barbour, *Religion in an Age of Science* (San Francisco: Harper and Row, 1990), 16.

I have argued before that all religious (and certainly all theological) language always reflects the structure of our interpreted experience.[12] In science too our concepts and theories can be seen as products of an interaction in which nature and ourselves play a formative role. The personal dimension of this relational knowledge does not at all take away from its validity and objectivity, which is warranted by a communally shared expertise. Our search for legitimate knowledge always takes place within the social context of a community, and individuals who share a certain expertise make up this community and help, challenge, critique, and confirm one another. If we relate to our world epistemically through the mediation of interpreted experience, our attempts to locate theology in the ongoing and evolving interdisciplinary discussion acquire new depth and meaning. It also brings us a few steps closer to answering Wayne Proudfoot's challenge to somehow reconstitute theology as genuine inquiry.[13] Not only are important epistemological overlaps like our shared quest for intelligibility, the shaping role of personal judgment, the process of progressive problem solving, and experiential accountability thus identified, but also the locus of important differences between disciplines is revealed in what William R. Stoeger has called the "focus," the "experiential grounds," and the "heuristic structures" of different disciplines.[14] What this means for theology and the sciences is that the differences between these various modes of inquiry are far more subtle than just differences in objects of study, language, or methodology. The differences revealed in interdisciplinary discussion are often radical differences in epistemological focus and in experiential scope.

Stoeger thus argues for a necessary discussion of foci, experiential grounds, and interpretative scope, because it is here that the differences between the disciplines as ways of knowing and modes of inquiry are found. But what is meant by the focus and the experiential grounds, or

12. J. Wentzel van Huyssteen, "Critical Realism and God: Can There Be Faith after Foundationalism?" in *Intellektueel in Konteks: Opstelle vir Hinnie Rossouw,* ed. A. A. van Niekerk (Pretoria: HSRC Publishers, 1993), 253-65.

13. Wayne Proudfoot, "*Regulae fidei* and Regulative Idea: Two Contemporary Theological Strategies," in Sheila Greeve Davaney, ed., *Theology at the End of Modernity: Essays in Honor of Gordon Kaufman* (Philadelphia: Trinity Press International, 1991), 113.

14. William R. Stoeger, "Contemporary Cosmology and Its Implications for the Science-Religion Dialogue," in *Physics, Philosophy and Theology: A Common Quest for Understanding,* ed. Robert J. Russell et al. (Vatican State: Vatican Observatory, 1988), 232ff.

what I would rather call the experiential scope, of a discipline? For Stoeger the focus of a discipline indicates the primary aspect of experienced reality to which a discipline gives attention, and which provides its primary point of reference.[15] The experiential focus of a discipline is the type of data, of phenomena, or of experience to which the discipline appeals, which it analyzes, and on which it reflects in arriving at and justifying its conclusions, and in testing and modifying its models.[16]

This difference in foci, experiential scope, and heuristic structures obviously gives rise to the different languages, contexts, and methodologies of diverse disciplines, and as such makes meaningful interdisciplinary communication and understanding very difficult. But the difficult and demanding process of entering the interdisciplinary conversation by attempting to raise an authentic personal voice in a complex, pluralist situation is just what a postfoundationalist model of rationality hopes to facilitate. In interdisciplinary discussion, those of us who utilize diverse methodologies and techniques, and also at the same time have very different foci while appealing to very different experiential grounds and heuristic structures, are attempting to understand and appreciate one another's points of view and commitments. As members of specific epistemic communities who would like to plausibly claim some form of expertise in our own fields of inquiry, we hope to discover in disciplines other than our own — and often in the hazy interfaces between disciplines — some clues, indications, or forms of persuasive evidence that will help us push forward the limits of our own disciplines.[17] For theology to take part in this process of critical synthesis and creative, interdisciplinary communication, it first has to show why it should be taken seriously as a discipline with its own focus, experiential scope, and heuristic structures.

How do important differences as well as significant similarities between theology and other sciences become more intelligible by focusing on their respective foci, experiential scope, and heuristic structures? In the natural sciences, broadly speaking, the focus is on detailed, reproducible behavior, on patterns of structure and behavior of physical, chemical, and biological systems, as given by systematic and controlled observation and experiment and by precise measurement. Taking the

15. Stoeger, 233.
16. Stoeger, 234.
17. See Stoeger, 232.

next step, that is, examining the limitations, horizons, and presuppositions of the natural sciences, already implies a move into the realm of philosophical reflection.[18] The focus of philosophy is essentially on the knower, on the experience of knowing, evaluating, and acting, and on the structure of what is known. In the broadest sense of the word this experiential scope of philosophical reflection finally touches on the limits of our experience, and at this point philosophy begins to open itself to the scope of theological reflection. In both theology and the sciences we therefore indeed relate to our world epistemically through the mediation of interpreted experience, but for the Christian believer this interpreted experience will now often be *religious* experience, where the experiences of genuine love, faith, or permanent commitment may be deeply revelatory of what is believed to be beyond these experiences.

However different the foci, experiential scope, and heuristic structures between theology and the other sciences may be, a postfoundationalist model of rationality has already revealed remarkable epistemological overlaps because of the shared resources of human rationality. Therefore, in spite of important differences in focus and experiential scope, we are now on our way to recognizing some remarkable parallels in the values that shape the rationality of both theology and science. Ian Barbour has already revealed some powerful comparisons between the structures of scientific and religious/theological thought, and now proceeds by pointing to data and theory as possibly the two most basic components of scientific reflection.[19] Barbour is joined there by Nancey Murphy, who has very persuasively argued that data and theory play an equally important and crucial role in theological reflection.[20] The data of theological reflection that emerge here are judgments that result from communal discernment, religious experience, tradition, and Holy Scripture as the classical text of the Christian tradition.[21] The experiential scope of religious reflection especially points to religious experience, story, and ritual, and to the fact that religious beliefs, and the commitments they constitute, have explanatory functions similar to that of scientific theories.

18. See Stoeger, 236ff.

19. Barbour, *Religion in Age of Science*, 31f.

20. Nancey Murphy, *Theology in An Age of Scientific Reasoning* (Ithaca: Cornell University Press, 1990), 130-173.

21. See also J. Wentzel van Huyssteen, *The Realism of the Text* (Pretoria: UNISA, 1987).

The postfoundationalist acknowledgment that we relate to our world epistemically only through mediation of interpreted experience at this point clearly surfaces in remarkable parallels between, on the one hand, the epistemic structure of science as revealed in the theory-laden-ness of data and the fact that all scientific theories are therefore under-determined by facts and, on the other hand, the epistemic structure of religious cognition as an equally unmistakable form of interpreted experience.[22] Just as all scientific observations are always theory-laden, so too all religious experiences are always interpretation-laden. For theology, as a reflection on interpreted religious experience and thus on the epistemic structure of religious cognition, this is the definitive move beyond foundationalism: if our beliefs are the results of our interpreted experiences, then the content of these beliefs (for instance, the notion of divine revelation) can never be merely given — immediately or directly — in the experience itself. The possibility that religious cognition could in any way be directly experiential is therefore ruled out; not because in some reductionist way divine action is ruled out in principle, but because any claim to such direct experience presupposes an immediate givenness that has been shown — in Kuhnian and post-Kuhnian analyses of both ordinary knowledge and scientific knowledge — to be totally impossible.

The interpretation-laden character of religious experiences therefore leads to the conclusion that the structure of religious cognition is indeed that of interpreted experience.[23] In this sense one could also say that the models and the metaphors of the basic religious language of a specific religious tradition are always used to construct creatively (but in continuity with the scope of the tradition) our religious beliefs. These religious beliefs in turn correlate with and point to certain experiences and, in a sense, explain them. And as in the scientific model, the religious model is drawn from the familiar realm of the experienced perceptual world. In this sense it could be claimed that what gives empirical meaning to scientific theory are scientific models and observations, and what

22. See William A. Rottschaeffer, "Religious Cognition as Interpreted Experience: An Examination of Ian Barbour's Comparison of the Epistemic Structures of Science and Religion," *Zygon: Journal of Religion and Science* 20, no. 3 (1985): 265-82.

23. See Ian G. Barbour, *Myths, Models and Paradigms: A Comparative Study in Science and Religion* (New York: Harper and Row, 1974), 122-26.

gives experiential meaning to our religious beliefs are the religious models and the way they help to interpret experience.[24] It is thus the interpretation that provides (valid) religious meaning. Religious cognition, as the basis of theological reflection, therefore indeed has the structure of interpreted experience.

For scientific modes of cognition the theory-ladenness of data means not only that theories always influence our observations in many ways, but that due to the focus and specific experiential scope of a discipline, even the object observed may be altered by the process of observation itself. This is particularly problematic in the microworld of quantum physics and the complex world of ecosystems, where we also end up being not detached observers separate from observed objects, but participant observers who are part of an interactive system.[25] That we relate to our world epistemically through the mediation of interpreted experience thus reveals remarkable overlaps between theology and science. In contemporary physics, for example, the role of the observer as participant becomes essential when we realize that quantum phenomena are given never in themselves, but only in terms of a measurement made by an observer. What is thus given is never an object in itself, but an object in relationship, in interaction with the observer.[26] Because we relate to our world epistemically only through the mediation of interpreted experience, the observer or the knower is always in a relationship to what is known, and thus always limited in perspective, in focus, and in experiential scope.

In this sense beliefs are both brought to experience and derived from it, and our interpreted experience thus becomes the matrix within which meaning and knowledge arise.[27] Our world is thus experienced in direct relation to our active engagement with it, in terms of what phenomenologists have called "intentionality".[28] The religious dimension of our experience, however, transcends other dimensions by providing what Jerry Gill has called the "hinge" by means of which they

24. See Rottschaeffer, 271.

25. See Barbour, *Myths*, 33f.

26. See Stoeger, 237.

27. See Jerry H. Gill, *On Knowing God* (Philadelphia: Westminster Press, 1981), 19.

28. Maurice Merleau-Ponty, *Phenomenology of Perception* (London: Routledge and Kegan Paul, 1962), xviiff.

are integrated and through an ultimate commitment endowed with deeper meaning.[29] Because of this mediated structure of the religious dimension of our experience, other experiences thus provide the context for our religious awareness. All our knowledge therefore takes place in, and is constituted by, a relationship: every knower, from the theoretic scientist interacting with abstract symbols to the skillful athlete judging the angle and speed of a ball, acquires and employs his or her knowledge in relational participation with that which is known.[30] Religious experience can therefore be thought of as arising out of, and yet as transcending, the physical, social, moral, and aesthetic dimensions of reality. What is revealed here is the continuity between human awareness in general and religious awareness in particular, and thus also an experiential basis for the postfoundational epistemological overlaps already identified between theological and scientific modes of knowing. Religious experience thus depends on complex sets of beliefs, and although an insistence on the immediacy of religious experience may often seem descriptively accurate, such a description will by itself, because of the interpreted nature of religious cognition, always be theoretically inadequate.[31]

From Fideism to Postfoundationalism

Part of the problem of the shaping of rationality in theological reflection is precisely the fact that religious experience may often seem to be immediate and noninferential, while in reality it never is independent of concepts, beliefs, and practices. And if we always relate to our world epistemically through the mediation of interpreted experience, then our experience will always be theory-laden and tradition-specific. With this the profound and comprehensive ramifications of a religious commitment become clear: the criteria for identifying a specific form of religious consciousness as such will always include not only a reference to

29. Gill, 69.
30. See Gill, 91.
31. See Wayne Proudfoot, *Religious Experience* (Berkeley: University of California Press, 1985), 3ff.

a whole framework or network of concepts, but also to a specific belief about how the experience is to be explained.[32] This, however, will have important implications for any postfoundationalist critique of theological assumptions. Precisely because all religious experience is intentional or transactional,[33] it is always already interpreted in terms of the preexisting patterns of the belief-systems we are already committed to. This then is the necessary tension we must hang on to: language gives us access to experience, while experience in turn predetermines linguistic expression. This is also the reason why the impact of a religious experience can best be accounted for by the fact that the criteria for identifying an experience as religious are always going to include reference to a very specific explanatory claim.[34] Thus, once more, it is revealed why religious beliefs and faith commitments always already include in themselves important values and value judgments that shape the rationality of theological reflection.

From this, crucially important conclusions have to be drawn. Not only are religious beliefs and practices interpretations of our experiences, which as such again become objects of interpretation; as interpretations of our experiences, religious beliefs also assume explanatory roles.[35] In a postfoundationalist model of rationality, hermeneutics and epistemology will therefore always go together very closely. To say, therefore, that there is no such thing as an uninterpreted experience is to say that all observation is theory-laden, and that again is to assume a concept of interpretation that reaches deep into the pragmatic, cognitive, and evaluative dimensions of a postfoundational epistemology. Proudfoot says it well: Our tacit theories and hypotheses have already played a constructive role in the perceptual judgments that make up our experience.[36] To say, therefore, that experience is always interpreted is to say that all our experience assumes particular concepts, beliefs, hypotheses, that is, judgment skills about ourselves and the way we relate to our world through theological and scientific reflection. Thus, too, the fiduciary rootedness of human rationality is revealed.

32. See Proudfoot, *Religious Experience*, 14.

33. See Jerome A. Stone, *A Minimalist Vision of Transcendence: A Naturalist Philosophy of Religion* (Albany: SUNY, 1992), 130.

34. See Proudfoot, *Religious Experience*, 216.

35. See Proudfoot, *Religious Experience*, 41.

36. See Proudfoot, *Religious Experience*, 61.

The distinguishing mark of religious experience in this sense would therefore be the individual's judgment that the experience, and the beliefs that constitute the experience, can be accounted for only in religious terms. Why anybody would identify an experience as a religious experience could of course be explained in many ways, for example, historically, psychologically, culturally, or epistemologically. But what is to be explained here is *why* we understand what happens to us in religious terms, and this requires the evaluation of the commitments and the tacit value judgments we bring to our experiences, as well as contextual conditions, and the network of concepts, theories, and beliefs that may support the plausibility of our judgments to identify our experiences in religious terms in the first place. Our judgments about the causes of our respective experiences therefore account for the difference between one of us having a religious experience and the other not.[37] In this sense an explanatory commitment is always embedded in the criteria we use to judge or identify an experience as religious. An interest in explanations, and the value judgments we bring to them, is therefore not an alien element illegitimately introduced into the study of religious experience: those of us who identify our experience in religious terms are seeking the best available explanations for what is happening to us.

Thus, once more, the rationality of the quest for intelligibility in theological reflection is revealed, and along with that the fact that through the crucial epistemic skill of responsible critical judgment, theological reflection too may claim reasons for specific theory choice through an ongoing progress of progressive problem solving. Locating theological reflection within the context of interdisciplinary reflection is possible especially because religion and science, within the context of our typically Western culture at least, are both part of the same interrelated intellectual conceptual structure.

This explains why modes of critical thought that are at home in contemporary science, contemporary culture, and common sense should indeed have a bearing on our assessment of the plausibility or rationality of religious belief. Foundationalist as well as nonfoundationalist attempts to deal with the justification of theory choice in philosophical theology have typically resulted, on the one hand, in inferential

---

37. See Proudfoot, *Religious Experience*, 231.

procedures that completely lose the experiential basis of religious reflection or, on the other hand, in nonfoundationalist attempts to evade the issue of the justification of religious belief altogether. This fideist view that religious beliefs are commitments that as such cannot be justified has become especially popular in some forms of contemporary postmodern and postliberal theologies.

Some philosophers of religion relate much of the current fideism in philosophy of religion and in philosophical theology directly to Wittgenstein's celebrated notion of language games, which as forms of life cannot and need never be justified.[38] Fideism, as a blind, uncritical commitment to a set of beliefs, could of course be at the heart of both foundationalist and nonfoundationalist models of rationality. What happens in the fideistic move, however, is that an ultimate faith commitment in, for instance, the Christian God, is first isolated in a very definite protective strategy and then equated to a commitment to a very specific set of foundational beliefs. Often, however, fideism and nonfoundationalism also collapse into one another when, for instance, religion, morality, or science would each claim to have internal criteria of intelligibility peculiar only to itself. The fideist move, where any account of religious faith, practices, or experiences is nonfoundationally restricted to the perspective, worldview, beliefs, and judgments of the subject alone, is thus equally revealed as a protective strategy[39] where the subject's own experience and explanation is never contested, and the need for transcommunal or intersubjective evaluation is never taken seriously.

Several dubious and problematical assumptions lie at the heart of all forms of theological and philosophical fideism. In her discussion of the problem of fideism, Nancy Frankenberry identified some of these assumptions as follows:

1. Forms of life, when considered as a whole, are not subject to criticism;
2. Each mode of discourse is in order as it is, for each has its own criteria and sets its own norms of intelligibility, reality, and rationality;

38. See Nancy Frankenberry, *Religion and Radical Empiricism* (Albany: SUNY, 1987), 11f.

39. ͤ e Proudfoot, *Religious Experience*, 197.

3. There is no Archimedean point or common ground in terms of which a philosopher can relevantly criticize whole modes of discourse;

4. Commitment is prior to understanding, intracontextual criteria take precedence over extracontextual considerations, and confessional functions can substitute for and finally supersede cognitive meaning.[40]

In a postfoundational model of rationality this isolation of religion and modes of religious cognition becomes completely unacceptable. If in both theology and science we relate to our world epistemically through the mediation of interpreted experience, and if different modes of intellectual inquiry all share in the same rational resources and thus facilitate significant epistemological overlaps between different modes of cognition, then it becomes impossible to oppose the rationality of religion to that of science in the way that theological fideism would need to survive plausibly.

Furthermore, the fideist strategy is simply not capable of consistently evading the issue of truth or falsity of religious discourse once it recognizes that truth claims made by different theologies (and even more so, different religions) often conflict with one another. An uncritical retreat to a fideist commitment,[41] or to religious forms of life or narratives, therefore seriously challenges the epistemic status of theological reflection as a credible partner in the contemporary interdisciplinary discussion. And on this point Roger Trigg was right to warn that Wittgensteinian fideism easily slides into conceptual relativism.[42] Within a fideist context all commitment and religious faith therefore has to be blind or arbitrary.[43] What is more, it is clear that the notion that religious systems have their own autonomous principles and their own unique decision procedures not only is a denial of the interdependence of religious cognition and other forms of human cognition, but also is fundamentally inconsistent with a postfoundational holist

40. Frankenberry, 11.

41. See William W. Bartley, *The Retreat to Commitment* (London: Chatto and Windus, 1964).

42. Roger Trigg, *Reason and Commitment* (Cambridge: Cambridge University Press, 1977).

43. See Frankenberry, 12.

epistemology, which claims a network of interrelated intersubjective or transcommunal criteria for its statements.

Certainly the most serious limitation of any fideist epistemology, however, is its complete inability to explain why we choose some viewpoints, some language games, or some networks of belief over others, and why we believe that some in fact offer better and more plausible explanations than others. This not only brings us back to the crucial epistemic role of critical judgment in all human cognition, but also clearly suggests the need for some form of transcommunal or intersubjective criteria in theological reflection. There is obviously more to the matter of using religious language than just understanding and adopting the internal workings of some specialized linguistic system that is not answerable to anything or anybody outside itself.[44] There obviously also is more to the making of commitments than just being embedded in forms of life that never can be questioned. Religious language and theological theories are human conventions, and as such are closely interwoven with the way we relate epistemically to our world through the mediation of interpreted experience. They are the results of creative intellectual construction, and along with the commitments they serve to express, they too should be examined and critiqued. If this does not happen, fideist epistemologies will be misused as ideological shelters and protective strategies for immunizing religious beliefs and theological theories from critical examination, refutation, or revision. Nancy Frankenberry goes even further and states that the work of some fideists is dominated by the same conservative attitudes that also characterize some forms of evangelical Christianity: in the end, both groups embed their arguments in assumptions that reinforce dogmatism and serve to insulate from criticism precisely those already established standards, frameworks, or activities that have come to be the most controversial in society.[45]

In contemporary religious epistemology, theologians and philosophers of religion (even those who would not call themselves empiricists), in an attempt to move beyond the dilemma of an absolutist foundationalism and a relativist nonfoundationalism/fideism, have increasingly come to depend on concepts like experience and experiential account-

44. See Frankenberry, 13.
45. Frankenberry, 13.

ability. In her own form of radical empiricism, Nancy Frankenberry has already creatively broadened the scope of what can be regarded as religious experience by arguing that sensing, perceiving, willing, doing, wondering, feeling, inferring, judging, and imagining are all modes of what we normally would call experience.[46] Thanks to both Frankenberry and Proudfoot it has also become abundantly clear what kind of protective strategies are invoked when appeals are made to direct or immediate religious experiences. The fact that appeals to immediate religious experiences, and therefore also appeals to self-authenticating notions of divine revelation, have become almost universally suspect does not, however, take away from the serious problems created for theology by our claim that — as in science — we have no uninterpreted experiences. Does this mean, for instance, that we can never have direct experiences of God, but only experiences interpreted in a theistic manner?

It seems that Jerome Stone was right: in a sense one's concept of experience will indeed entail one's concept of meaning, which in turn will determine one's concept of religious cognition.[47] So why do some of us choose traditional forms of Christian faith, others minimalist visions of transcendence, and still others naturalism? With this, the challenge to postfoundational theology becomes even more profound: could an even stronger claim ever be warranted, that even a minimalist vision of transcendence in the end may still be empowered to point to something more, and maybe even to a personal God? The notion of a personal God may serve to make sense of (and thus may be experientially more adequate to) great swathes of experience that without this notion would simply baffle us.[48] Elizabeth A. Johnson points to this in her recent groundbreaking study on divine presence and transcendence: at the root of all religious imagery lies an experience of the mystery of God, potentially given to us in all experience where there is no exclusive zone, no special realm, that alone may be called religious. In this way the historical world potentially becomes a sacrament of divine presence and activity, even if only as a fragile possibility.[49]

46. Frankenberry, 31f.
47. Stone.
48. See John Polkinghorne, *Reason and Reality* (Philadelphia: Trinity Press International, 1991), 98.
49. Elizabeth A. Johnson, *She Who Is* (New York: Crossroad, 1993), 124.

It has now become abundantly clear that, because of the nature and implications of interpreted experience, no general epistemological account can ever be given of the way in which such a transcendent possibility may, for some, become a plausible experienced reality. A postfoundational model of rationality does, however, leave us an important epistemic opening: we can pragmatically point to the fact that throughout history, and in various cultures — including our own — human beings have found it helpful, if not necessary, to make room for a transcendent interpretation of the natural dimensions of our world and ourselves. This then is what we mean by the experiential accountability of religious faith: it seems to be fruitful, within specific cultural contexts and the ongoing dynamic flow of traditions, to view the nature of this religious awareness as based in a relational interaction between humans and God.[50] Our commitment to a mind-independent reality called God thus would arise not only *from* experience, but in a very specific sense also *for* experience, that is, for making optimal sense of our experience.

A postfoundationalist model of rationality should therefore include an interpretation of religious experience that transcends pitfalls like the kind of dualism that would set up "natural" against "supernatural" and then demand a reductionist choice between the two. Surely our choices here cannot be restricted to either the dualist notion of seeing the divine as always interrupting or intruding on the natural, or the reductionist option of a completely naturalist interpretation of experience.[51] Precisely because of the transactional and relational nature of all interpreted experience, religious experience can indeed be thought of as arising out of, and yet transcending, the social, ethical, moral, and aesthetic dimensions of reality. Because of this, Jerome Stone's transactional realism[52] may prematurely be giving up on what may be discovered — contextually and through traditioned experience — about the scope and the richness of the presence of transcendence in the natural world. For the postfoundationalist our only epistemological access to God, and to what is interpreted as divine initiative and continued action, would be through the human side of what we may want to see as our relationship

---

50. See Gill, 122.
51. See Gill, 117ff.
52. Stone.

with God. This interactionist understanding of religious experience not only leaves room for the notion of divine activity, but may eventually even be said to entail it.[53]

The postfoundationalist choice for the relational quality of religious experience thus opens up the possibility of interpreting religiously the way that we believe God comes to us in and through our manifold experiences of nature, persons, ideas, emotions, places, things, and events. And because of this religious quest for ultimate meaning, each dimension and context of our experience contains within itself not just a potential element of minimalist transcendence, but an element of mystery, which when responded to may be plausibly said to carry with it the potential for divine disclosure. With this we have also arrived at possibly the most crucial and telling difference between theology and the sciences. This element of mystery is unique to the experiential scope and focus of theology and very definitely sets it apart from the very focused empirical scope of especially the natural sciences. As such it also has to be distinguished from what normally we see as lack of information in any given field, or as yet unsolved problems in a specific field of inquiry.[54] Not just in religion, but also in theology as a reflection on religious experience, this mystery is to be thought of as that which in principle may remain inexplicable within all of the complex dimensions of our experience.

It is also the element of mystery in all religious reflection that has often led to claims that theology and the sciences, if not in conflict, should at least be seen as incommensurably different paradigms from one another. This element of mystery, when followed by a religious commitment, does indeed again seem to force theology out of the shared domain of interdisciplinary discussion and now confronts us with the serious question, Are deep and personal convictions radically opposed to, and different from, ordinary and scientific forms of knowledge, and does this again imply a radical difference between scientific and theological rationality? The postfoundationalist notion of rationality for which I have argued above claims, of course, the exact opposite: we should be able to enter the pluralist, interdisciplinary conversation with our full personal convictions and at the same time be theoretically empowered to step beyond the

53. See Gill, 120.
54. See Gill, 122.

ions and boundaries of our own contexts or forms of life. How do
owever, in this discussion justify the pragmatic move of choosing for
or ..gainst a commitment, a theory, a model, a tradition?

Tradition, Commitment, and Pluralism

To try to answer this question adequately, I now want to take the ramifications of the fact that we relate to our world epistemologically only
through the medium of interpreted experience one step further by
exploring what it might mean that interpreted experience is always
contextual and as such determined — epistemically and nonepistemi-
cally — by living and evolving traditions. We saw earlier that responsible
judgments and progressive or problem-solving theory choices ultimately constitute the true nature of rational reflection. This implies that
not just our rational beliefs, but also any plausible notion of problem-
solving progress, are therefore located within the context of living,
changing, and developing traditions. Any time we choose to modify or
replace a theory with another theory, the change is progressive if and
only if the later version is a more progressive problem solver than its
predecessor.[55] The real meaning of intellectual progress is then found
— in fallibilist terms — in our ability to find good enough reasons for
choosing one theory or framework of ideas above another. Larry Laudan
also convincingly argued that it is these more general, global theories,
rather than only the more specific ones, that turn out to be our primary
tools for understanding and appraising progressive theory choices.[56]
These comprehensive or global frameworks of theories, because of the
interpreted nature of all human cognition, form an essential part of the
structure of all forms of human cognition. Kuhn called them paradigms,
Lakatos called them research programs, and Laudan calls them research
traditions. These research traditions are, as we saw, complex and comprehensive frameworks, and when carefully analyzed always reveal a

---

55. See J. Wentzel van Huyssteen, *Theology and the Justification of Faith: Constructing Theories in Systematic Theology* (Grand Rapids: Wm. B. Eerdmans, 1989), 172ff.

56. Larry Laudan, *Progress and Its Problems: Towards a Theory of Scientific Growth*
(London: Routledge and Kegal Paul, 1977), 71f.

network of conceptual, theoretical, instrumental, and metaphysical commitments that give the research tradition its particular identity.

No postfoundationalist notion of rationality would ever claim that these broader traditions, unlike specific theories, are in any way directly testable or justifiable. This does not mean, however, that they are outside the problem-solving process. Because a progressive or successful research tradition leads one, through its component theories, to the adequate solution of an increasing range of empirical and conceptual problems, the tradition itself could claim a very specific form of theoretical and experiential adequacy. The degree of this adequacy, of course, tells us nothing about the truth or falsity of the tradition itself,[57] but rather points to pragmatic criteria for choosing — through responsible judgment — between frameworks of thought, frameworks that may in reality be very different from one another. We thus saw that the role of critical judgment in all cognition not only implies a distinctly pragmatic move, but also enables us to retain the idea of intersubjective rational appraisal and the idea of progress in a clearly postmodernist and postfoundationalist way.

Research traditions, like all traditions, are historical creatures.[58] As such they are created and articulated within a particular intellectual milieu, and like all other historical institutions, they wax and wane.[59] We have seen before that theology and science, in spite of important differences in their foci and experiential scopes, also share important epistemological overlaps because of shared rational resources, the important epistemic role of responsible rational judgment, and the possibility of progressive theory choices. We also saw that in both theology and the sciences we relate to our worlds epistemically through the medium of interpreted experience. This interpretation of experience, however, always takes place within the comprehensive context of living and evolving traditions, and these traditions are epistemically constituted by broader paradigms or research traditions.

Because of their historical nature, research traditions in all modes of human knowledge can change and evolve through either the internal

57. See Laudan, 82.
58. See Delwin Brown, *Boundaries of our Habitations: Tradition and Theological Construction* (New York: SUNY, 1994), 24ff.
59. See Laudan, 95.

modification of some of their specific theories or a change of some of their most basic core elements. Larry Laudan correctly points out that Kuhn's famous notion of a "conversation" or paradigmatic revolution from one paradigm to another[60] can most probably be better described as a natural evolution within and between research traditions. Traditions, however, not only imply ongoing change and evolution, but also exhibit continuity. In this sense Delwin Brown is right in maintaining that in any adequate theory of traditions, continuity and change would be primary categories.[61]

To understand what continuity and change might mean in the dynamic of evolving traditions, Laudan — like Lakatos — suggests that certain elements of a research tradition are sacrosanct and can therefore not be rejected without repudiation of the tradition itself. Unlike Lakatos, however, Laudan insists that what is normally seen as sacrosanct in traditions can indeed change with time.[62] Lakatos and Kuhn were right in thinking that a research tradition or paradigm always has certain nonrejectable elements associated with it. They were, however, mistaken in failing to see that the elements constituting this core can actually shift through time. From this Laudan concludes: "By relativizing the 'essence' of research tradition with respect to time, we can, I believe, come closer to capturing the way in which scientists and historians of science actually utilize the concept of tradition."[63]

This reveals again not only the radical historical nature of all research traditions, but also the fact that intellectual and scientific revolutions take place not necessarily through complete shifts, but through the ongoing integration and the grafting of research traditions. From this we can now glean the following characteristics of research traditions:[64]

> First, because we belong to history, tradition is constitutive of the present and finally explains why we relate to our world epistemically only through the mediation of interpreted experience.

---

60. T. S. Kuhn, *The Structure of Scientific Revolutions* (Chicago: University of Chicago Press, 1970), 92ff.

61. D. Brown, 24f.

62. Laudan, 99.

63. Laudan, 100.

64. See also D. Brown, 44f.

Second, research traditions — like all traditions — are not re-
ducible to the activities of individuals and groups within them,
but neither do they have reality except as they are instantiated
by the epistemic communities (the "experts") of specific traditions.
Third, research traditions are dynamic, evolving phenomena that
live precisely in the dialectic of continuity and change.
Fourth, as such, they are never isolated, because the borders sepa-
rating traditions from the milieus are usually, if not always,
exceedingly porous.[65]
Fifth, all traditions have sacrosanct elements that, even if they shift
or change over time, form the canons of traditions. These
canons serve as the source of creativity as well as the principle
of identity of traditions.

These characteristics of research traditions now take us back again to a
problem that, while exceedingly difficult for theology to deal with, has
become impossible to ignore if we want to move beyond the extremes
of both foundationalism and nonfoundationalism: Are we ultimately,
and fideistically, the prisoners of our research traditions and commitments? And if not, why do we choose to commit ourselves — often
passionately — to only certain traditions, theories, viewpoints? In trying
to answer these complex and challenging questions, I will argue that,
first, we should be able to enter the pluralist, interdisciplinary conversation between research traditions with our full personal convictions,
while at the same time stepping beyond the strict boundaries of our
own intellectual contexts; and, second, we can indeed in interdisciplinary discussion justify our choices for or against a specific research
tradition. As we saw earlier, the fact that broader research traditions can
as such never be directly tested or justified does not mean that they are
outside the problem-solving process.

65. See D. Brown, 26.

A Christian Voice in a Pluralist Conversation?

We already saw that when a progressive or successful research tradition leads to the adequate solution of an increasing range of empirical and conceptual problems, the tradition itself can claim a high degree of theoretical and experiential adequacy. It also has become abundantly clear that, as far as a postfoundationalist notion of rationality is concerned, the degree of this adequacy tells us nothing about the truth or falsity of the tradition itself, but rather points to pragmatic criteria for choosing — through responsible judgment — between often very diverse frameworks of thought. The role of judgment in all forms of human cognition thus not only points to a distinctly pragmatic move, but also opens the door — through the critical role of the epistemic community of experts — to intersubjective rational appraisal and progressive theory choice.

What could this postfoundational move now mean for theological reflection? An intriguing attempt to move beyond the objectivism of foundationalism and the radical relativism of nonfoundationalism, and to identify a distinctly Christian voice in the contemporary pluralist American culture, is found in an argument put forward by William C. Placher.[66] Thanks to its confusing and unfortunate title, this book starts out on the wrong foot, and *Unapologetic Theology* indeed seems to suggest that an "assertive" theology, not caring about the rules of responsible conversation, might turn out to be the only way to speak "Christianly" today. The most important reason for this confusion is, however, not so much the book's title as Placher's claim that Christians ought to speak in their own distinct voice without worrying about finding philosophical "foundations" for their claims.[67] Later in the book it becomes clear that Placher's concern does not so much seem to be the problem of philosophical or theological foundationalism, but rather that too much philosophical or epistemological awareness will give philosophy a "priority" over theology. With this, however, Placher bypasses the epistemological ramifications of recognizing the shared ra-

---

66. William C. Placher, *Unapologetic Theology: A Christian Voice in a Pluralist Conversation* (Louisville: Westminster/John Knox Press, 1989).

67. Placher, 13.

tional resources and epistemological overlaps between the structure of religious cognition and other forms of human knowing.

Placher wants Christians both to be authentic partners in the pluralist conversation between diverse research traditions and also to remain faithful to their own vision of things for reasons internal to the Christian faith. However, when Placher begins to argue against theology's intellectual isolation and hopes for making "wider connections while still speaking faithfully in one's own voice",[68] he has already moved beyond any nonfoundationalist "unapologetic theology" into what I have consistently called the third option of a postfoundationalist rationality. In our pluralist and often fragmented postmodern culture, an adequate Christian apologetics could hardly still be about just adopting and assimilating the language and assumptions of our culture.[69] On the contrary, good apologetics today is precisely about finding an authentic and committed voice in a pluralist conversation. In fact, for Placher, too, Christians have reasons internal to their own tradition for seeking out members of *other* traditions for serious dialogue.[70]

Although Placher's initial anti-philosophical remarks remain puzzling and unfortunate, it should not detract from the fact that he seriously engages with contemporary theology, philosophy, and science, and thereby inadvertently clears the way for a postfoundational epistemology in theology. By now proposing authentic interdisciplinary conversation as a model for meaningful interaction between theology and culture, theology and science, theology and philosophy, and different research traditions in theology, Placher already moves beyond his own self-confessed postliberal leanings.[71] This is eminently clear from the structure of this work, which is developed exactly around the specific implications that an interdisciplinary conversation will have for the relation between religion and science, for the dialogue with different research traditions and other religions, and — last but not least — for theological method.

By locating theology in the heart of the interdisciplinary conversation, Placher wants to develop a theological "middle ground" by moving

68. Placher, 13.
69. Placher, 11f.
70. Placher, 166.
71. Placher, 20.

beyond various forms of (nonfoundationalist) relativisms like the Wittgensteinian fideists' image of cultures as self-contained worlds that never
interact, postliberalism's theological isolationism, and neopragmatism's
historicism. Because of theology's interdisciplinary location, conversation now becomes possible even in the absence of any claims to universal
rules. For Placher a genuine conversation involves conversation partners
who come to the conversation with all their beliefs, prejudices, and
presuppositions intact. In developing this interactionist position,
Placher's viewpoint — although he never explores these possibilities —
now reveals remarkable epistemological similarities to what I identified
as a postfoundationalist notion of rationality. Even with widely divergent viewpoints, we do share similar resources of human rationality,
and because of these epistemological overlaps there may be an overlap
of beliefs that provides a place or common ground for a particular
conversation to begin.[72]

In his very recent *Boundaries of our Habitations: Tradition and Theological Construction*, Delwin Brown too takes up some of these issues and
proposes a constructive historicism where theology retrieves its trans-
contextual obligation precisely by being the caregiver of tradition.[73]
Seeing tradition as the matrix of creative theological reflection may help
us to develop a form of theological thinking that would be both culturally
and religiously more effective, by achieving an integration of inheritance
and imagination in theological reflection that is as adequate as possible.
The central theme of Brown's book thus develops around an exploration
of the idea that tradition is one type of cultural strategy, one way of
negotiating chaos and order, or — as I would put it — one way of facili-
tating responsible critical judgment in our theory choices.

Both William Placher's and Delwin Brown's views on transcontex-
tual conversation and evaluation will be significantly strengthened when
supported by the kind of postfoundationalist epistemology I have outlined above, which also has close affinities with what religious epistemol-
ogist Andy F. Sanders has recently called "traditionalist fallibilism."[74] I
would put it as follows: We begin our conversations by bringing our

72. Placher, 106.

73. D. Brown, 111-55.

74. Andy Sanders, "Traditionalism, Fallibilism and Theological Relativism," *Neder-
lands Theologisch Tijdschrift* 49, no. 3 (July 1995).

fallible views and judgments to those who traditionally make up our epistemic communities (the "experts"). In a postfoundationalist evaluation of the beliefs, opinions, and viewpoints that hold our commitments, the epistemic movement thus goes from individual judgment to expert evaluation to intersubjective conversation. Because each judgment and each rhetorical argument always takes place in some community, and each community has a particular tradition and history, the broader research tradition(s) in which communities are embedded will now epistemically shape (but not completely determine) the questions one asks, the assumptions one can make, and the arguments one will find persuasive. For theology this interdisciplinary location not only opens the way to genuine conversation, but also reveals a judgment about how theology should be done and the criteria to which theological claims should be obligated. Delwin Brown puts a similar conclusion succinctly: Theology, even specifically Christian theology, is answerable to canons of critical inquiry defensible within the various arenas of our common discourse, and not merely within those that are Christian.[75]

The fact that there are no more foundationalist, universal, cross-cultural, or interreligious rules for theology does not therefore necessarily mean that all criteria are now always going to be strictly local or exclusively contextual. If none of our criteria were to be acceptable beyond the boundaries of a research tradition, the giving of rational reasons beyond the boundaries of any tradition would be impossible.[76] The crucial problem for a theology located in interdisciplinary conversation therefore remains the following: Is it at all possible to make sensible and rational choices between different viewpoints and alternative research traditions? At this point Larry Laudan's admonition to scientists and theologians comes to mind: unless we can somehow articulate criteria for choice between research traditions, we have neither a theory of rationality nor a theory of what progressive growth in knowledge should be.[77] In theology, as in other forms of inquiry, providing warrants for our views thus becomes a cross-cultural obligation.[78] Remarkable parallels have again surfaced here between theology and the sciences: in both theology and

75. D. Brown, 4f.
76. D. Brown, 6.
77. Laudan, 106.
78. D. Brown, 6f.

science we should be able to identify some criteria to warrant our theory choices, and neither scientific nor theological knowledge can ever claim demonstrably certain foundations for making these choices. Epistemic similarities between theology and the sciences do not mean, of course, that scientific knowledge is "just like" theology, but it does mean that methods in science do not provide a uniquely rational and objective way of discovering truth. In both theology and science good arguments should therefore be offered for or against theory choice, or for or against the problem-solving ability of a research program. Obviously, our good arguments and value judgments rest on broader assumptions and commitments that can always again be challenged. This does not mean, however, that any opinion is as good as any other, or that we can never compare radically different points of view.[79]

The postmodern challenge always to critique our own assumptions certainly means that there are no universal standards of rationality against which we can measure other beliefs or research traditions. The fact that we lack a clear and "objective" criterion for judging the experiential adequacy or problem-solving ability of one tradition over another does not, however, leave us with a radical relativism, or even with an easy pluralism. Our ability to make rational judgments and share them with various and different epistemic communities also means that we are able to communicate with one another meaningfully through conversation, deliberation, and evaluation. Sharing our views and judgments with those inside and outside our epistemic communities can therefore lead to a truly postfoundationalist conversation, which we should enter not just to persuade, but also to learn from. In Placher's terms: Such a style of inquiry can provide a way of thinking about rationality that respects authentic pluralism — it does not force us all to share the same assumptions, but it finds ways we can talk with one another and criticize our traditions while standing in them. In this sense genuine pluralism ought to allow for conversations between people who may enter the conversation for very different reasons.[80] This means that even if we lack universal rules for rationality, and even if we can never judge the reasonableness of statements and beliefs in isolation from their cultural or disciplinary contexts, we can still meaningfully engage

79. See Placher, 51.
80. Placher, 117.

in cross-contextual evaluation and conversation and give the best available cognitive, evaluative, or pragmatic reasons for the responsible choices we hope to make.

Conclusion

In our quest for the values that shape rationality in theology and science, a broader and richer notion of human rationality with its distinct cognitive, evaluative, and pragmatic resources was revealed. Whether in faith, religion, theology, or the various sciences, we have good reasons for hanging on to certain beliefs, good reasons for making certain judgments and moral choices, and good reasons for acting in certain ways. In theology, as a critical reflection on religion and religious experience, rationality implies the ability to give an account, to provide a rationale, for the way one thinks, chooses, acts, and believes. Here too theory acceptance has a distinct cognitive dimension. When we asked, however, what besides belief is involved in theory-acceptance, the pragmatic and evaluative dimensions of theory-acceptance were revealed.

I have therefore claimed that the quest for intelligibility and ultimate meaning in theology is also dependent on broader resources than just the purely cognitive, that is, on the evolving nature of the epistemic and nonepistemic values that have shaped theological rationality through its long history. But what does this concretely imply for theology? At the very least it implies that the realist assumptions and faith commitments of experienced Christian faith are relevant epistemic issues that deserve to be taken seriously in interdisciplinary discussion. By doing this, theology could in fact move away from the absolutism of foundationalism, as well as from the relativism of nonfoundationalism. This can further be achieved by showing that, because theology is an activity of a community of inquirers, there can be no way to prescribe a rationality for that activity without also considering its actual practice, along with the way this reflective and traditioned practice grows out of the way Christian believers live a daily life of faith. The interdisciplinary location of theology has then, in a very specific way, revealed how the explanatory role of interpreted experience in theology can be adequately appreciated in terms of experiential epistemology.

Chapter Two

Critical Realism and God:
Can There Be Faith after Foundationalism?

A S ONE LOOKS BACK OVER THE PAST FEW DECADES TODAY, THE SIXTIES
stand out as an accepted — albeit controversial — icon of cultural
change. Those years indeed changed our world: not only through the
fragmented extremes exemplified by Woodstock in the United States of
America and Sharpeville in South Africa, but also through a tremendous
intellectual challenge to those of us who were students of philosophy
at the University of Stellenbosch at the time. For some of us the hopeless
struggle to combine a living faith with an impotent, outdated theology
coincided with the arrival of Hennie Rossouw as a new lecturer in
philosophy. Hennie dutifully guided us through A. E. Loen's *De Vaste
Grond*. He also, however, took the (then) daring step of opening our
searching minds and critical souls to existentialist and phenomenologi-
cal thinking. This afforded me, as Hennie's first M.A. student, an intellectual context for identifying my very own most basic theoretical problem: the loss of all foundations (or "truth") once one moved beyond
the safe haven of the reigning theological paradigm.

This problem, which I could only much later identify as the problem
of the shaping of rationality in religious/theological reflection, has
stayed with me in one way or another ever since. In its contemporary
postmodern guise the problem reads as follows: Can there be a life of
committed Christian faith after moving beyond the absolutism of foundationalism and the relativism of antifoundationalism? I believe a
plausible, and very helpful, postfoundationalist model for theistic belief

can be found in a carefully constructed critical realism. After all, the model of rationality we choose to live by very much determines our intellectual context.

To juxtapose critical realism and God in this way turns out to be especially challenging for anyone concerned with the epistemic values that shape our religious and theological reflections. Critical realism, of course, is neither a theological nor a scientific thesis; it is a philosophical, or even more accurately, an epistemological, thesis about the goals of scientific knowledge and the implications of theoretical models in science.[1] Hence it should not be seen as a theory about truth, but rather as a theory about the epistemic values that shape scientific rationality. In theology, critical realism should be seen as a response to the question, What sort of philosophical account is possible of the aims and the structure of religious/theological reflection and of the epistemic attitudes presupposed by this kind of reflection?

This very specific epistemological focus distinguishes critical realism from the many realisms that dot the history of philosophical thought. In this article I therefore want to argue that in theology critical realism has a quite limited claim: it purports to explain why it makes sense not to abandon some of the Christian faith's most basic realist assumptions. Critical realism thus will turn out to be at least in part an empirical thesis and not just a metaphysical claim about how the world must be. From this it follows that a choice for critical realism in theological reflection does not necessarily imply a choice for some form of realism in either the social or the natural sciences. Philosophers of science have convincingly argued that there can be no undisputed and monolithic notions of reality or of explanation in science. The objects of our interest dictate not only different strategies but also different views on what could be regarded as adequate forms of explanation in the different sciences. The crucial question now is whether theology in any way exhibits a rationality comparable to the rationality of scientific reflection.

With this in mind, I want to explore the possibilities of critical realism as a response to the postmodern challenge to the rationality of religious dialogue and theistic belief. Within the broader context of a

1. See E. McMullin, "Realism in Theology and Science: A Response to Peacocke," *Religion and Intellectual Life* 2 (1985): 41.

postfoundationalist, holist epistemology, critical realism can be re-trieveds for religious and theological reflection. Viewed in this way, critical realism may become a valuable epistemological tool for evalu-ating the explanatory role of religious commitment and also for highlighting the fact that the rationality of religious/theological reflec-tion is shaped not only by pragmatic or empirical criteria, but also by the cognitive and evaluative dimensions of human knowledge. This focus on the epistemic values that shape the rationality of religious reflection might show that there is more to our religious and theological language than just what happens to be useful to us. On this view critical realism can become an important epistemological tool for any attempt to intellectually move beyond the dilemma of foundationalism versus antifoundationalism in theological reflection.

It is therefore meaningful to talk about critical realism and God only when we talk about the aims of theological knowledge and about the epistemic attitudes presupposed by a religious faith commitment. As in the case of scientific knowledge, the question here is what aim our religious reflection has, and also how much shall we believe when we accept a theory: Is the proper form of theory acceptance the belief that the theory as a whole is true, or is it something else?[2] I should like to propose that to accept a theory in theology is to believe that it is experientially adequate and that what the theory says about what is intelligible to us is highly probable.

I

The current focus on critical realism is not only symptomatic of the fact that in philosophy of religion and theology the special challenge posed by the cognitive aspects of religious faith just won't go away; it also shows us why contemporary philosophy of science has become the most important link in the debate on rationality in religious and scien-tific reflection.

I have dealt extensively with the complex nature of critical realism

2. See Bas. C. van Fraassen, *The Scientific Image* (Oxford: Clarendon Press, 1980), 17f.

in post-Kuhnian philosophy of science elsewhere.[3] I have also argued against the uncritical, superficial transference of realism in science to the domain of religious belief and to theology as reflection on the claims of this belief. In a qualified or weak form of critical realism in theology, the focus is only on the very limited epistemological conviction that what we are provisionally conceptualizing somehow really exists. "Critical realism and God" in this context becomes an attempt to find a promising and suggestive hypothesis that can help us deal with some of the traditionally realist assumptions of the Christian faith within a postmodern context. A qualified or weak form of critical realism, therefore, does not at all offer a strong defense of theism, but attempts to deal with and make more plausible the cognitive claims of religious language and theological reflection.

In rejecting the claim that religious language provides only a useful system of symbols that can be action guiding and meaningful for the believer without being in any sense reality depicting in its cognitive claims, the critical realist also wants to avoid both the insular comfort of theological foundationalism and the arbitrariness of antifoundationalism, as attempts to say how religious language can claim to be about God at all. Critical realism in theology thus makes a proposal about the provisionality, but also about the reliability, of theological knowledge. Without losing the validity of the fact that all our knowledge is always socially contextualized, critical realists — with good reasons, but not on compelling grounds — claim reference for their tentative proposals. A critical realist viewpoint is indeed realist because, in the process of theological theorizing, this model enables us to recognize the cognitive and referential nature of analogical language as a form of indirect speech. It is also, however, critical because theological language should retain its openness and provisionality throughout the ongoing process of theological theorizing.

Against this background it should already be clear why critical realism has developed into one of the most important positions in the current philosophy-of-science debate. It not only highlights the role of

---

3. J. Wentzel van Huyssteen, *The Realism of the Text* (Pretoria: UNISA Publishers, 1987); "Experience and Explanation: The Justification of Cognitive Claims in Theology," *Zygon* 23, no. 3 (1988); *Theology and the Justification of Faith: Constructing Theories in Systematic Theology* (Grand Rapids: Wm. B. Eerdmans, 1989).

metaphorical reference in scientific theory formation while at the same time honoring the provisionality and sociohistorical nature of all knowledge, but it also enables us to retain the ideals of truth, objectivity, rationality, and intellectual progress in a radically reconstructed way. Certainly the strength of the critical realist position lies in its insistence that both the objects of science and the objects of religious belief often lie beyond the range of literal description.[4] In their respective quests for intelligibility, the scientific and theological enterprises share alike the groping and tentative tools of humankind: words, ideas, and images that have been handed down, which we refashion and reinterpret for our context in the light of contemporary experience.[5] "Realism" in "critical realism" thus refers to the attempt at reliable cognitive claims about domains of reality that lie beyond our experience, but to which interpreted experience is our only epistemic access. As communities of faith come to experience the reality and intelligibility of God and interpret these experiences linguistically, they use models and metaphors to access and express interpreted religious experience.

Critical realism, in this sense, is an empirical thesis since its credibility acceptance as a belief system is determined on experiential grounds. Also, in theology our rational inquiry and quest for intelligibility will always include a response to what we experience, and experiential adequacy thus becomes one of the most important epistemic values that shape the rationality of theological reflection. The high degree of personal involvement in theological theorizing not only reveals the relational character of our being in the world, but epistemologically implies the mediated and interpretative character of all religious commitment, which certainly is no irrational retreat to commitment, but on the contrary reveals the committed nature of all rational thought, and thus the fiduciary rootedness of all rationality. In a sense one's concept of experience will therefore entail one's concept of meaning, which in turn will determine one's concept of knowledge.

On this view religious experience, and the way we define it, serves as a matrix out of which meaning and knowledge arise as bases for

4. See McMullin, 47.

5. See Arthur Peacocke, *Intimations of Reality: Critical Realism in Science and Religion* (Notre Dame: University of Notre Dame Press, 1984), 51.

theological theorizing. The theory-ladenness of all data in the sciences therefore parallels the interpreted nature of all religious experience. This also means, however, that the underdetermination of theories by data is epistemologically as important in theology as in the other sciences. Furthermore, the use of metaphors and models in religious cognition — a use that parallels that in scientific cognition — also argues for the claim that the structure of religious cognition is that of interpreted experience. Models also provide a way of speaking of the unknown in terms of the known; and as comprehensive interpretive networks, they open up new dimensions through their suggestiveness and fertility.

In my attempt to focus on experiential adequacy as perhaps the most important epistemic value for theological rationality, theology has emerged, in the broadest sense, as a reflection on religious experience. This is consistent with the important postfoundationalist challenge to retrieve religious experience as a valid methodological starting point for theological reflection. In terms of a qualified form of critical realism, it now becomes possible to construct an imaginative approach to theological reflection that begins with ordinary human experience and reflection and then moves from there to religious affirmations about the nature of reality. On this view critical realism in theology implies a fallibilist, experiential epistemology that not only opens up new common ground between religion and science, but also confronts the current challenge to incorporate theology and science in the broader interdisciplinary dialogue. On this view critical realism is also consistent with a holist epistemology that not only challenges the traditional barriers between philosophy of religion and philosophical theology, but also enables us to explore the presupposed continuity between a Christian theology and the general enterprise of understanding our world rationally. A holist approach such as this will then be concerned with both the integration of our experience and an analysis of what believers experience as the ultimate in every experience.

II

In a review of my recent book, J. Wesley Robbins[6] applauds this holism but then sees it waiver and backslide, because a commitment to the Christian faith apparently necessitates the postulate of a correspondence between words and reality. For Robbins, this goes hand in hand with Christian theist/realist claims, which, according to him, have already caused more trouble than they are worth. Robbins therefore projects life without this belief and justifies this pragmatist commitment by its ultimate usefulness.

Robbins's critique eminently focuses the complex challenge of postmodern thought to a theology that wants to move beyond the insular comfort of epistemological foundationalism. Not only do we have to take seriously the postmodern trilemma of trying to keep together, as a meaningful whole, a sense of continuity with the Christian tradition, a respect for and celebration of pluralism, and a resistance to any authoritarian (also epistemological) domination,[7] but postmodern thought challenges us to explore again the presupposed continuity between Christian theology and the general enterprise of understanding our world rationally. Much of contemporary theological reflection has in fact been shaped decisively by postmodernism's fragmentation, indeterminacy, and intense distrust of all universal or "totalizing" discourses.[8] Not only theology, however, but also postmodern philosophy of science has moved away from conceptions of linear progress, absolute truths, and the standardization of knowledge. Joseph Rouse recently argued for a postmodern philosophy of science that, along with feminist readings of science, joins trust in local scientific practice with suspicion toward any global interpretation of science that claims to legitimize that trust.[9]

6. J. Wesley Robbins, review of *Theology and the Justification of Faith* (by Wentzel van Huyssteen) and *Explanation from Physics to Theology* (by Philip Clayton), *Zygon* 27, no. 2 (1992): 225-31.

7. See Mark Kline Taylor, *Remembering Esperanza: A Cultural Political Theology for North American Praxis* (New York: Orbis, 1990), 31ff.

8. See David Harvey, *The Condition of Postmodernity* (Oxford: Basil Blackwell, 1989), 9f.

9. Joseph Rouse, "The Politics of Postmodern Philosophy of Science," *Philosophy of Science* (1991): 58.

It is precisely in the light of this challenge that I want to develop a holism that is consonant with a fallibilist, experiential epistemology. This epistemology articulates and defends the cognitive claims of our religious beliefs, but not in terms of so-called universal standards of rationality. Of course, religious beliefs should not be treated differently from scientific, philosophical, or other beliefs. Epistemologically speaking, there is nothing unique about religious beliefs; like other beliefs they can be assessed to determine whether they are useful, useless, meaningful, true, or false. And in the assessment of our beliefs critical realism — at least in the sense that I have used this term — certainly rejects the "objectivity" of all foundationalism and aims for the truthfulness granted by intersubjectivity instead.

To reject foundationalism in theology, however, is not to embrace nonfoundationalism without any further ado — in any case not a type of nonfoundationalism or antifoundationalism that claims that one should engage in theological reflection without paying attention to the epistemic values that specifically shape theological rationality. Generally speaking, the nature of rationality consists of the intelligent pursuit of certain epistemic values, of which intelligibility is the most important. The source for this quest for intelligibility, however, is never only pragmatic but always at least cognitive and evaluative as well.[10] What this means is that in postmodern theology, too, we should have good reasons for hanging on to our beliefs, good reasons for our evaluations and moral choices, and good reasons for acting in certain ways. Within a postfoundationalist, holist epistemology the three go together as a seamless whole and merge in the common task of uniting the "best reasons" for belief, choice, and action. For this reason, Robbins is not very convincing on the fate of theism.[11] Projecting a life on pragmatist premises alone (and thus eschewing the cognitive claims of religious beliefs) not only fundamentally challenges his own holism when epistemology is finally emptied into pragmatist hermeneutics, it also illustrates that not all kinds of postmodern thought should be accepted uncritically; even pragmatism can conceal an oppressive neopositivist bias towards the cognitive claims implicit in religious and theological statements.

10. See Nicholas Rescher, *Rationality: A Philosophical Inquiry into the Nature and Rationale of Reason* (Oxford: Clarendon Press, 1988).
11. See Robbins, 231.

Presupposed in all of this is Robbins's erroneous assumption that even a weak qualified form of critical realism necessarily implies a strong correspondence theory of truth. But these two need not go together at all. The epistemic purpose of metaphorical language is not to transcend the world of human experience but rather to set limits to the range of our language. Such limits establish a domain for human knowledge, and our subjective encounter of the world is therefore of the same order as our re-creation of the world in language. Our "words" are here not seen as derivative of an "objective" world and consequently do not find truth in correspondence with such a world. This is obviously not a denial of the existence of an extralinguistic world, but an affirmation of the reality of the world as encountered in language, and of the language of our inter-preted experience as our only epistemic access to this world. The epistemic implications of this is not "quite useless"[12] at all, but point to the fact that there is more to our religious and scientific language than just whatever happens to be useful to us. This selective discrimination against the cognitive dimension of religious experience turns out to be perhaps the most important challenge to a critical realist program in theology.

III

In the current discussion on the nature and status of religious and theological beliefs, some postmodern theologians disturbingly enough embrace a postmodernism of reaction[13] that calls for a "postliberal" return to orthodox or neo-orthodox epistemic values and confessional traditions. This should alert us to the fact that postmodernism is a complex phenomenon and that no position in theology or philosophy of religion should be accepted uncritically just because it claims to be postmodern. Postmodernism challenges theologians to account for the fact of Christianity[14] and to rediscover the explanatory role of religious

---

12. Robbins, 231.

13. See Peter C. Hodgson, *God in History: Shapes of Freedom* (Nashville: Abingdon Press, 1989), 29.

14. See P. G. R. De Villiers, "The End of Hermeneutics? On New Testament Studies and Postmodernism," *Neotestamentica* 25, no. 1 (1991): 115.

experience in postfoundationalist theology. In this sense, the postmodern theological project is to reaffirm and revision faith in God without abandoning the powers of reason.[15] In this sense, too, critical realism, as an epistemological tool, helps to focus on the epistemic values that shape the rationality of religious reflection.

When focusing on problems related to theological rationality, we will do well to understand postmodernism not merely as a radical departure from modern thought. The key to moving to a postfoundationalist position that moves beyond the alternatives of foundationalism and antifoundationalism lies not in radically opposing postmodern thought to modernity, but in realizing that postmodern thought shows itself in the constant interrogation of foundationalist assumptions and thus in always interrupting the discourse of modernity.[16] As such the postmodern incredulity towards global metanarratives need not lead to the end of the possibility of dialogue, but rather through the relentless criticism of intellectual conceit and uncritical dogmatism to a continuation of all conversation. Seen in this way, modern and postmodern thought are unthinkable apart from each other, and postmodern thought is not only modern thought coming to its end. In fact, when postmodern thought challenges foundationalist assumptions in theology, a fallibilist, experiential epistemology can develop that is highly consonant with the qualified form of critical realism that I have been proposing earlier in this paper.

In her *Theology in the Age of Scientific Reasoning*, Nancey Murphy not only demonstrates that both theologians and philosophers of religion need a thorough knowledge of the cognitive aspects of religious belief, but also presents her own interpretation of the work of philosopher of science Imre Lakatos as a model for postmodern theology.[17] In this program she embraces a nonfoundationalist interpretation of religious experience as "theological data" for a postmodern Lakatosian theology, but at the same time rejects critical realism as a meaningful epistemological model for dealing with the cognitive implications of

15. See Harvey, 41.
16. See Gary John Percesepe, "The Unbearable Lightness of Being Postmodern," *Christian Scholar's Review* 20 (1991): 120-25.
17. Nancey Murphy, *Theology in the Age of Scientific Reasoning* (Ithaca: Cornell University Press, 1990).

religious belief. The basic question, of course, is, How is one in general to distinguish between religious experiences that represent encounters with God and those that do not? For Murphy the Christian church, in a long history of communal decisions and judgments, provides a rich treasury of answers to just these questions.[18] It is within this context that she proposes that the crucial data for theology are the results of Christian discernment. Citing William Alston, Murphy correctly states that somehow what goes on in the experience of leading the Christian life indeed provides some ground for Christian belief and makes some contribution to the rationality of Christian faith.[19]

A serious challenge to this view, however, involves not only the reliability of these communal discernments, but the need to justify conceptualizing experience in theistic categories in the first place. In glaring contrast to this critical question, Murphy includes the existence of God as the presupposed and untouchable hard core of her theological research program. Whether Murphy's version of postmodern nonfoundationalism manages to move beyond a postliberal neoconservatism and its inherent fideism is unlikely. By radically opposing modern and postmodern thought, Murphy cuts herself off from maybe the most distinctive trait of postmodernism: its relentless criticism of foundationalist assumptions.

Since Murphy never challenges communal consensus and its limited and restricted epistemic scope, this leads to her uncritical inclusion of these basic Christian beliefs, or communal discernments, as unassailable hard-core beliefs in her theology. The fact that this move might lead to a subtle form of foundationalism that may not at all be consistent with Murphy's proposal for a postmodern theology leads me to her rejection of critical realism. She has important difficulties with this position. As a problematic position philosophically, it not only gives no clear account of how theology and science might interact, but also implies the "outrageous" claim to have some knowledge of reality apart from our ordinary human ways of knowing.[20] No sophisticated and qualified form of critical realism, however, would ever make this strong, dated, and truly foundationalist claim. As we saw earlier, a modest and qualified

18. Murphy, 132.
19. Murphy, 159.
20. Murphy, 197.

form of critical realism takes seriously the holist epistemology of current postmodern and postfoundationalist thought and makes tentative claims through the epistemic access provided by interpreted religious experience. The problem, of course, is that Murphy sees any attempt to define a relation between language and the world as "modern," as opposed to a "postmodern" position where words like "real" and "exists" would be restricted only to the meaning they obtain from being used within certain current linguistic frameworks.

I do believe, however, that there is a third, postfoundationalist, option here. In critical realism the epistemic function of language is not at all to transcend the world of human experience, but indeed to set the limits to the range of religious and theological language. A weak form of critical realism, which would seek epistemic warrants for the basic realist assumptions that a theology like Murphy's just accepts as the hard core of a program, claims that one's subjective encounter of the world is of the same order as one's re-creation of the world in the language of interpreted experience. This is an epistemic affirmation of the fact that, whatever the "real world out there" might or might not be, this reality is always encountered in the language of interpreted experience. This, however, makes Murphy's allegation that critical realism makes an "outrageous" claim to have some knowledge of reality "apart from our ordinary ways of human knowing" completely unintelligible.[21]

IV

Critical realism thus has a modest and limited claim in the broader theological enterprise: it seeks epistemic warrants for the basic realist assumptions that religious people live by and thus tries to determine the epistemic values that shape religious and theological reflection. This obviously implies that the realist assumptions and explanatory commitments of experienced Christian faith are relevant epistemological issues within our postmodern context. By taking these issues seriously, theology can move away from the absolutism of foundationalism as well as from the relativism of antifoundationalism. This can be a achieved by

21. Murphy, 198.

arguing that, because theology is an activity of a community of en-
quirers, there can be no way to prescribe a rationality for that activity
without considering its actual practice.

Taking this kind of religious experience seriously is taking the pragmatic and empirical dimension of the Christian faith seriously. This
again would explain why critical realism in theology is at least in part
an empirical thesis that purports to explain why it makes sense to be
committed to this faith, and as such can therefore claim experiential
grounds for its acceptance as an explanatory theory in theology. Thus
critical realism proposes that interpreted experience not only is the sole
legitimate source of information about our world, but also is the sole
legitimate source of information about how we should learn about our
world.[22]

This also points to the philosophical reason why critical realism in
theology will have to take seriously the epistemological role of Christianity's classic text and the way this has been inextricably interwoven
with ongoing religious experience and communal discernments that
have shaped the intellectual history of theological thought through the
long history of the Christian faith. But also, the way in which the
epistemological problem of shaping of rationality challenges theology
to transcommunal explanations and warrants has to be taken as seriously if theology wants to move beyond fideism. A postfoundationalist
theological program can, by means of a fallibilist, experiential
epistemology, properly aim for justified beliefs and for a tentative and
provisional knowledge of what Christians have come to call God. What
is retrieved here is not only a more nuanced way of dealing with the
cognitive claims of religious and theological reflection, but also the
important insight that rationality can never be reduced to scientific
rationality, and scientific rationality can never be reduced to natural
scientific rationality. As a broader, holist approach a fallibilist, experiential program of postfoundationalist critical realism can, however,
again link theology, philosophy of religion, and the sciences in their
common search for intelligibility.

22. See Michael Devitt, *Realism and Truth* (Oxford: Basil Blackwell, 1991), 149.

Chapter Three

Truth and Commitment in Theology and Science: An Appraisal of Wolfhart Pannenberg's Perspective

IN A SPECIFIC SENSE THE *LEITMOTIV* OF WOLFHART PANNENBERG'S work has always been his conviction that the Christian faith, and especially theology as a reflection on this faith, has a universal credibility in our age. Any discussion on issues regarding theology and science in Pannenberg's thought will therefore have to deal with this central theme and driving force behind his work.

This essay approaches this theme in terms of the problem of rationality in theology and science. The shaping of rationality in both theology and science will therefore form the framework for dealing with the philosophical problems of truth, objectivity, and commitment in Pannenberg's impressive and ever-expanding body of thought. I am convinced that only by clarifying this central epistemological perspective can one deal with the way Pannenberg relates theological reflection to the other sciences. Pannenberg's views on truth, justification, and objectivity — as reflected especially in his monumental work *Wissenschaftstheorie und Theologie*[1] — are not only important but also often sadly lacking from many discussions concerning his perspective on the significance of the sciences for theology as such.

---

1. W. Pannenberg, *Wissenschaftstheorie und Theologie* (Frankfurt am Main: Suhrkamp, 1973).

I therefore want to deal with Pannenberg's views on truth and justification in theology and then from that distil a model of rationality typifying his work. This obviously will have implications for his views on objectivity and on the relationship between theology and science, but also for the idea of progress in theology and science. Through this effort, I hope at the same time to fulfill the complex task of analyzing what it might mean for theology to demonstrate that the data as described by the sciences are provisional versions of objective reality and that the data themselves contain a further and theologically relevant dimension.

What Pannenberg says regarding the data provided by a nontheological anthropology[2] is certainly also true of the data provided by contemporary nontheological science: theologians should not undiscriminatingly accept the data provided by science and make these the basis for their own work, but rather must appropriate them in a critical way. For me this "critical appropriation" means *not* asking the wrong questions, such as where science ends and where theology begins.[3] It does, however, imply an analysis (from a philosophy-of-science point of view) of models of rationality that determine how both theology and science work and whether these two might perhaps share a common or analogous epistemology on the level of intellectual reflection. Only in this sense could I personally understand what it might mean to lay theological claim to data described by the sciences.[4]

Pannenberg has of course always and correctly maintained that a credible doctrine of God as creator must take into account scientific understandings of the world.[5] Theological talk about God as creator remains empty if it cannot be related to a scientific description of nature. This statement alone secures the direct relevance of the rationality of science for the rationality of theology. Pannenberg senses this when he states that theological assertions concerning the world, although not formulated on the same level as scientific hypotheses, must be related

2. W. Pannenberg, *Anthropology in Theological Perspective* (Philadelphia: Westminster Press, 1985), 18.

3. See J. S. Wicken, "Theology and Science in the Evolving Cosmos: A Need for Dialogue," *Zygon* 23, no. 1 (1988): 49.

4. See Pannenberg, *Anthropology,* 19f.

5. W. Pannenberg, "The Doctrine of Creation and Modern Science," *Zygon* 23, no. 1 (1988): 3f.

to scientific reasoning as such.[6] Determining whether this is possible or not is what this essay is all about.

Philosophy of Science and the Epistemological Claims of Theology

In the light of the problem of rationality in theology and in science, it is quite clear that no theologian dealing with these issues can evade the questions of the epistemological status and validity of theological statements in terms of contemporary philosophy of science. Although there have always been theologians who questioned the nature of theological thought, few contemporary ones have purposefully taken up the challenge of justifying theology within the wider context of philosophy of science.

In the context of current discussions of these problems, the lead was undoubtedly taken by Wolfhart Pannenberg, who has opted, from a concern with problems specifically raised by the philosophy of science, for a patently argumentative theology[7] rather than any form of dogmatistic *axiomatic theology* based on the preconceived and unquestionable certainties so typical of positivism. Pannenberg has always been remarkably outspoken about systematic theological models in which the critical question of theorizing in theology is totally neglected. In such models, a particular concept of revelation may so uncritically and ideologically assume an authoritarian character that it consciously rejects any critical examination or justification.

The fundamental reasons for his broad approach may be found in the earliest development of his thought, long before his well-known book on the nature of theological science.[8] In "Die Krise der Schriftprinzips,"[9] Pannenberg already makes the point that systematic theology is always shaped by the tension between two seemingly divergent

---

6. Pannenberg, "Doctrine of Creation," 7.

7. See Wentzel van Huyssteen, *Teologie van die Rede* (Kampen: J. H. Kok, 1970).

8. Pannenberg, *Wissenschaftstheorie.*

9. W. Pannenberg, "Die Krise des Schriftprinzips," in *Grundfragen Systematischer Theologie. Gesammelte Aufsätze* (Göttingen: Van den Hoeck and Ruprecht, 1967), 11-12.

trends. We recognize, on the one hand, theology's commitment to its religious source, namely God as revealed in Jesus Christ and testified to by Holy Scripture, and on the other, theology's assumption that it has a universal character, transcending all specific themes as it strives towards truth itself (precisely because it would make statements about God). This universality emanates from the fact that reality, in its all-encompassing totality as God's creation, not only is dependent upon and committed to God, but is in its profoundest sense incomprehensible without God.[10]

In Pannenberg's view it goes without saying that theology is ultimately, fully, and most profoundly concerned with God's revelation in Jesus Christ. Precisely as God's revelation, however, that revelation can be properly understood only if we realize that all knowledge and anything we might regard as "true" or as "the truth" must have some bearing on that revelation. As the Creator, God not only is creatively responsible for everything in our reality, but is greater than our present, created reality. Therefore, any aspect of that reality is correctly (albeit provisionally) understood only in relation to God's final revelation.

Given the universality of the concept of God as logically implied in the concept of creation, Pannenberg has consistently maintained that systematic theology can never fall back on a *special* and epistemologically isolated *revelationist position*. It has therefore always been clear to him that theology could never exist purely as a "positive church theology," isolated from the other sciences. Although such a *ghetto theology* might ensure an unproblematic coexistence with philosophy of science and the other sciences, it would have a radically negative impact on the universality implicit in the concept of God.

In the broad spectrum of theological disciplines, systematic theology in particular is directly concerned with this universal perspective. As such, it is committed to facing the problem of rationality. This raises the question of the broad fundamentals that theology shares with other sciences and of what constitutes the unique character of theological reflection. In addition, systematic theology becomes the area in which theology itself must be able to account critically for its own credibility and for the validity of its conceptual paradigm.

Specifically for the sake of the truth of the Christian message, sys-

10. Pannenberg, "Krise des Schriftprinzips," 11.

tematic theology must take up the task of formulating and founding its concept of science in a confrontation with the perceptions of contemporary philosophy of science, and thus with alternative concepts of the nature of science. For the sake of its intellectual integrity, theology can on no credible grounds claim *privilege* in its pursuit of truth. If it did try to claim such a privileged position, it would be able to do so only by founding its thematics on arbitrary, irrational, or authoritarian grounds. This tactic would in turn become the target of renewed criticism of theology itself.

In his debate with philosophy of science, Wolfhart Pannenberg scrutinizes logical positivism and its pervasive effect on diverse scientific disciplines and pointedly rejects both the positivist unitary ideal for all sciences and the positivist influence that causes science to be constantly oriented and formulated on the model of the natural or "mature" sciences.[11]

Ultimately, however, Pannenberg's relationship with critical rationalism and with Kuhn's paradigm theory will be crucial to an evaluation of his views of theology and science. Although critical rationalism undoubtedly had a decisive influence on his thought and he consistently reveals links with Popper's thought, it is Thomas Kuhn's paradigm theory, in particular, that has guided him in the later phase of his enquiry. In his reflections on the nature and identity of theology he sought to liberate systematic theology not only from the one-sided demands of a positivist concept of truth, but also from a too rigorous falsification criterion of critical rationalism, precisely in order to leave room for a claim to "scientific" validity in theological statements and theories. Whether Pannenberg has in fact succeeded in doing so, and how these various elements of his thought are interrelated, will have to be closely examined.

First, Pannenberg points out that Karl Popper, in his attempt to find a meaningful demarcation criterion that would transcend the one-sidedness of the positivist verifiability criterion, gave a central place to the falsifiability of theories in his model of the philosophy of science.[12] In doing so, Popper was looking not merely for a way to separate science and metaphysics, but also for a broad criterion by which the social

11. Pannenberg, *Wissenschaftstheorie*, 28ff.
12. Pannenberg, *Wissenschaftstheorie*, 43.

sciences would be able to subject their hypotheses and theories to the falsification test.[13] Having outlined the well-known arguments by Bartley, Pannenberg proceeds to discuss further themes from critical rationalism without coming back specifically to the demands of Bartley's pancritical rationalism. However, it is clear that Pannenberg is strongly concerned about Bartley's sharp criticism of theology, namely that it too readily falls back on an irrational fideistic premise as a final basis for argument. In an evaluation of Pannenberg's theoretical model we shall have to consider whether he has in fact avoided having his own thought definitively structured by the critical rationalist model. The crucial question will be to what extent Bartley's demand for a *commitment to noncommitment* has determined Pannenberg's development of his own answer to the question of objectivity and truth in theology and science.

In the context of examining the origin of theological statements, these problems will come to a head as we proceed to ask critical questions about the role and function of the theologian's own conceptualized subjective *commitment*. At this stage we may begin to pose a central critical question to Pannenberg: *How does he justify his view of the role of the theologian's personal religious commitment in the process of theorizing in theology, and his definition of truth and objectivity in theology and science?*

In a discussion of the possibility of justification in theology, Pannenberg examines in detail the main demands of critical rationalism.[14] Our purpose is to determine not only the nature of the model of rationality Pannenberg adopts, but also its origins. In this regard, it is important to appreciate that Pannenberg follows Popper in his view that inductive reasoning and the principle of verification offer us no solution to the question of scientific knowledge. A general rule is always applicable to an infinite number of instances; however, only a limited number of those infinite instances can be known at any given time. In Popper's view, therefore, generalizations can never claim absolute certainty, and for that reason the strict verification of postulated general laws is also impossible.

The basic propositions that must now act as objective criteria in the

13. Pannenberg, *Wissenschaftstheorie,* 44ff.
14. Pannenberg, *Wissenschaftstheorie,* 52ff.

process of scientific thought (and in terms of which falsification might be possible), however, must be testable on an intersubjective level, according to the principles of critical rationalism. An examination of critical rationalism will show that, with Popper, the old positivist ideal of value-free, objective knowledge has been turned into intersubjective correspondence. *Objectivity* thus becomes the characteristic of a certain group (realized by mutual criticism), a social matter that can no longer be founded purely on so-called a-theoretical, self-evident "facts."

In this sense, basic propositions are data accepted on the grounds of a group's decision or agreement and may therefore also be called *convictions.*[15] The very objectivity operating here as a criterion is, however, dependent on the group that accepts it as objective, and would therefore also be subject to change.

Pannenberg makes the further point that the implications of this type of consideration make it very difficult to distinguish absolutely between scientific and metaphysical statements.[16] In fact, if the concepts and language in which experiences are scientifically described are a matter of convention, there can be no compelling reasons for presumptuously barring the concept of God from the exclusive circle of scientifically admissible statements. Pannenberg argues that Popper's concept of the theory-ladenness of all observation, and his acknowledgement of the conventional nature of so-called objective statements, must ultimately lead to failure in Popper's attempts to draw sharp distinctions between scientific and metaphysical statements. In Pannenberg's view, scientific statements are thus in themselves ultimately founded on general worldviews of a profoundly philosophical and/or religious nature.

This in itself implies, as Thomas S. Kuhn was to demonstrate so clearly, that hypotheses cannot be empirically tested within the framework of theoretically neutral observations. All testing must form part of a process Kuhn calls *paradigm articulation.* In the terms of philosophy of science I would put it as follows: The personal involvement of the scientist, in the paradigm out of which he or she lives and works, always plays a role, not only in the so-called context of discovery, but also in the context of justification.

---

15. K. Popper, *The Logic of Scientific Discovery* (London: Hutchinson, 1968), 106.
16. Pannenberg, *Wissenschaftstheorie,* 56.

This conclusion Pannenberg reached in his own fashion, and in my view correctly, as far as critical rationalism is concerned. This shows Pannenberg's[17] spiritual affinity with Thomas S. Kuhn's thought. Kuhn pointed out that even in the natural sciences the testing of hypotheses does not normally consist of direct attempts to falsify them, but of comparisons of the capacities of various theories for providing meaningful solutions to certain problems.[18] Pannenberg would agree here that the capacity for integrating and giving meaning to available data, and thus for providing solutions to puzzles, is the primary principle in the testing of both strictly scientific and theological hypotheses.

Therefore Pannenberg, partly under Kuhn's influence, opts for a rationality model that attempts to transcend the bounds of critical rationalism in order to allow for critical enquiry on a much wider front. We may now assess his view of the epistemological status and validity of theological statements and the extent to which critical rationalism determines his own conceptual model.

Theological Statements as Hypotheses

Pannenberg's debate with critical rationalism has had a lasting impact on the evolution of his own thought regarding the nature of theological science. In particular, Bartley's[19] and Albert's[20] criticisms of theology infuse his thinking on this theme. Albert's reproach that systematic theologians fall back too readily on a supposedly unique and esoteric epistemology as an ideological immunization against criticism, and Bartley's related reproach that theologians evade critical scientific questions by retreating to an irrational position of faith, ultimately become the focal points of Pannenberg's attempt to for-

17. Pannenberg, *Wissenschaftstheorie*, 57-60.

18. T. S. Kuhn, *The Structure of Scientific Revolutions* (Chicago: University of Chicago Press, 1970), 192.

19. W. W. Bartley, *The Retreat to Commitment* (London: Chatto and Windus, 1964), 215f.

20. H. Albert, *Trakat über kritische Vernunft* (Tübingen: J. C. B. Mohr [Paul Siebeck], 1968), 104ff.

mulate a credible theory of theology.[21] Pannenberg rejects out of hand any authoritarian axiomatic theology that uncritically takes its stand on prepostulated dogmatic certainties, which he sees typified in Karl Barth's positivist revelatory response to the demands Heinrich Scholz had made of systematic theology. Thus Pannenberg could state that if the reality of God and God's revelation or the liberating act of God through Jesus Christ is to function epistemologically as a preestablished datum in theological theorizing (and thus as a theological premise), theology can no longer be concerned with knowledge or science, but merely with the systematic description or exposition of what might be regarded as the "true dogma" or "proper doctrine" of a church.[22]

If the premises of such a theology are finally exposed to criticism it is, ironically, its very conception of God and revelation that stands exposed as a subjective and arbitrary mental construct. Pannenberg rightly objects to any such reduction of the object of theology to the religious consciousness of the believer. An allegedly direct theological premise in God and God's revelation offers no escape from this problem.

Clearly, Pannenberg believes that creditable theological argument is possible only if one acknowledges that no theologian can formulate meaningful statements without being involved, somehow, in the epistemological question of the criteria for truth. This is the case because theological statements aim to be meaningful, valid, and comprehensible, and also to lay a provisional claim to truth and reality-depiction.

This implies, however, that theological statements purport to be testable in principle, even if it does not require that they must be confined to a specific form of testing.[23] For Pannenberg, then, the fact that theological statements claim to be true, and therefore (logically) try to exclude untruth, implies that such statements, too, must come within the ambit of rational criteria. And for Pannenberg the concept of "hypothesis" also belongs in this context.

Pannenberg sees as hypotheses only those assertions that, as statements on a particular issue, are distinguishable from the issue as

---

21. See Wentzel van Huyssteen, *Theology and the Justification of Faith: The Construction of Theories in Systematic Theology* (Grand Rapids: Wm. B. Eerdmans, 1988), 95ff.

22. Pannenberg, *Wissenschaftstheorie*, 271.

23. Pannenberg, *Wissenschaftstheorie*, 277.

such.[24] The hypothetical nature of assertions implies that any given assertion may be true or false, and thus also implies the possibility for checking or testing. Pannenberg maintains that logical positivism was quite correct on this point, except, of course, in its one-sided restriction of examination to a particular type of testing, namely that of sensory observation.[25] In principle, however, it remains true that an assertion that cannot be tested, at least in principle, cannot be a valid assertion.

This brings us to Pannenberg's typically *realist* claims. In terms of the contemporary debate in philosophy of science, theological statements (and even statements of faith) are not merely expressions of a certain religious commitment, but contain an *element of assertion,* reality depiction, or reference, which is needed to make such a commitment possible. Even the simple assertion *I believe* makes sense only if there is Someone to believe in. In my view Pannenberg is therefore justified in concluding that all statements of faith in this sense have a *cognitive* core.

Given the logical implications of assertions, the questions philosophy of science asks about the epistemological status of theological statements must culminate in the question of the object of systematic theology. At this point the question whether theology in fact has an object leads naturally to the question of the testability of theological assertions, which for Pannenberg means testability of the claims to truth in theological statements.

Pannenberg rightly suggests that this confronts the theologian with the most rigorous demand of all.[26] Conscious of Bartley's and Albert's stringently rationalistic criticism, he maintains that the systematic theologian dare not evade this most strict of all epistemological demands by retreating to an irrational religious commitment. Any such immunization of theological premises against criticism must ultimately rebound on the systematic theologian with redoubled force, since the very statements he or she makes could then no longer be taken seriously.

24. W. Pannenberg, "Antwort auf Gerhard Sauters Überlegungen," *Evangelische Theologie* 40, no. 2 (1980): 171.

25. W. Pannenberg, "Wie war ist das Reden von Gott?" in S. Daecke and N. Janowski, eds., *Grundlagen der Theologie* (Stuttgart: Kohnhammer, 1974), 31.

26. Pannenberg, *Wissenschaftstheorie*, 34.

The Object of Theology: God as a Problem

In reply to the question about a specific and coherent object-field for theology, Pannenberg would answer without hesitation: theology is the science of God.[27] In fact, Christian faith obviously depends entirely on God's reality, and therefore no systematic theology could be satisfied with regarding itself as a limited, narrow *science of Christianity*. To Pannenberg this would be unacceptable in terms of both religious and cultural history. Systematic theology cannot evade the question of the implication of its statements: God reveals God as a reality and as such forms the object of theology. Theology must examine the truth of these statements precisely because they are hypotheses.

Given the universal implications of the concept of God, theology as a science of God has no finally demarcated field of study or "object-area." Furthermore, God as object provides the intrinsic structural unity of theology. A difficult question remains, however: Is it in any way possible to test theological statements, whether as direct or as indirect assertions, about God? After all, assertions about God cannot be tested against their immediate object, not only because the reality of God has become so problematic in our time, but also because it would surely contradict God's divinity if God became a *present object*, accessible to human scrutiny. Clearly, assertions about God cannot be tested against their purported object. For Pannenberg the question of God's reality, and thus also the question of the truth of Christianity, can be posed only within the broader framework of a science having as its theme not only Christianity or the Christian faith, but the reality of God.

For Pannenberg this becomes possible in the context of a theology of religions that transcends the narrower bounds of theology as the science of Christianity.[28] Therefore any theologian sensitive to the questions asked by contemporary philosophy of science realizes not only that the concept of God forms the thematic focus of all his or her enquiries but also that God, as a problematic concept, has in fact become the object of a wider critical theology.[29] In his formulation of such a premise for systematic theology, and in his identifying an object for

---

27. Pannenberg, *Wissenschaftstheorie*, 299f.
28. Pannenberg, *Wissenschaftstheorie*, 229.
29. Pannenberg, *Wissenschaftstheorie*, 301.

systematic theology, Pannenberg consistently takes serious note of Bartley's and Albert's critical-rationalist repudiation of any subjectivistic,
fideistic religious commitment.

The critical question that must be put to Pannenberg at this point
is whether making "God as a problem" the premise for theology really
meets the concerns of critical rationalism. It seems that what we have
here, especially in the so-called context of justification, is merely a
concession to Bartley's and Albert's criticism and (especially to Bartley's
commitment to noncommitment.) This concession, however, not only
fails to solve the problem of a fideistic axiomatic theology, but ultimately
also fails to confront the vital question of the intrinsic role of the
theologian's subjectivity (his or her *ultimate commitment* and its conceptualization) in the theorizing of theological reflection. These problems play a crucial role in the development of Pannenberg's model for
theology and can, in my view, be attributed directly to the conflict
between the influence of critical rationalism and the influence of
Kuhnian elements in his thought.

We have seen that, for Pannenberg, the conception of God as object
of theology links directly with the problematic role of the concept of
God in our wider experiential world. For him — at least in the first,
broad phase of his theology — God can therefore be the object of theology only as a problem, not as an established datum.

But can this problematic concept of God be defined more closely,
or does it remain an abstract hypothesis in theology, untestable against
the object of its statements? According to Pannenberg, that concept can
in fact be defined more closely. The fact that reality is totally dependent
on God (if God is indeed really God) is, after all, a minimum requirement for the concept of God. For that reason Pannenberg can give more
content to the hypothesis of God, maintaining that if God is real, God
must be the all-determining reality. And although the concept of God
can in itself not be tested or verified directly against its object, it is in
fact possible to assess that concept in terms of its own implications.
Thus the concept of God, which as a hypothesis includes the idea of
God as an all-determining reality, becomes testable by its implications
for human experience of reality.[30]

In Pannenberg's view, the concept of God that would ultimately be

30. Pannenberg, *Wissenschaftstheorie*, 302.

most successful and solve the most problems in the meaningful integration of human experience would be the one that had validated itself convincingly. Assertions about God are, therefore, testable by their implications for our experience and understanding of reality.[31] Such assertions are testable by analyzing whether their content does indeed give maximal sense and meaning to our present, finite reality. Pannenberg's approach very much concerns the "theology and science" debate, for it implies that nothing in our finite reality can be fully understood outside its relationship to the living God. Obversely, one might expect this concept of divine reality to open up a much more profound understanding of all that exists, to provide knowledge that would have been impossible without it.

Insofar as both of these demands could be met, Pannenberg maintains, one might speak of a validation of theological statements. This justification is done not by criteria alien to the concept of God, but through a kind of proof provided by God. But since our knowledge of surrounding reality is incomplete and unrefined, and since our experience of it is tentative and ambivalent, the concept of God remains (in terms of philosophy of science) a mere hypothesis. Given the finite and tentative nature of our theological choices, the concept of God can therefore never be finally justified by our experience of ourselves and of the world.

Pannenberg thus maintains[32] that we can never abandon "truth," which functions as a regulative principle at the end of an indefinite process of enquiry.[33] And since truth (in both theology and science) is accessible only in anticipation, science cannot exclude the broader context of history nor, ultimately, of philosophy and theology.

This brings us to the essence of Pannenberg's thesis: Since in our time access to the concept of God is no longer direct and self-evident, it can be achieved only indirectly, through our human self-concept and our experiential relationship with surrounding reality.[34]

---

31. See B. J. Walsh, "A Critical Review of Pannenberg's *Anthropology in Theological Perspective*," *Christian Scholar's Review* 15, no. 3 (1986): 248.

32. Pannenberg, "Wie war ist das Reden von Gott?" 36.

33. See J. V. Apcynski, "Truth in Religion: A Polanyian Appraisal of Wolfhart Pannenberg's Theological Program," *Zygon* 17, no. 1 (1982): 54.

34. See Pannenberg, *Anthropology,* 15f.

By this means Pannenberg sought to develop a problem range within which theological statements might be evaluated (hence the so-called context of justification for theology). Assertions about God (for instance about God as the Creator) may therefore be measured, on the one hand, against the handed-down ideas that have accumulated within a certain religious doctrine of creation, and on the other hand, against the problems confronting such inherited concepts (like the doctrine of creation) in terms of the natural sciences and of the philosophy of science in our time.

Rationality and Ultimate Commitment

The influence of Bartley's criticism and pointed rejection of any retreat to commitment is clearly evident in Pannenberg's development of his own conceptual model. For Pannenberg, divine revelation cannot be pre-annexed by any particular religion, and set up against others as the only true revelation. Only a religious option that had in advance immunized itself against all critical reflection[35] could unproblematically identify God's revelation with its own religious tradition, and set it up as an absolute against all other traditions.

This brings us to the most problematic element of Pannenberg's epistemology. Although he shares Thomas S. Kuhn's view of the paradigmatic determination of our thought, he seems to remain caught up in the critical rationalist demand for a specific noncommitment in the evaluation of theories in the so-called context of justification. Ultimately, this provides no means of thematizing, and even less of resolving, the problem of the role of the theologian's subjective religious commitment in the construction of his or her theories.

On this point Pannenberg concedes that theology, like all other sciences, does not approach its object without presuppositions or values, as a kind of *tabula rasa*.[36] Theologians obviously tackle their subject with a certain interest, which also implies opinions and presuppositions that may relate to the religious communities to which they belong. They

35. Pannenberg, *Wissenschaftstheorie*, 322.
36. Pannenberg, *Wissenschaftstheorie*, 323.

may even be Christians, which might either stimulate questioning or act as a restraint on the unbiased evaluation of their object and their own tradition.

Against this background, Pannenberg could say that the theologian's subjective religious commitment may fall in the *context of discovery*, but definitely not in the *context of justification*.[37] His conception of the context of discovery is the all-inclusive historico-sociological framework that produces a certain science; the context of justification, on the other hand, is the objective theoretical framework within which specific criteria have an explanatory and evaluatory function in respect of theological statements. Confusing the two contexts, for example by converting a personal religious commitment into the premise for rational argument (and at the same time claiming intersubjective validity for that argument), is in Pannenberg's view a fatal mistake.

This attempt by Pannenberg to claim objective criteria for a scientific theology's context of justification is, on the one hand, a clear echo of Bartley's *"people can be engaged without being committed,"*[38] and thus reveals the lasting effect of critical rationalism on the structure of Pannenberg's thought.[39] Nevertheless, Pannenberg himself had earlier pointed out that this would make critical rationalism untrue to its own principles: basic or objective criteria in terms of which testing (and therefore falsification) becomes possible must surely be testable intersubjectively, according to the principles of critical rationalism. By failing to recognize this, Popper allowed the old positivist ideal of value-free, objective knowledge to be surreptitiously twisted into intersubjective correspondence. In critical rationalism, therefore, objectivity ultimately becomes a conventional matter, no longer dependent on so-called a-theoretical facts. In fact, Pannenberg pointed out that the allegedly "objective" basic propositions of critical rationalism could be seen as conventions precisely because of their intersubjective determination. He also noted that the implications of that determination made it impossible to draw such sharp critical rationalistic distinctions between scientific and metaphysical statements.[40]

37. Pannenberg, *Wissenschaftstheorie*, 323.
38. Bartley, 217.
39. See also Apczynski, 52ff.
40. Pannenberg, *Wissenschaftstheorie*, 54ff.

Thus Pannenberg concedes not only that the nature and origins of scientific and of theological statements are rooted in the socio-cultural context of the individual researcher (the context of discovery), but also that theological statements as such (the context of justification) are founded indirectly on general worldviews. In my view such statements are also deeply rooted in the scientist's subjective religious commitment.

Two points can be made about Pannenberg's attempt to separate the theologian's subjective commitment from the theoretical *context of justification*. First, he has abandoned Thomas S. Kuhn's concept of paradigm articulation, for which he had formerly opted and which now confronts his own demand for a context of justification without a personal commitment. Second, he has shunned the problematic question of how the theorizing implied by the theologian's subjective religious commitment may be revealed (not to mention somehow temporarily suspended) and rationally accounted for, precisely to prevent its becoming an uncritical and irrational immunization tactic in critical reasoning.

Pannenberg's intentions are clear: to conceive the theological enterprise — different as it might be from the other sciences — as fundamentally continuous with empirical science. What is then needed here is an analysis of the shaping of rationality in both theology and in science. As far as theology goes, we must point out that a pretheoretical commitment cannot simply be equated with irrational religious choices. On the contrary, the form in which that commitment manifests itself in religious statements and viewpoints must be exposed to critical argument. If that is done, the question of the relationship between our scientific statements again becomes the focus of our enquiry. Only thus will it become clear that a personal religious commitment does not necessarily (*contra* Bartley and Pannenberg) imply "unscientific" or irrational thought.

In this reaction to the way the concept of revelation is formulated and abused in most forms of confessional theology (as immunization against criticism), Pannenberg tries to follow the wider program of a comparative theology of religions. He even maintains that such a theology is ultimately based on the tradition of biblical Christianity.[41] A definitive, final vindication or justification of theological statements is, however, unattainable, and is even sharply distinct from the nature of

41. Pannenberg, *Wissenschaftstheorie*, 326.

pretheoretical religious certainty. On the other hand, a provisional vindication of theological hypotheses may be attained inasmuch as they may lend (at least tentatively) maximal meaning and clarity to our experiences. In my view, however, such provisional vindication of theological statements and theories is possible only if we can think from a paradigm that enables us to handle such criteria. This must also be founded on a paradigm choice that cannot be suspended temporarily and theoretically but that refers consciously to a critically responsible basic conviction or religious commitment.

From the above it follows that the theologian's personal commitment, if rightly understood and credibly accounted for in terms of contemporary philosophy of science, need not stand in the way of a scientifically acceptable model of rationality for theology. Although Pannenberg (in my opinion) does not account for the role of the theologian's personal religious commitment in theological theorizing, his incisive and highly original debate with contemporary philosophy of science enables us to pursue this discussion with greater confidence and credibility.

Conclusion

The theologian must realize that the questions raised by religious reflection are not those raised by science. Accepting that different kinds of knowledge are involved in the practices of science and theology, and that neither can provide the content of the other's knowledge, does not mean *that they do not inform the context within which their respective knowledge is to be constructed.*[42] In this sense, Pannenberg rightly claims that science provides an essentially incomplete epistemology for understanding nature. However, the claim that scientific data contain a further and theologically relevant dimension should never be rooted in the search for the line where science ends and where theology begins, for this is the wrong question.[43]

---

42. See Eileen Barker, "Science as Theology: The Theological Functioning of Western Science," in *The Sciences and Theology in the Twentieth Century* (Notre Dame: University of Notre Dame Press, 1981), 276.
43. See Wicken, 49.

The epistemological problem of claiming a theologically relevant dimension for scientific data reveals the common adherence of theology and all other sciences to the problem of rationality, as we have seen. This problem compels the theologian and the believing scientist to deal with the role and function of an ultimate religious commitment in the construction of theories in both theology and science. It also challenges us to evaluate the role of justification and explanation in both theology and science.

The relationship between *explanatory power* and *truth* has always been a central issue in the understanding of science.[44] Philosophers of science have also convincingly pointed out that there can be no undisputed and monolithic notions of "reality" or of "explanation" in science; the objects of our interest dictate not only different strategies, but also different views on what could be regarded as adequate forms of explanation. But the central questions remain: Does theology exhibit a rationality comparable to the rationality of science, and how plausible can an explanatory justification of the cognitive claims of theology be?

I think that the rationality of science and theology is in each case determined by certain goals and criteria, that is, by certain epistemic values. In both theology and science, whatever their other differences might be, the supreme value that determines rationality seems to be *intelligibility*. What is real for theology and for science is not the observable but the intelligible,[45] and in both theology and science beliefs and practices are attempts to understand at the deepest level, where understanding can be construed as seeking the best explanation.[46] What is at stake, therefore, is not only the general epistemic status of religious belief, but also the implications this will have for the epistemic and rational integrity of theological discourse as such.

At the same time, the high degree of personal involvement, that is, of faith and commitment in religion and theology will present a very special challenge to any theory of rationality meant to apply to both

44. E. McMullin, "Explanatory Success and the Truth of Theory," in Nicholas Rescher, ed., *Scientific Inquiry in Philosophical Perspective* (New York: Lanham, 1986), 52.

45. See Ian G. Barbour, *Issues in Science and Religion* (New York: Harper and Row, 1971), 170.

46. See Wayne Proudfoot, *Religious Experience* (Berkeley: University of California Press, 1985), 43.

theology and science. Because of this personal dimension, the contextuality of religious experience, and the cognitive claims that arise from this, I would argue for a theory of rationality in theology that encompasses both *experiential adequacy* and *epistemological adequacy.*

The central role of experience and explanation in the justification of the cognitive claims of theology finally implies that the very important distinctions between *commitments, an ultimate commitment, beliefs,* and *religious faith* should always be maintained. I am also convinced that no strong form of justification is possible for a commitment to an ultimate commitment (that is, the search for maximal meaning in life), outside of the way of life in which that commitment plays a part. This is no retreat to irrationalism, because experiential and epistemological adequacy (and not justified certainty) makes a commitment and its resulting beliefs and propositions valid and responsible. This suggests that the beliefs that are implied in a commitment should in principle always be open to criticism. This does not go against what could be called the certainty of faith from the perspective of religious experience. It does, however, imply a highly critical sensitivity towards the construction of theories in theology and certainly prevents any form of dogmatism in theological theorizing.

In a critical realist model of rationality in theology, the beliefs implied in a commitment to an ultimate religious commitment could never be justified by any foundationalist doctrine of justification. However, it might indeed be possible to provide good or adequate reasons for *not* giving up a commitment and its implied propositional beliefs. Beliefs are therefore never just the "frills on a commitment,"[47] but can in a process of explanatory progress offer good reasons why it would make more sense (i.e., be more rational) to be committed to a certain way of life than not to be committed to it. In this sense there is no contrast between scientific and religious beliefs, nor between a commitment to realism in science or a commitment to critical realism in theology.

We could therefore say that all commitments must involve beliefs (are propositional), which might eventually turn out to be true or false. On this view — which is also my own — it is therefore not enough to

47. See R. Trigg, *Reason and Commitment* (Cambridge: Cambridge University Press, 1977), 36.

maintain that beliefs have a "truth" that is relative only to a group, a society, or a conceptual system. Obviously a conceptual framework or paradigm could involve beliefs that are only true within this context, but eventually we are confronted with the meaningfulness or provisional truth of the paradigm as such, as well as being committed to a certain set of beliefs. Such a commitment should be based on beliefs that are themselves external to the system. This is what I tried to indicate throughout as *epistemological adequacy:* beliefs that function as criteria for rationality or epistemic values in a critical realist approach to theorizing in theology and in science.

Post-Kuhnian philosophy of science has shown us that there can be no sharp line of demarcation between scientific rationality and other forms of rationality.[48] In fact, rationality in science relates to the "reasonableness" of a more basic kind of rationality that informs all goal-directed action. Within this broader context, theology seeks as secure a knowledge as it can achieve, a knowledge that will allow us to understand and, where possible, to construct theories as better explanations. In the end this epistemic goal of theology will determine the shaping of rationality in theology. And if in both theology and science we want to understand better and explain better, then surely the rationality of science in the broader sense is directly relevant to the rationality of theology. This epistemological consonance between theology and the other sciences thus suggests what it might mean for theology to demonstrate that the data as described by the sciences are provisional versions of reality and that the data themselves contain a further and theologically relevant dimension.

48. See Wentzel van Huyssteen, *Teologie as Kritiese Geloofsverantwoording* (Pretoria: RGN, 1986), 63ff.

Chapter Four

Is the Postmodernist Always a Postfoundationalist? Nancey Murphy's Lakatosian Model for Theology

M ODERN THOUGHT HAS LEFT THOSE OF US WHO DO THEOLOGY WITH little or no choice when it comes to finding a plausible methodological starting point for contemporary theological reflection. Whether we like it or not, we have all become part of modernity's "flight from authority."[1] This obviously implies liberating ourselves from all the different types of foundationalisms that we have learned to associate with the broad spectrum of biblical, traditional/revelational, and doctrinal authorities that used to be so "helpful" and readily available in attempts to justify the truth of our theological claims.

The flight from authority in modern thought coincided with a rediscovery of the role of religious experience in theological reflection. Wayne Proudfoot has recently argued that ever since the Enlightenment theologians and scholars of religion have increasingly come to depend on the concept of religious experience.[2] Religion, of course, has always been an experiential matter and never just a set of doctrinal or credal statements, or a cluster of rites and rituals. The biggest challenge for

---

1. Jeffrey Stout, *The Flight from Authority: Religion, Morality, and the Quest for Autonomy* (Notre Dame: University of Notre Dame Press, 1981).

2. Wayne Proudfoot, *Religious Experience* (Berkeley: University of California Press, 1985).

nonfoundationalist thought, however, will be to retrieve religious experience as a valid methodological starting point for theological reflection. As philosophical theologians, we might want to phrase the question as follows: Is it possible to construct an imaginative approach to theological reflection that begins with ordinary human experience, explores possible "signals of transcendence"[3] to be found in it, and then from there moves on to explanatory religious affirmations about the nature of reality?

The way these problems have now been phrased raises questions about the either/or of foundationalism vs. nonfoundationalism, and reveals that here we not only are dealing with modernity's challenges to theological reflection, but have in fact already moved into the even more complex challenge of contemporary postmodern thought. For the theologian this challenge translates into the following questions:

> Do we still have good reasons to remain convinced that the Christian message does indeed provide the most adequate interpretation and explanation of one's experience with God, of the world, and of one's self?
>
> If so, would these reasons be epistemological, ethical, or pragmatic?
> Does it still make sense within a postmodern context to be committed to the fact that the universe as we have come to know it ultimately makes sense in the light of Sinai and Calvary?[4]

Such a faith commitment would at least have to be able to show convincingly that it never implies being irrational or authoritarian, or intolerant towards other views of the world. This requirement arises not only in a postmodern world, but also in a world that has been fundamentally changed by an all-pervasive scientific culture.

For theology today, an all-important focus of its dialogue with contemporary culture is not only the challenge of moving beyond the insular comfort of theological foundationalism, but also and precisely its uneasy relationship with the sciences. In fact, as theologians we are now confronted with a double challenge.

3. Peter Berger, *The Heretical Imperative: Contemporary Possibilities of Religious Affirmation* (New York: Anchor Books, 1980), ix.

4. See Berger, 165.

First, we have to deal with the postmodern trilemma of trying to keep together, in a meaningful whole, a sense of continuity and tradition, a respect for and celebration of pluralism, and a resistance to any form of authoritarian (also epistemological) domination.[5] This challenge does not call for a benign balancing act, but rather for a serious engagement, which may entail a radical revisioning of the way we theorize about our most basic Christian commitments.

Second, postmodern thought challenges us again to explore the presupposed continuity between Christian theology and the general human enterprise of understanding the world rationally. Much of contemporary theological reflection has been shaped decisively by postmodernism's fragmentation, indeterminacy, and intense distrust of all universal or "totalizing" discourses.[6] Not only theology, however, but also postmodern philosophy of science has moved away quite dramatically from positivist and technocentric conceptions of scientific rationality, with its resulting beliefs in linear progress, absolute truths, and the standardization of knowledge. Joseph Rouse[7] has argued for a postmodern philosophy of science that, along with feminist readings of science, joins trust in local scientific practice with suspicion toward any global interpretation of science that claims to legitimize that trust.

Postmodern thought in both theology and science thus centers around the radical rejection of all dominating global narratives of legitimation, and as a result embraces pluralism and diversity. A crucial and increasingly controversial theme throughout the development of twentieth-century philosophy of science has been the justification for interpreting the history of science in terms of a modernist story of progress or rational development.[8] Postmodern philosophy of science highlights this by its combination of respect for the local context of inquiry and a resistance to any global interpretation of science that could constrain local inquiry. At the same time, of course, it raises serious political issues by sharply focusing on the autonomy and cultural authority of the

5. See Mark Kline Taylor, *Remembering Esperanza: A Cultural-Political Theology for North American Praxis* (New York: Orbis, 1990), 31ff.

6. See David Harvey, *The Condition of Postmodernity* (Oxford: Basil Blackwell, 1989), 9f.

7. Joseph Rouse, "The Politics of Postmodern Philosophy of Science," *Philosophy of Science* 58 (1991).

8. See Rouse, 610.

sciences. The concern to uphold the political autonomy and cultural authority of successful scientific practice is part of the modernist legacy of logical positivism, which had always claimed the epistemic and cultural primacy of mathematical physics by showing that mathematics exemplified the very structure of rational thought, and that sense experience can be the only basis for knowledge of the world.[9]

Postmodernism's embracing of pluralism, and the resulting rejection of grand metanarratives that supposedly globally legitimize the cultural dominance of scientific thought, indeed has serious implications for the theology and science discussion. The fundamental question, "Is postmodern religious dialogue possible today?"[10] now translates into an even more complex question: Is any meaningful dialogue between postmodern philosophy of science and postmodern theology possible, or does the pluralism and localization of postmodern discourse (once more!) confront theologians, philosophers, and scientists who share some common quest for human understanding with near complete epistemological incommensurability? Disturbingly enough, some postmodern theologians seem to accept just this in their enthusiastic embracing of a postmodernism of reaction[11] that calls for a "post-liberal" return to orthodox or neo-orthodox epistemic values and confessional traditions. This should alert us to the fact that postmodernism is a complex phenomenon and that no position in either theology or philosophy of science — just because it claims to be postmodern — should be accepted uncritically. Postmodernism challenges theologians to account for the fact of Christianity[12] and to rediscover the explanatory role of religious experience in postfoundationalist theology. In this sense the postmodern theological project is to reaffirm and revision faith in God without abandoning the powers of reason.[13] Obviously this will imply a careful revisioning of what "powers of reason" might

9. See Wentzel van Huyssteen, *Theology and the Justification of Faith: Constructing Theories in Systematic Theology* (Grand Rapids: Wm B. Eerdmans, 1989), 3-10; Rouse, 613.

10. See Gary L. Comstock, "Is Postmodern Religious Dialogue Possible?" *Faith and Philosophy* 6, no. 2 (1989): 189ff.

11. See Peter C. Hodgson, *God in History: Shapes of Freedom* (Nashville: Abingdon, 1989), 29.

12. See P. G. R. De Villiers, "The End of Hermeneutics? On New Testament Studies and Postmodernism," *Neotestamentica* 25, no. 1 (1991): 155.

13. See Harvey, 41.

mean today, and of the values that shape theological and scientific rationality in a postmodern world.

At this point it should now be clear that the postmodern challenge to the theology and science dialogue invites a serious and critical countercritique: If postmodern thought's anti-metanarrative stance is equated with an uncritical bias towards the broader epistemological problem of the shaping of rationality in religious reflection, a few epistemological eyebrows should be raised. Even a postmodern position can mask a repressive and intolerant neopositivist epistemology. The crucial question will therefore be, Can we, as postmoderns, successfully deal with the problem of the shaping of rationality in theology and the sciences?

With this question in mind, the following statement by Gary Comstock gains special epistemological significance: Postmoderns or not, we are uncomfortable with the idea — whether loosely derived from the Bible or from the canons of modern thought — that the same universal principles undergird every particular conversation.[14] This skepticism is, of course, well-founded, since too many conversations and interreligious dialogues have in the past been decided in advance by our patriarchal, sexist, classist, or racist metanarratives. In a postmodern world we therefore worry about efforts to plan and build one world, one conversation for humankind, one story for humanity. For the theology and science dialogue this has serious implications: If our trusted metanarratives cannot be trusted anymore to provide the basis for religious and interreligious conversation, how can they provide the basis for the all-important dialogue between theology and science? Will our postmodern skepticism allow us still to trust in the ability of language to somehow "hook up" with the world? Will postmodern religion still provide us with a certainty of faith that will manage to "weigh us down" while celebrating pluralism, or will we be doomed to the "unbearable lightness of being postmodern?"[15] Can the postmodern Christian manage to (epistemologically at least) move beyond foundationalism? In other words: Is the postmodernist always also a postfoundationalist?

Comstock argues that for postmodern religious dialogue "something like the old rules" — perhaps even metanarratives — might be

14. See Comstock, 190.
15. Gary John Percesepe, "The Unbearable Lightness of Being Postmodern," *Christian Scholar's Review* 20 (1991).

needed to keep the conversation going, and that there is a "weight" that must be borne when believers speak seriously about religion. Comstock, however, eschews defining the problem of the explanatory role of an ultimate faith commitment and hopes for the ideals of truth, goodness, and consensus to emerge as rules for our postmodern dialogue.[16] Epistemologically, however, this is not enough to prevent this dialogue from eventually ending in nihilism.

Not only when focusing on problems of religious and theological dialogue, but also when dealing with the theology and science debate, we will do well to understand postmodernism as not only a radical departure from modernism. The key to moving beyond the mutually exclusive problems of foundationalism and nonfoundationalism, and further on to postfoundationalist thought, lies not in radically opposing postmodern thought to modernity in a false dichotomy, but in realizing that postmodern thought shows itself precisely in the constant interrogation of foundationalist assumptions and thus always interrupting the discourse of modernity.[17] The postmodern incredulity towards global metanarratives therefore need not lead to the end of the possibility of dialogue, but indeed — through the relentless criticism of intellectual conceit and uncritical dogmatism — can lead to a continuation of all conversation. Seen in this way, modern and postmodern thought are unthinkable apart from each other, and postmodernism is not simply modern thought coming to its end. In fact, when postmodern thought shows itself best in the interrogation of foundationalist assumptions, a fallibilist, experiential epistemology develops that not only can be seen as the hallmark of postmodernism, but also just might open up a new common ground for the current dialogue between theology and science.

II

In the current discussion between theology and science, only a few scholars have shown sensitivity for the difficult challenge and special demands posed to theology and philosophy of science by current post-

---

16. Comstock, 195.
17. See Percesepe, 120-25.

modern thought. One such scholar, who is both a theologian and a philosopher of science, is Nancey Murphy. The recent publication of her *Theology in the Age of Scientific Reasoning*[18] is a welcome addition to the growing literature on theology and science, and in more than one way typifies the complexity of trying to relate theological and scientific thinking in a postmodern context. In this important book she not only convincingly demonstrates that both theologians and philosophers of religion need a thorough knowledge of the cognitive aspects of religion, but also shows us why contemporary philosophy of science has become the most important methodological link in the current theology and science debate. In doing this she tries to vindicate her claim that theology, too, in its scientific reflection on religious experience, can creatively come forward with novel facts. Her own highly original and creative interpretation of the Lakatosian model for theology in itself becomes a novel and challenging postmodern way of dealing with the troubled relationship between theology and science. True to her postmodern sensibilities, Murphy's book espouses a holist epistemology that transcends the traditional boundaries between theology, philosophical theology, and philosophy of religion, and centers on the problem of assessing the theologian's claims to rationality (although she never explicitly deals with the problem of rationality as such). It is especially significant to note that Murphy apparently wants to avoid the fideism of some forms of postmodern "narrative theologies" by her stated assumption that in this age of agnosticism and atheism, the Christian community has an obligation to provide rational support for its belief in God "in accord with the going standards of evidence."[19] What is meant by "rational support" and "the going standards of evidence," and whether her model lives up to this claim, will have to be evaluated carefully. This will help us determine the validity and reliability of the program that is presented to us in this volume.

In this book, Nancey Murphy sets out to dispel skepticism regarding Christian belief, so widespread since Hume and the rise of modern science. She accepts Jeffrey Stout's verdict that theology can no longer validly appeal to traditional sources of authority in order to establish

---

18. Nancey Murphy, *Theology in the Age of Scientific Reasoning* (Ithaca: Cornell University Press, 1990). See my review in *Zygon* 27, no. 2 (June 1992).

19. Murphy, 192.

its credibility,[20] and sets out to demonstrate theology's commensurability with current scientific probable reasoning. She thus argues for the rationality of Christian belief by carefully demonstrating the similarities of theological reasoning to scientific reasoning and even claims that theology is (potentially, at least) methodologically indistinguishable from the sciences.[21] She concludes that a nonfoundationalist approach to theology guided by current philosophy of science is indeed possible and then justifies this by drawing on new historicist accounts of science, particularly that of Imre Lakatos.

According to Lakatos, scientists work within a research program consisting of a fixed core theory and a series of changing auxiliary hypotheses that allow for prediction and the explanation of novel facts. Futhermore, Lakatos claimed that the history of science is best understood not in terms of successive paradigms, as it is for Thomas Kuhn, but rather in terms of competing research programs that could be either progressive or degenerating.[22] In Lakatos's view, scientific rationality requires a specification of a criterion for choice between competing research programs. A research program always consists of a set of theories and a body of data. One such theory, called the "hard core," is central to the research program. Next to this core theory is a set of auxiliary hypotheses that together add enough information to allow the data to be related to the hard core theory. These auxiliary hypotheses form a "protective belt" around the hard core theory and can be modified when potentially falsifying data are found.[23] Murphy competently summarizes this when she says, "A research program, then, is a series of complex theories whose core remains the same while auxiliary hypotheses are successfully modified, replaced, or amplified in order to account for problematic observations."[24]

Like Kuhn, Lakatos distinguished between mature and immature science. In mature science a research program includes both a negative and a positive heuristic. The negative heuristic is simply the plan to

20. Stout.

21. Murphy, 198.

22. Murphy, 59.

23. See Imre Lakatos, "Falsification and the Methodology of Scientific Research Programmes," in Imre Lakatos and Alan Musgrave, eds., *Criticism and the Growth of Knowledge* (Cambridge: Cambridge University Press, 1970), 132ff.

24. Murphy, 59.

avoid falsification of the hard core and as such, implies a "hard core" of beliefs that either could be unconscious, could be assumed without question, or could be treated as if they were irrefutable. The positive heuristic includes plans for the future development of the program and thus implies a long-term research policy. This gives rise, in the course of research, to a protective belt of auxiliary hypotheses (e.g., scientific models and answers to possible refutations), which, as such, are falsifiable.[25] Against this background, programs of research can over a long period of time be either fruitful or unfruitful. Hence Lakatos's distinction between progressive and degenerating research programs.

Lakatos's answers to two of the main problems of philosophy of science can now be stated as follows:

1. Regarding demarcation, Lakatos claimed that we have "science" whenever there is a series of theories whose empirical content increases as the auxiliary hypotheses are modified to avoid falsification; and we have "mature science" whenever these content-increasing modifications are in accordance with a preconceived plan.
2. Regarding confirmation, Lakatos claimed there are objective reasons for choosing one program over another when the former has a more progressive record than its rival — that is, a greater demonstrated ability to anticipate novel facts.[26]

Murphy now argues that similar patterns of probable reasoning can be used to justify theological claims. She then sets out to support this claim through historical analyses of theological research programs such as those of Wolfhart Pannenberg and of the Roman Catholic Modernists, who, in her view, already come close to satisfying the philosophical demands of Lakatos's methodology.

In what may be the most original part of the book, Murphy develops a characterization and analysis of what can be regarded as "theological data" for a postmodern Lakatosian theological model. This chapter indeed focuses Murphy's program on what I would regard as one of the

---

25. See Philip Clayton, *Explanation from Physics to Theology* (New Haven: Yale University Press, 1989), 50f.

26. Murphy, 61.

most central issues for philosophical theology today. Theologians who want to approach theological methodology from an antiauthoritarian and postfoundationalist viewpoint, precisely in our scientific age, will have to select from the manifold of religious experience those elements that claim to yield some form of knowledge of God. The theologian therefore not only must have access to religious experience, but also should formulate criteria for the proper means of distinguishing valid and reliable knowledge claims for theology.

Drawing on the rich history of spiritual discernment in the works of Jonathan Edwards, Ignatius Loyola, and the Anabaptist traditions, Nancey Murphy takes up this challenge and develops her crucial and thoroughly postmodern idea of communal discernment as perhaps the most typical of Christian epistemic practices. Against this background, Murphy claims that the most pressing requirement in a search for suitable data for theology is to find ways to distinguish data that have a bearing on the nature of God and those that bear only on the psychology or history of religion.[27] For Murphy, suitable data for theology would be the results of Christian discernment, that is, judgments regarding the involvement of God in assorted events in the life of the church, and would therefore focus on moral and devotional practices. However, crucial data for theology could also include scriptural texts, historical facts, sociological and anthropological data, and perhaps even facts from the natural sciences.[28]

Murphy also stresses that the categories of appropriate data must be determined by the content of the research program itself, especially by its positive heuristic and by auxiliary hypotheses of a methodological nature. On this view facts of the devotional and moral life of the church can now also function as data for theological reflection, and as such, provide the data that serve to confirm theological doctrines. The basic question of course is, How is one to distinguish between religious experiences that represent encounters with God and those that do not? For Murphy the Christian church, in a long history of communal decisions and judgments, provides a rich treasury of answers to just these questions.[29] It is within this context that she proposes that the crucial data for theology are the results of Christian discernment.

27. Murphy, 130.
28. Murphy, 130.
29. Murphy, 132.

On the basis of the practice of communal discernment, participants in a wide assortment of Christian communities select certain observable events in ordinary church life and then designate them as acts (or words) of God. It is these discernments, resulting from Christian communal consensus, that form an important and often overlooked category of data for theology. It is also this practice of making knowledge claims about God's activity in the human life on the basis of discernment that Murphy calls a Christian epistemic practice.[30] An adequate set of criteria for discernment in the Christian church includes the following: (1) agreement with the apostolic witness, (2) production of a Christlike character in those affected, which means specifically freedom from sin and manifestation of the fruits of the Spirit, and (3) unity in the community based on prayerful discussion.[31] When these criteria are met, the authentic work of the Spirit can be recognized with reasonable certainty, and theologians can then proceed to claim it as data for theological research programs.

The following critical question, however, has to be put to Murphy: Are her criteria appropriate to their explicitly stated purpose?[32] If her goal is to meet the challenge of probable reasoning, then not only her Lakatosian methodology, but also the data that feed into it, must conform to scientific epistemic standards.

And on this latter point Murphy is suspect. In the light of Hume's and Stout's challenge, precisely the status of the apostolic witness and of the authority of Christ is in doubt. Murphy is therefore unjustified in making Scripture a criterion for judgment since she gives no reasons why it should have even a formal authority.[33] This is not to say that the authority of Scripture *can* not be warranted on the basis of probable reasoning, but only that Murphy *does* not do it. And the same is true of her other two criteria for data identification. This leads one to suspect that these criteria have their epistemic foundation in a deeper and prior commitment. This obviously raises the specter of an epistemological foundationalism that would not at all be commensurable with Murphy's

---

30. Murphy, 159.

31. Murphy, 152.

32. I am indebted to James A. Moos for his insightful contributions on this specific issue.

33. See Wentzel van Huyssteen, *The Realism of the Text* (Pretoria: UNISA, 1987), 30f.

attempt at probable reasoning, and at a holist, nonfoundationalist epistemology. It furthermore raises the critical question about whether a model from the natural sciences (in this case that of Imre Lakatos) can succesfully be utilized to determine the rationality of theological reflection? Using the methodological framework of Lakatos's model to locate theist assumptions, and assumptions on the authority of Scripture and the Spirit, in the unassailable hard core of a theological program certainly does not guarantee probable reasoning. What is more, in contradiction to Murphy's explicit goal, it demonstrates that in its methodology theology is not at all indistinguishable from the sciences,[34] but could in fact turn out to be very different from the sciences. But if this were true, theologians would ultimately have to concede to Hume's and Stout's challenge. A crucial question for theologians can now be phrased as follows: If we can agree that faith in God is neither an epistemic virtue or an epistemic vice, and therefore does not make the object of faith "more probable,"[35] how will it be possible to get out of the vicious circle of fideism to some form of transcommunal criteria that may determine what could be regarded as data for a Christian theology?

In spite of the fact that Murphy attempts a nonfoundationalist theology by seeing religious experience as primary data for theological research programs, her model lacks a well-developed theory of experience. Such a theory might have enabled her not only to focus on religious experience as data for theological reflection, but also to highlight the explanatory role of religious experience. And because of the meaning-giving role of experience and the analogous role of experiential claims in science, precisely the explanatory role of experience can become the decisive link in the theology and science debate. From this it is clear that within a holist, postmodern epistemology, a theory of experience is always a further refinement of one's theory of rationality. In our quest for theological intelligibility, religious experience guides us not only in finding ultimate meaning in our lives, but also ultimately in connecting the religious quest for understanding with our general quest for understanding the world rationally. In the postmodern theology and science discussion, an adequate theory of experience thus becomes a crucial issue.

34. Murphy, 198.
35. See Clayton, 143.

Murphy, citing William Alston, correctly states that somehow what goes on in the experience of leading the Christian life provides some ground for Christian belief and makes some contribution to the rationality of Christian belief.[36] Because we are convinced that somehow God is acting in our lives, we are more justified than we would have been otherwise. Murphy claims that the results of Christian discernment can serve as data for theology despite the fact that such data always inevitably involve interpretation. However, the question of the reliability of these communal discernments, and the need to justify conceptualizing experience in theistic terms in the first place, raises serious challenges to this view.

Murphy, however, not only argues the need for communal discernment and the need to make more frequent and determined use of this practice,[37] she also argues for a degree of objectivity in these communal judgments. "Objectivity" for her just means that others under similar circumstances and experience will see the same thing, which again is a matter of degree. Thus, the process of Christian discernment not only satisfies the requirement of providing suitable data for theology, but is for her also a replicable process. Not only can it be repeated, just as scientists repeat experiments, but it can also produce novel facts. Murphy concludes that theological facts do not differ all that much from scientific facts in this regard.[38] The replicable process of Christian discernment or community consensus can, however, hardly be so directly compared to the disciplined control of the scientific experimental context. At most, it demonstrates that both scientific and theological facts are theory-laden, that they function within the context of traditioned experience, and that degrees of objectivity exist and are always context-bound. However, Murphy's analysis does not help us solve the epistemological problem of trying to formulate transcommunal criteria for the truth claims and realist assumptions in theological reflection.

Murphy does state that although the results of Christian discernment meet all the standard requirements of scientific data, they will not be of the same quality (reliability, replicability) as those of the natural

36. Murphy, 159.
37. Murphy, 166.
38. Murphy, 168.

sciences.[39] She qualifies this by stating that as such, they may more justly be compared to those of the human sciences, but unfortunately, she does not expand on this. Thus, by evaluating the data of theological reflection, she argues that Lakatos's model gives us a workable criterion for choosing between competing scientific programs. But because theological programs have been shown not to function at all like scientific research programs in Murphy's model, Lakatos's criterion of relative empirical progress could hardly be used to adjudicate between competing theological theories or schools. In the end, we are left with no idea how one of Murphy's most startling claims could ever be justified: that the more acceptable — and progressive — theological program(s) may claim to provide (superior?) knowledge of God and of God's relation to the world.[40]

Murphy's attempt at a Lakatosian theology finally runs into its most serious problems when she proposes a convention for postmodern philosophical theology and radically opposes modern thought to postmodernism. Postmodern theologians are those whose presuppositions are postmodern rather than modern and who have removed themselves decisively from modern conceptual space.[41] Against the background of a discussion of Thiemann's and Lindbeck's work, she defines the typically postmodern change as:

1. from foundationalism to holism in epistemology;
2. from the modern emphasis on reference and representation to an emphasis on language as action, and meaning as use;
3. from individualism to communal thinking and consensus.

Whether Murphy's version of postmodern nonfoundationalism manages to move beyond postliberal neoconservatism and its inherent fideism to a postfoundational framework with room for transcommunal criteria is unlikely. By radically opposing postmodernism to modern thought, Murphy cuts herself off from perhaps the most distinctive trait of postmodernism — its relentless criticism of foundationalist assumptions. Lakatosian theology in this mode inevitably becomes (epistemo-

39. Murphy, 173.
40. Murphy, 174.
41. Murphy, 201.

logically at least) completely insulated, with no possibility of true inter-subjective communication. Without any intersubjectivity, however, one of the most salient features of the Lakatosian program falls away — the ability to progress by choosing critically between competing research programs. If we are to accept a definition of rationality as an ultimate quest for intelligibility, or even just follow Lakatos in his notion of competing research programs, it becomes inevitable that we compare the rationality of explanations in various and different contexts, and therefore, also between the contexts of theology and science. This, again, touches the heart of Murphy's crucial notion of communal discernment — not only because of the troublesome question of how reliable these communal discernments in the history of the Christian church(es) are (even if, as Murphy claims, they are replicable by the same religious or faith group), but simply because of their limited and severely restricted epistemic scope. For explanatory progress in theological reflection, Murphy appeals to communal consensus. What a theology in discussion with agnosticism and atheism needs, however, is to show its ability to demonstrate transcommunal or intersubjective explanations, for this is what really challenges the shaping of rationality in postmodern theology, especially in the theology and science debate.

In the end a holist epistemology implies more than communal discernment and communal consensus for contemporary theological reflection. It also demands a broader intersubjective coherence that goes beyond the parameters of the experience and reflection of just the believing community. If Nancey Murphy's proposed convention for a postmodern theology cannot demonstrate this, the serious problem of how a Lakatosian theology would escape the charge of fideism remains unresolved.

Closely linked to this is the question whether the Lakatosian model — so specifically suited to determining empirical progress in the natural sciences — can adequately cope with the broader and more complex problem of meaning as highlighted by the social sciences. Murphy initially tries to disarm all forms of foundationalism in her central argument. But when she designates the presupposed existence of God as "hard core" for a theological research program (à la Lakatos), and then adds that this hard core will always typically contain reference to God,[42]

42. Murphy, 194.

the important hermeneutical problem of the metaphorical and epistemic function of religious language is raised. Moreover, the very distinction between "hard core beliefs" and others that can be regarded as auxiliary hypotheses, within an attempt at a holist postmodern theology, inevitably raises the specter of some surreptitious form of foundationalism.

The fact that incorporating Lakatosian "hard core beliefs" within a theological research program suggests a subtle form of foundationalism, which is not consistent with Murphy's general proposal for a postmodern theology, leads me finally to her quarrel with critical realism. She has important difficulties with this position. She claims that as a problematic position philosophically, it gives no clear account of how theology and science might interact, and furthermore implies the "outrageous" claim to have some knowledge of reality apart from our ordinary human ways of knowing.[43] No sophisticated form of critical realism, however, would ever make this strong, dated, and truly foundationalist claim. A modest and qualified form of critical realism, on the other hand, can take seriously the holist approach of current postmodern and postfoundationalist thought and make tentative claims through the epistemic access provided for us by the metaphorical nature of human language.

The problem, of course, is that Murphy sees any attempt to define a relation between language and the world as "modern," as opposed to a "postmodern" position where words like "real" or "exists" would be restricted to the meaning they obtain from being used within certain linguistic frameworks. I do believe, however, that there is a third option here. In critical realism the epistemic purpose of metaphorical language is not to transcend the world of human experience, but indeed to set limits to the range and scope of our theological and scientific language. Such limits establish a domain for human knowledge. A weak form of critical realism (which takes the realist assumptions of the Christian faith seriously) claims that one's subjective encounter of the world is of the same order as one's re-creation of the world in language. Language here, therefore, is never seen as a derivative of an "objective" world, and consequently does not find truth in correspondence with such a world. This, of course, is not a denial of the existence of an extralinguistic

43. Murphy, 197f.

world, but is an epistemic affirmation that this reality is mostly encountered in language. This, however, makes Murphy's allegation that critical realism makes an "outrageous" claim to have some knowledge of reality "apart from our ordinary ways of human knowing"[44] completely unintelligible.

It is in this sense that critical realism in theology would seek epistemic warrants for precisely the basic realist assumptions that a Lakatosian theology like Murphy's wants to work with (compare the existence of God as the presupposed "hard core" of Murphy's theological research program). In doing this, critical realism in theology would take seriously precisely the role of Christianity's classic text and the way religious experience and communal discernment have shaped the history of theological ideas right through the long history of the Christian faith. But the way that the philosophical problem of rationality challenges theology to transcommunal explanations also has to be taken as seriously if theology hopes to become a worthy partner in the current debate with the sciences.

The inclusion of God in the hard core of a research program is therefore not only inconsistent with the rejection of a qualified form of critical realism. It could also reveal a retreat to an esoteric fideist commitment that might firmly bar the way of theology to the reality about which it proposes to make statements. In the extreme form of this view, religious beliefs have no need for explanatory support and can in the end be seen as just part of a groundless language game. However, when theological beliefs become a species of belief whose truth is discovered only by means of criteria internal to the language game itself, this leads not only to a relativistic understanding of justification, truth, and knowledge, but to an epistemological relativism that would be fatal for the cognitive claims of theological statements — precisely in an age of postmodern scientific reasoning. Postmodernism in theology can therefore never settle for a mere laid-back pluralism. Lakatos was right: We should indeed have criteria to help us choose between competing research programs. Postmodern theology has already shown us that we have a choice in opting for contexts that can politically be good, better, best, or, of course, oppressive and therefore bad.[45] And if this is true

44. Murphy, 198.
45. See Taylor.

ethically, pragmatically, and politically, then surely it must also be true epistemologically. But to have this kind of scope, theology cannot afford to isolate itself from the sciences, but should develop transcommunal, intersubjective criteria in its quest for intelligibility. Murphy opts for progressive research programs that are marked by their ability to produce novel facts. But if the criteria for judgment and for choosing research programs are relative to particular faith communities, progress can never be assessed, and honest choices would be hard to make.

Is the postmodernist, then, always also a postfoundationalist? In theology, at least, this often hardly seems to be the case. In fact, the postmodernist might even turn out to be a crypto-fideist.

Nancey Murphy is certainly right in asserting that theology can constitute knowledge that is on a par with the epistemic status of scientific knowledge. It is as important, however, to realize that a postfoundationalist theology can, by means of a fallibilist, experiential epistemology, properly aim for justified beliefs and for a tentative and provisional knowledge of what Christians have come to call God.

Chapter Five

The Realist Challenge in Postmodern Theology: Religious Experience in Jerome Stone's Neo-Naturalism

IN CONTEMPORARY RELIGIOUS EPISTEMOLOGY THEOLOGIANS AND philosophers of religion have increasingly come to depend on the concept of religious experience. Today this approach is accepted and even embraced by many scholars who normally would not call themselves empiricists. Of course religion has always been an experiential matter and never just a set of credal statements or a collection of rites and rituals. Wayne Proudfoot has recently and persuasively argued that this turn to religious experience since the Enlightenment has been motivated in large measure by a very specific wish to free religious doctrine and practice from dependence on metaphysical beliefs and ecclesiastical institutions.[1]

Although religious experience seemed and still to a large extent seems to be fairly pervasive, the concept of religious experience is as vague as it is elusive. In a striking image Nancy Frankenberry sees the concept of religious experience as both slippery and overworked at the same time, and as entering our discussions like a ghostly shadow: haunting the premises, but still unreal and elusive.[2] One of the more far-

1. Wayne Proudfoot, *Religious Experience* (Berkeley: University of California Press, 1985), xiii.
2. Nancy Frankenberry, *Religion and Radical Empiricism* (Albany: SUNY, 1987), 189.

91

reaching implications of this has been that both philosophers of religion and philosophical theologians — instead of evaluating the empirical basis of religious beliefs and of theological theories and doctrines in experience — have focused increasingly on a study of the conditions or warrants for the justifiability of holding basic religious beliefs. In theology this inevitably led to the foundationalisms of both natural theology and a brand of naive realist theologies that still finds justification in self-authenticating and supernaturalist concepts of revelation.

I

An exciting attempt to move beyond those well-known dilemmas is found in Jerome Stone's recent book, *A Minimalist Vision of Transcendence: A Naturalist Philosophy of Religion*.[3] What Stone wants to do in this book is precisely to clear a space for the renewed interest in the role of religious experience. In doing this he not only wants to reveal the weaknesses of foundationalism and fideism in religious epistemology, but especially wants to show how the problems of faith, theism, and realism look different when approached from the standpoint of naturalism, and how an empiricism generously conceived can form the basis of a public ecotheology.

For the philosophical theologian this kind of focus on the role of religious experience opens up rather difficult but also exciting methodological and epistemological challenges. The question of how our beliefs are related to concrete experiences is central to this form of radical empiricist naturalism. In the end, however, the focus of this challenge will be the crucial epistemological question: how do epistemic values such as interpreted experience, personal commitment, and experienced tradition really shape the rationality of religious and theological reflection?

In his focus on religious experience Stone is intensely aware of the pervasive presence of ambiguity in our daily existence: an ambiguity not only in what happens to us, but also in the way we respond. Stone

---

3. Jerome Stone, *A Minimalist Vision of Transcendence: A Naturalist Philosophy of Religion* (Albany: SUNY, 1992).

is therefore skeptical of theological and metaphysical answers to the problems confronting us in religious experience, and in the end opts for a minimalism that — to put it in Langdon Gilkey's apt words in his foreword to Stone's book — "learns from both the theologians, whom he admires, and the wary naturalists, whose critical agnosticism he shares."[4] What is quite remarkable in this book is his accord with those who articulate a presence of transcendence in our everyday experience. This explains at least some of his appreciation for and limited agreement with some of the more important theological traditions of our century. But he consistently remains a strict minimalist: any theological or metaphysical explanation for the presence of this transcendence in our experience remains forbidden.

Stone calls this view a neo-naturalistic philosophy of religion, combining a vision of this-worldly transcendence with an attitude of openness in inquiry and action. Crucial to this view is his minimalist model of the divine, and Stone locates himself between believers and non-believers: not as confident as the humanists in their anti-theism, but also not able to make the affirmations of most theologians. He also explicitly joins hands with the recent revival of radical empiricism in religious thought as a viable third option to foundationalism and antifoundationalism. When lamenting the lack of the experience of transcendence in our Western culture, Stone eschews all traditional God-talk and focuses instead on the divine aspects of contemporary experience.[5] This project is therefore about retrieving experiences of transcendence in secular life and about developing a theory of this-worldly transcendence, a theory that might uncover transcendent resources of renewal and judgment that might be available to us within secular life itself.

For his theory of this-worldly transcendence Stone develops a minimalist model of the divine, a tentative conceptualization of what might be affirmed of God when we cannot make a full ontological affirmation of an ultimate reality anymore. In this he is amazingly — and typically — honest: he acknowledges that the ontological reticence underlying his naturalism is a metaphysical position and needs whatever justification a metaphysical position can get.[6] Stone's faith in naturalism as an

---

4. Stone, ix.
5. Stone, 1ff.
6. Stone, 7.

adequate explanation for religious experience will eventually have to be challenged precisely at this level of discussion.

Stone's intended third alternative beyond theism and secular humanism is especially fascinating since he very consciously wants to contribute to the current discussion on realism in philosophy of religion and contemporary philosophy of science. He therefore very explicitly raises the question of what sort of reality might correspond to our thoughts about God.[7] His minimalist answer to this reads as follows: "the transcendent is the collection of all situationally transcendent resources and continually changing ideals"[8] that we experience. Maximalist theologies, in their attempts to use that concept of God to affirm some kind of unity in the real and ideal aspects of transcendent resources, affirm just too much. Stone hence rejects the extravagant conceptual claims of maximalist theisms, especially any claims of unity for the transcendent. His minimalist vision of transcendence therefore remains with an affirmation of the plurality of the presence of the transcendent in secular life.

Stone's model thus asserts transcendence without ultimacy. What is affirmed is that there are real creative processes transcendent in a significant sense to our ordinary experience, and that there are ideals that we may call transcendent. This model therefore is a long way from affirming an intelligent purposiveness to a transcendent creator, since purposiveness presupposes a unity of individuality, that is, a personal God capable of entertaining such a purpose. Stone does call the three elements of his model transcendence, the real, and the idea — elements that correspond to the three most basic characteristics of religious experience: transcendence, blessing, and challenge.[9] His minimalist vision is thus transformed into a philosophical reconception of the object of religious experience. Stone's situationally transcendent resources (for example: a moment of unexpected healing) furthermore not only are always relative to a personal and temporal point of view, but can only be explained in resolutely naturalistic terms. Within this minimalist context transcendent resources are not signs of the divine, but part of whatever there is of the divine that we can know. Hence moments of

7. Stone, 10.
8. Stone, 17.
9. Stone, 13.

extremity and of despair, as moments of real transcendence, are not bearers of grace but are gracious themselves.[10]

Closely aligned with the real aspect of transcendence is its ideal aspect: defined minimally, this is a set of continually challenging ideals insofar as they are worthy of pursuit. In an intriguing, and certainly at least epistemologically controversial, move, Stone takes the pursuit of truth as a paradigm of the ideal aspect of the transcendent.[11] The concept of "truth" continues to function for him as a goal in relation to which our theories are but approximations. As such, truth is an ideal never fully attained, but, like a kind of *focus imaginarius*, functions as a continual demand that we push toward.

For Stone the divine (or God) is the collection of situationally transcendent resources and continually challenging ideals of the universe, that is, the sum of the worthy and constructively challenging aspects of the world. Stone's model hence articulates a concept of this-worldly transcendence. The question, of course, remains whether this transcendent could in any sense be the same as God? In answering this Stone wants to move beyond a mere "yes" or "no." On the one hand he acknowledges that it is a long way from traditional and even revised beliefs about God; on the other hand this transcendent can function in a person's life much as the traditional God. Whether one then chooses to call the transcendent by the traditional name of God is a matter of personal choice and context.[12] For Stone, however, a minimal requirement would be to stop short of affirming any ontological unity.

It has now become abundantly clear, I think, that Stone's approach is characterized by a functional justification for using minimalist religious language. In this his naturalism relies on a phenemenology of the transcendent, and the resulting focus is on a pluralistic understanding of the divine.

10. Stone, 15.
11. Stone, 16.
12. Stone, 18.

II

When we now move to a more critical assessment of Stone's proposal, the focus will be on one fairly simple question: How religious is the religious experience that follows this clear and well-argued-for minimalist vision of transcendence? I hope to make clear that I have no problems with Stone's carefully constructed theory of experience as such. What does, however, seem to be problematical is the way epistemic decisions are made in advance — decisions that in the end determine the boundaries between maximalist and minimalist forms of theism.

Stone's proposal has never been that the transcendent is God, but that the "transcendent" and "God," minimally understood, share the same reference to transcendent resources and challenges. The transcendent may in reality be more than what our experience shows: there may be unity, ultimacy, and intelligent purposiveness. There is, however, not enough support for these affirmations for us to make them as publicly responsible assertions, nor to take them as the basis for personal faith. This brings to mind Langdon Gilkey's remark in the Foreword he wrote for this book, where he points to Stone's reticence on the extra-human grounds for confidence and religious faith, and wonders how he can stay as serenely confident and doggedly hopeful as he wishes to be.[13] Stone's model is sophisticated, genuine, and to a certain extent even moving. Ultimately, however, it is highly individualistic, and one wonders if it could withstand the criticism that it is elitist, even escapist, and ultimately may function as one more example of the remarkable creativity of our Western scholarship. Stone's book, however, demands much more serious attention than this.

What I am therefore struggling with in trying to understand this minimalist vision of transcendence is how such a generic concept of the divine, without at some point being immersed in the language of a living religious tradition, can avoid becoming not only acontextual (even ahistorical), but also too remote, too empty, in a word, too generic. It is precisely at this point that I again raise the question, How *religious* is religious experience within the context of this radical empiricism? For a model of transcendence to be, religiously speaking, experientially adequate, it has to relate somehow to an ultimate commitment of faith,

13. Stone, x.

that is, if it wants to avoid the label of being intellectually highly esoteric. Of course Stone wants to avoid this. The key question for him is not whether a person uses language about God, but whether a person is open to transcendent resources and demands. But if Stone wants to avoid ultimacy, what would be the distinctive trait of this religious self-actualization that would go beyond and distinguish it from, say, psychological self-actualization?

When the term "God" is adequately understood, so Stone argues,[14] it will be found to refer to inner-worldly transcendent resources. It can, however, be convincingly argued that the belief in the inadequacy of natural explanations to account for all our experience may be more invariant across cultures than the belief in any specific God.[15] Stone's minimalist vision hence seems to be grounded in a prior commitment to and faith in a naturalist metaphysics, and not in whether the minimalist vision of transcendence is experientially adequate to the way in which religious people of various stripes live their lives.

Closely linked to this issue is the fact that Stone does not really show why maximalism fails, but only why highly restricted — and already problematic — arguments for maximalist positions on theism fail.[16] He renounces the full ontological affirmation of the transcendent that normally is contained in such religious notions as Brahman or God. He does, however, acknowledge that the major traditions provide a clue to the notion of the transcendent that is useful. The reason for this minimalism is his faith in naturalism, but the position taken on the broader spectrum between minimalism and maximalism remains vague, a line to a certain extent even arbitrarily drawn. Stone's faith in naturalism gives each of the themes of his empiricist philosophy a carefully constructed agnostic boundary, which is, however, never completely crossed precisely because of his accompanying — and intriguing — commitment to realism. Because of his generic minimalist vision of transcendence, however, Stone can also stop short of asking what the "MORE," the religious aspect of reality his notions are referring to, in fact is.

Stone concedes that no rigorous proof for the adequacy of his or

14. Stone, 20f.
15. See also Proudfoot, 77.
16. Stone, 28ff.

any other model can be given.[17] An ontological position cannot be proved, but it can indeed be argued for. Helpful arguments for Stone would be arguments on clarity, empirical fit, and especially pragmatic adequacy. I have no problems with clarity and pragmatic adequacy, but how a naturalistic minimalist vision can manage empirically to fit (or be experientially adequate to) the way religious people live their every-day lives — normally in commitment to some extra-human grounds for their faith — remains unclear to me, except if it is meant all along only for a selected intellectual few. Stone's view on God is a stance of ontological modesty, but he also wants to argue that this view is indeed the most adequate. Stone realizes that his position of ontological re-straint is in itself an ontological position.[18] It remains highly question-able, however, whether this position can be argued for on the basis of his radical empiricism only. The reasons and the place for pinning down the boundaries of Stone's minimalism thus remain unclear. His model retains a notion of the transcendent. In fact, the model explicates and nurtures experiences of the transcendent without making too many assertions about it. This model, then, is "for those who operate in the critical mode."[19] But, then again, is this enough for living a day-to-day life of faith?

III

A critical evaluation of Jerome Stone's work will benefit greatly if we now focus on an all-important concept in his philosophical naturalism, namely, transactional realism. Stone wants to enter the present debate about realism in philosophy of religion and in philosophy of science by defining his radical empiricism as a transactional realism.[20] This trans-actional realism is also an anticipatory realism, or a realism of hope that sees correspondence between idea and object not as a constitutive, but as a regulative principle.

17. Stone, 27.
18. Stone.
19. Stone, 33.
20. Stone, 130ff.

This transactional realism implies a fallibilist epistemology and is an attempt to revise or correct theories, visions, ideas, or images by further exploration of experience. Within this context Stone opts for an approximate concept of truth where pragmatic adequacy is our only guide. In this transactional realism tentative assertions are made about realities, assertions that we believe — not on compelling grounds, but with good reasons — are more adequate to these realities than other assertions. In Stone's own words: "The realities which we dimly perceive and the theories which we develop concerning them, when subject to appropriate scrutiny, are worth the risk of living by, despite our propensity to error and fantasy."[21]

This form of realism, as a self-critical, culturally aware empiricism, is in fact Stone's postfoundationalist move beyond the certainty and despair of foundationalism, relativism, and cultural provincialism.[22] It is deeply rooted in his radical empiricism, and also in the crucial importance he attaches to sensitive discernment, the historical rootedness of all empirical inquiry, and the transactional nature of experience.

Stone develops a theory of experience (and of religious experience) in which experience is seen as a transaction, a transaction between "self" (as a combination of social choices and genetic legacies) and "world" (as both construct and reality). As such, experience is a complex interaction between language and lived feelings, between organism and environment. From this can be gleaned Stone's focus on interpreted experience as an epistemic value that shapes the rationality of (also) religious reflection. There are no points of "pure" experience here that could be used as epistemological anchors or sure foundations to solve our quest for religious certainty. With this Stone moves remarkably close to the current views on critical realism in religious and theological reflection. We are indeed never out of touch with our world, that is, it is not language all the way down.[23] Also in our religion we are therefore not adrift on a linguistic sea, but experience is a relational transaction, and interpreted experience reveals that language is part of this transaction.

When Stone, however, finally discusses the historical rootedness of

21. Stone, 132.
22. Stone, 135.
23. Stone, 128.

all inquiry,[24] the problems we raised earlier in this paper are back to haunt us: can a minimalist naturalistic view, which eschews theistic explanations for religious experience, indeed provide adequate explanations for what is experienced as the essentially religious in religious experience? Stone is right: a theory of experience has to affirm — both in theory and in practice — that all experience and all inquiry is historically rooted. A generous empiricism such as Stone's will therefore recognize that present experience is, to a large degree, a reconstruction of past experience. Hence experience is a chain or series of interpretations, informed but also restricted in its range by the past.

This means — and Stone would agree — that our experiences of the divine also are always rooted in the past.[25] Going beyond the foundationalist confines of cultural provincialism, Stone moves from theism to minimalism and radical empiricism. But what really warrants this move? The only apparent answer, again, seems to be prior metaphysical commitment to naturalism. This of course is fine, but if so, what we have here is not just an argument for great experiential adequacy, but also a prior commitment to, or faith in, naturalism.

This naturalism determines the minimalist vision of transcendence completely. Stone, of course, would be happy with that, but ironically it also sets limits to his transactional realism. This is nowhere more clear than when Stone points to the crucial referential aspect of religious language.[26] This referential function of what Stone calls the translucent domain of the language of devotion[27] is indeed a key point in his religious naturalism. Stone's focus on the referential function of religious language sets him apart from expressivists and antirealists in philosophy of religion and thus serves to justify his realist stance. The reference, however, is not to an ontological ultimate, but to the divine aspects of our experienced world.

In this way Stone's arguments claim reference along with experiential adequacy by exploring experience and by discovering transcendence in experience. The crucial question, of course, is how does this model lead us — through experience and reference — to discover a

24. Stone, 142ff.
25. Stone, 143.
26. Stone, 157ff.
27. Stone, 158.

minimalist transcendence in experience? And again the answer can only be, because the model itself is already a naturalist one, and is working as a grid to determine this minimalism. Of course, if it is true of even an interactionalist model like Stone's that all our experience is in the end preceded by a commitment to a specific paradigm, it raises serious problems for all of us who are trying to construct plausible models in religious epistemology. It also may point to the fact that there might be more epistemic values involved in the shaping of the rationality of religious reflection than we think.

Postmodern thought challenges those of us who are Christian theologians to account for the fact of Christianity. Jerome Stone's important book shows that it also challenges us to rediscover the explanatory role of religious experience in postfoundationalist theology. I agree with Stone that religious language can never be seen as just a useful system of symbols that can be action guiding and meaningful for the believer without having to be referential or reality depicting in any stronger sense of the word.

Within Stone's minimalist model, however, the divine functions as a placemaker,[28] and not as the move, which he would consider illegitimate, beyond the available evidence to an ontological ultimate. This transactional realism and the accompanying notion of reference may be the most intriguing notions of Stone's minimalist vision, but they are also where this model is at its most vulnerable. When in moments of extremity, moments of defeat or despair, joy or victory, we reach a profound awareness of our own limits, what will the language and experience of our limitation refer to? For Stone the reference is to generic resources of minimalist transcendence, which is at the same time a (bold?) step outside any particular religion. Stone's initial embracing of pluralism might indeed have allowed for the ultimate and even passionate commitment to truth that many of the historic religions presuppose. But could his move to a generic minimalist vision of the divine really be consonant with postmodernism's celebration of true pluralism?

Stone is right when he argues that any plausible form of realism in religious epistemology should always be an empirical thesis since its credibility and acceptance as a belief system can be determined only on

28. Stone, 40.

experiential grounds. In theology, too, our rational inquiry and quest for intelligibility will always include a response to what we experience. Empirical fit, or experiential adequacy, thus becomes one of the more important epistemic values that shape the rationality of theological reflection. The high degree of personal involvement in religious and theological theorizing not only reveals the relational character of our being in the world, but epistemologically implies the mediated and interpretive character of all religious experience.

What is revealed here is the epistemic and explanatory role of an ultimate religious commitment, which certainly is no irrational retreat to commitment, but, on the contrary, reveals the committed nature of all rational thought, and hence the fiduciary rootedness of all rationality. Stone is right: in a sense one's concept of experience will indeed entail one's concept of meaning, which in turn will determine one's concept of religious cognition. With this the challenge to postfoundationalist theology becomes even more profound and can be stated as follows: Could it be that a minimalist vision of transcendence in the end may still be empowered to point to some form of ontological unity, and maybe even to a personal God? This notion of a personal God may serve to make sense of (and thus may be experientially more adequate to) great swathes of experience that without this notion would simply baffle us.[29] Elizabeth A. Johnson points to this in her recent groundbreaking study on divine presence and transcendence. At the root of all religious imagery lies an experience of the mystery of God, potentially given to us in all experience where there is no exclusive zone, no special realm, that alone may be called religious. In this way the historical world becomes a sacrament of divine presence and activity, even if only as a fragile possibility.[30] Our commitment to a mind-independent reality called God thus would not only arise *from experience,* but in a very specific sense also *for experience,* and would also be at least theologically consonant with the sacramental destiny that Stone's ecotheology wants to claim for our precious planet.

29. See John Polkinghorne, *Reason and Reality* (Philadelphia: Trinity Press International, 1991), 98.

30. See Elizabeth A. Johnson, *She Who Is* (New York: Crossroad, 1993), 124.

Part Two

Theology and Methodology

Chapter Six

Systematic Theology and Philosophy of Science: The Need for Methodological and Theoretical Clarity in Theology

A NYONE WHO CHOOSES TO BECOME INVOLVED IN THE PROBLEMS OC-cupying present-day systematic theology is immediately struck by the tremendous revival and renewal in the theological thinking of our time. This has given birth to new theologies, and in many instances to entirely new ways of practicing theology. But any optimism as to the possibility of exciting and accessible new alternatives in theological methodology soon evaporates when one faces the fact that the many, often discrepant, models in contemporary systematic theology can all be directly related to two problematical issues:

1. the ambivalence of the distinction between theology and faith in many cases, and
2. radical difference of opinion as to the nature and purpose of systematic theology as such.

Of course, it is no less true that the church and theology are both virtually in a missionary situation in the face of the secularized contemporary worldview. Hence the common denominator of these models is undoubtedly a profound desire to employ human reason in the cause of interpreting the gospel for modern people: a "concern for understanding" in which the intelligibility of the biblical message to this day and age is a top priority.

Yet the theologian is often caught in a crisis not only of self-understanding, but also of understanding the scientific task of theology. The fact that theology is commonly regarded as an ecclesiastical activity means that the theologian often has to contend with appalling insensitivity towards genuine problems posed by the philosophy of science, and is only too readily branded as either leftist or rightist, liberal or conservative, excessively scientific or not scientific enough. The situation becomes especially complicated when a theology chooses to see itself as a science, that is, when it attempts a critical and self-critical scrutiny of its own premises instead of simply and unquestioningly accepting the tenets of the Bible or some creed in an authoritarian way. When in the face of all this the distinction between personal faith and theology (or the language of faith and the language of theology)[1] is blurred and obscured, it puts paid not only to the search for methods and theories in systematic theology, but to the very recognition of the problem of what constitutes or ought to decide the nature and structure of theological propositions.[2] But this uncritical approach simply compounds the problem, since dogmatism[3] is all that such a theology can hope to convey. In other words, its statements could have cogency and meaning only for people who are already predisposed to adopt its subjective viewpoint. The result is invariably a typical "positional theology" in which the theologian proceeds predictably from preconceived axioms, thereby merely demonstrating his or her personal convictions.

But to practice theology in this way incurs a double reproach: in respect of traditional theology, doubt as to the possibility of any proper scientific theological practice; and in respect of a critical or

---

1. In this respect see J. W. van Huyssteen "Teologie en Metode," *Koers* 43, no. 4 (1978): 377ff., especially 396.

2. See S. M. Daecke, "Soll die Theologie an der Universität bleiben?" in W. Pannenberg, G. Sauter, S. M. Daecke, H. N. Janowski, *Grundlagen der Theologie — ein Diskurs* (Stuttgart, 1974), 7ff. Hereafter referred to as *Grundlagen*.

3. See Hans Albert's cynical comment: "Alles in allem bringen diese Vertreter der Theologie es fertig, kritisch und doch dogmatisch zu sein: kritisch in den Dingen, die ihnen nicht so wichtig sind, dogmatisch in denen, die ihnen wichtiger erscheinen." H. Albert: *Traktat über kritische Vernunft* (Tübingen, 1975), 129.

argumentative[4] theology, the reproach of being responsible for all the confusion, uncertainty, and doubt that beset the minds of the Christian community.

These two well-known objections present the systematic theologian with two fundamental questions: (1) Where does one find one's problems/questions? (2) Where does one find criteria for distinguishing good solutions or answers from bad ones? As regards the former, we could say that the theologian helps to find conscious and rational answers to the problems and doubts that beset the religious life of a Christian community.[5] This implies that systematic theology is not simply concerned with an introspective exploration of "academic" issues, but most consciously formulates the problems/questions that already exist in and preoccupy the human mind. It means that the theologian finds (or discovers) problems/questions at a level that precedes all theological inquiry, namely *religion* and *religious* experience.

This illustrates yet again that what we experience as events between God and humankind are still a long way from being theology.[6] Theology is, rather, a purely human activity restricted to people who formulate and *systematize the problems* surrounding every experience of God — those issues that accompany, and often jeopardize, our statements concerning God. To put it simply: One purpose of theology is to help the Christian community to solve its religious problems. In a stricter sense one could define it as a methodical process aspiring to insight and understanding in view of the fact that events between humankind and God often pose obstacles for the human intellect. From a philosophy-of-science point of view these can be stated only as problems.[7]

The community to which Christians ordinarily belong, the church, provides the context within which theological problems could arise. However, today Christianity is often manifested outside the established denominations, so that theologians may find legitimate theological

4. For positional theology and argumentative theology, see *Grundlagen*, 59.

5. See H. M. Kuitert, *Zonder geloof vaart niemand wel* (Baarn, 1974), 47ff.

6. See J. W. van Huyssteen, "Antwoord aan professor Adrio König," *Koers* 43, no. 4 (1978): 409.

7. See G. Sauter, "Theologie als Beschreibung des Rendens von Gott," in *Grundlagen*, 53.

problems outside the church as well.[8] Their field of inquiry extends even further, not only because theology often operates from universities, but also because theologians cannot avoid sharing the contemporary awareness of the problems of our age. This places them under an obligation to society as a whole — one that suggests the need for a self-understanding that would demand at least an unbiased testing of their credibility; hence a commitment to rationality.

It is in this regard that such eminent theologians as Gerhard Sauter, Harry Kuitert, and Wolfhart Pannenberg have repeatedly warned against the danger of an "ecclesiastical theology" that eventually proves to be no more than ghetto theology, citing its confessional doctrines as adequate grounds for withdrawing from the problems posed by the philosophy of science in our time. One could therefore contend that systematic theology has no justifiable claims to any methodological prerogatives in its search for truth. It is a human science because divine revelation is accessible to us only through our own dialogue concerning that revelation.

Hence theologians must formulate and substantiate their concept of science by dialogue and confrontation with other views on the subject. Inquiry into the construction of theological methods and theories, into the nature, quality, origin, and justification of theological methods and theories, and into the nature, quality, origin, and justification of theological propositions can be fruitful only if the theologian is *au fait* with both current theological problems and the complexities of present-day philosophy of science. Besides, the question of whether theology is a science is no sterile academic quibble, but originates from a commitment to account for one's faith in God. Hence it is not a facile technique for modernizing traditional theological viewpoints, but an attempt to keep abreast of the problems of our age.

A theological model that sets itself up as a critical or argumentative theology will automatically be "antiauthoritarian." This must not be interpreted naively as a denial of the authority of the divine revelation. By seeking theoretical and theological clarity concerning its own premises, critical theology does not denigrate the revelation any more than was the case in other or earlier situations. What it does mean is an insistence on theological and theoretical clarity and a warning against an uncritical approach to philosophical presuppositions when divine

8. See Kuitert, 99.

revelation is adopted as a premise in opposition to contemporary thinking. In any event, the theologian must bear in mind that the "positiveness" of the revelation, that is, divine revelation as the (supposedly) unmediated premise of a theological model, offers no alternative to theological subjectivism.[9]

The Challenge of the Philosophy of Science

Essentially, scientific study can be defined as an intellectual enterprise governed by the goal of trying to find solutions to problems.[10] It involves the collection of data that are used to elucidate a particular problem area. To qualify as scientific data, this knowledge must satisfy certain minimum requirements. Scientific knowledge is aimed at obtaining insight into problem situations, and this insight is then formulated as accurately and correctly as possible.

In this context contemporary theories in the philosophy of science make a distinction between the *context of discovery* and the *context of justification*.[11] The former is the framework within which a scientist finds problems, where he or she finds fresh ideas that furnish insight into a problem situation.[12] Eventually these ideas are formulated into statements about something (namely a problem situation), and these statements are known as *hypotheses.*

In its dialogue with philosophy of science, theology will have to establish whether its statements are valid, that is, whether they qualify as hypotheses. A hypothesis is more than just an educated guess. It is

---

9. Since any recourse to dogmatism is ultimately an act of arbitrary subjectivity, critical theology will always be on its guard against a naive approach towards subjective presuppositions — an approach that could easily result in uncritical sanctioning of traditional conceptions, hence subtly endowing these with "revelational authority." For more detail, see J. W. van Huyssteen, "God en Werklikheid," *Ned. Geref. Teologiese Tydskrif* 14 (July 1973); "Teologie en Metode," 377ff.

10. See R. P. Botha, *Generatiewe Taalondersoek. 'n Sistematiese Inleiding* (Kaapstad, 1978), 31ff.

11. See Botha, 104. See also G. Sauter, *Wissenschaftstheoretische Kritik der Theologie* (München, 1973), 267ff.

12. Botha, 104: "The context of discovery concerns the invention of ideas."

an assumption about something[13] or a statement concerning a particular object. Often the solution to a problem requires the forming of
several interrelated hypotheses, which together are known as a *theory,*[14]
whereas a theoretical description gives a picture or rendering of something that cannot be observed directly. Hence a *theoretical description* is
not simply a summary of a collection of data, but is given in terms of
descriptive statements.[15] In this sense theories can also be regarded as
hypotheses.

It is in this connection that we distinguish between the context of
justification and the context of discovery. The *context of justification*
concerns justifications as "reasons for knowing,"[16] that is, substantiating
why certain statements should be accepted or rejected. It is a matter of
the merit of ideas, implying rational inquiry into the grounds for accepting or rejecting them.[17]

In the dialogue between systematic theology and the philosophy
of science it is manifest that the latter does not merely want to
establish a "uniform ideal" for science.[18] Instead the emphasis is on
rational progress in systematic theology, which brings us to the issue
of its scientific nature. This by no means implies that theology must
be abandoned to the mercy of "science," ultimately to be swamped by
and to succumb to alien norms. In fact, if a given theological viewpoint were to posit that the criteria whereby theology qualifies as a
science are governed not by prevailing rules of philosophy of science,
but by theological norms, then all dialogue would be cut short automatically.[19] Any theology that dissociates itself from the general
philosophy of science in this way on account of the "nature" of its

13. Botha, 108: "In the sphere of the search for scientific insight a hypothesis is a
presupposition concerning the possible underlying structure of a problematic state of
affairs."

14. See Botha, 109.

15. See Botha, 128.

16. See Botha, 263.

17. See Botha, 105.

18. Sauter, *Wissenschaftstheoretische,* 13: "Ihr ist vielmehr daran gelegen, ein Forum
zu bilden, auf dem die Einzelwissenschaften ihre Zielsetzungen als gemeinsamen, aber
unterschiedlich zu bewältigenden Erfordernissen messen können."

19. The viewpoint of, among others, Karl Barth, who summarily rejected Heinrich
Scholtz's minimum requirements for scientific validity. See van Huyssteen, *Teologie en
Metode,* 386-91.

object, is patently guilty of Hans Albert's charge — using a "strategy of immunization."[20]

On the other hand, inquiry into the basic premises of theology from a philosophy-of-science point of view may help to determine critically the source of theological investigation (the "context of discovery"). It can also help to establish the structure[21] and scope[22] of theological statements. Furthermore, in systematic theology the theorist's definition and systematization of prescientific language — as opposed to scientific terminology — are of paramount importance, not only because this is a particularly difficult problem in theology where the two levels of language often mingle unobserved, but also because it usually highlights a definite polarity between the hypothetical nature of theological statements and the absolute certainty of the language of faith.[23]

Philosophy of science therefore raises the problems of the structure of systematic theological statements, the object of such statements, and their relationship to the language of faith. It also raises the tricky problem of how theological statements can be controlled and tested. After all, of all disciplines theology should be most profoundly concerned with "speaking the truth" as far as possible.

The Contribution of Gerhard Sauter

Although the problem of theology and the philosophy of science has forced itself on virtually every theologian of our age, the ones chiefly concerned with it are Gerhard Sauter, Wolfhart Pannenberg, and, in the Netherlands, Harry Kuitert.

20. Albert, 129.

21. Inquiry into the structure of a theological proposition means establishing whether it asserts reality, whether it is a presupposition about something (as distinct from the one who voices it) — that is, whether theological propositions qualify as hypotheses.

22. See Sauter, *Wissenschaftstheoretische*, 10: "Die Wissenschaftstheorie ist es um formal präzise Aussagen und um ihrem Sachgerechtikeit zu tun."

23. See H. N. Janowski, "Wissenschaft von Gott und Religionskritik," in *Grundlagen*, 121.

Gerhard Sauter in particular has devoted himself to the scientific nature of systematic theology. He is convinced that theologians can answer affirmatively such questions as, Is theology a science, does it belong in universities, and can it hold its own in the future?[24] The crucial point is that theology cannot simply claim scientific status unless this claim is based on a specific task and method in which its ways of obtaining and communicating knowledge are decisive criteria. The problem of the quality and reliability of theological statements is intimately linked with methodological procedure, hence with research technique and the possibility of demarcating a specific object or sphere for theological study.[25]

For Sauter the main problem posed by philosophy of science is the problem of constructing theories. He argues in favor of a theoretical analysis of theological ways of thinking, which will permit a positive, *critical* approach to the discipline.[26] Only thus can theology comply with the criteria currently regarded as optimally scientific without subjecting itself to strictures that may endanger its true nature. In this way Sauter tries to break away from the futile extremes of "rationalism" versus "authority." As an alternative to these theology must rely on its own tradition, the validity of which has long been established in the history of the transmission of ideas. This validity no longer needs to be rationally *legitimized;* it merely wants rational support.[27]

At the same time Sauter warns against a pseudoscientific adaptation in theological thinking, whereby theologians will decide for themselves what they represent without previously questioning the scientific validity of their findings. Hence the demand for a theological theory gives rise to a theological metatheory, which poses the ultimate problem of the very foundations of theology as such.

In answer to the authoritarian dogmatism of dialectical theology, Sauter posits his own analytical theoretical model.[28] In this he attempts

24. G. Sauter, *Theologie als Wissenschaft, Historisch-systematische Einleitung,* Theologische Bücherei no. 43 (München, 1971), 16.

25. G. Sauter, in *Grundlagen,* 63.

26. Hence Sauter advocates critical theology without allowing theology to be consumed by the fire of "anti-metaphysical rationality." Sauter, *Wissenschaftstheoretische,* 24.

27. Sauter, *Wissenschaftstheoretische,* 214.

28. G. Sauter, "Die begründung theologischer Aussagen — wissenschaftstheoretisch gesehen," *Zeitschrift für Evangelische Ethik* 15 (1971): 299.

to establish a theory of theology that does not base apodictic utterances on mere possibility, but actually founds them; which does not merely expound statements, but argues consistently for them; which does not simply proclaim and confess in faith, but is prepared to discuss both faith and the language of religion; which does not summarily embrace faith and revelation as unproblematical presuppositions of theological statements, but makes them the object of critical inquiry.

That which is experienced and formulated in faith must therefore ultimately be justified in a theological context. This demonstrates not only the difference between the language of faith and of theological statements, but also the difference between *theological statements* and the *truths* they wish to proclaim.[29] Hence we must draw a clear line between the reality that forms the object of theological statements and the different *themes* of theological language. The latter is itself an object of a theory of theology in terms of which theological propositions can be described. Accordingly Sauter claims that a truly scientific theory of theology would be primarily a critique of theological language.[30] For theologians this means a questioning of the *theory formation* on which their statements are based.

Sauter's next point is explicit: The theologian plies his or her trade because of an allegiance to and involvement with the truth to which he or she attests.[31] The theologian must scrupulously avoid inferring any direct ethical requirements from this, that is, uncritically establishing the norms of his or her own theological methods in terms of this allegiance. Such a misconception may well mean that the *assent* of the theological speaker and the listeners within a religious community is exalted to the status of theological truth. Once the boundaries between faith and theology become as fluid as all that, scientific theology is ruled out and the distinction between pulpit and university chair becomes a purely practical one. At the same time Sauter warns against the naivité of a certain type of theory of knowledge, in which the mere citation of a biblical text is made to serve as a basis for theological statements. As an exegetical method even the Reformed principle of *sola scriptura* could

---

29. G. Sauter, *Von einem neuen Methodenstreit in der Theologie?* (München, 1970), 63ff.

30. Sauter, *Wissenschaftstheoretische*, 225.

31. Sauter, *Wissenschaftstheoretische*, 230.

become no more than "exegetical positivism with kerygmatic preten-
sions."[32]

Sauter himself regards systematic theology as a tentative result of
reflection on Scripture, as well as the thinking concerning Scripture that
has evolved historically; theology's sole purpose is to make this tradition
intelligible and topical to contemporary humankind. In any case, theology as a critical discipline is feasible only when it regards itself as a
facet of Christian history and methodically recognizes its pretheoretical
origin. To Sauter's mind these are determinative factors when we come
to the question of how theological statements are formed, what object
they presuppose, and what "material" is used in their formulation.

This clearly demonstrates Sauter's approach to the context of discovery in theology. It is not just the theoretical context out of which the
systematic theologian derives his or her problems, but emcompasses
every factor that plays any part in theological concept formation. As
such it embraces not only the contents of Scripture and reflection on
this as it has evolved through history, but also the overall history of
Christianity.[33] To Sauter this means not only that all theological thinking
is historically determined, but that its horizon of thought must inevitably be the *church*. In arriving at its ideas theology is accordingly bound
also by the church.[34]

The "context of discovery" is therefore fundamental to theorizing
underlying such central theological concepts as revelation, history,
church, God, humanity, and so on. Sauter sees the analysis of these
theories as an inescapable task for any theologian.[35] The theologian
must, however, bear in mind that involvement with the object of his or
her thinking goes beyond mere theory. It is a religious involvement that
forms the basis of what Sauter calls *assertory propositions*.[36] He advocates
accepting this as a basic form of religious expression. Assertory propositions are not merely "convictions," but are a form of expression that

32. See "Die Begründung theologischer Aussagen," 300; *Von einem neuen Methodenstreit in der Theologie?* 36.

33. See "Die Begründung theologischer Aussagen," 301.

34. Hence to define the field of systematic theology requires inter alia a *theory of
the church*. See Sauter, *Wissenschaftstheoretische*, 226.

35. See "Theologie als Beschreibung des Redens von Gott," 51; Sauter, *Wissenschaftstheoretische*, 271.

36. Sauter, *Wissenschaftstheoretische*, 288.

has eliminated all doubt as to God's presence. As propositions, the language of faith does not concern the problem of "authority," but rather the "positiveness" of faith. In this sense systematic theology should formulate its propositions in keeping with those of the language of faith. Theological statements must therefore provide answers to questions posed within the context of the Christian language of faith.

Unlike Pannenberg and Kuitert, Sauter recognizes only such theological statements — and not those of the language of faith — as *hypotheses* requiring substantiation.[37] Theological propositions can assume the structure of the language of faith, but only then — as *theological propositions* concerning certain data — can they be substantiated. To Sauter's mind this implies that the theologian is charged not merely with developing his or her own ideas of faith, but also with marking out areas for religious insight.

He therefore wants to take statements of faith and subject them to rational inquiry for testing and justification. But this implies a clear-sighted consideration of the relationship between the *truths* and the *propositions* of theology, bearing in mind that the two are not interchangeable. It means that theological tests/controls must not be taken to the positivist extreme of demanding rational or historical universality.

The demand for testing or justification of theological propositions within a definite context of justification can be satisfied neither by invoking an empirical or quasi-empirical criterion of meaning,[38] nor by postulating a uniquely theological concept of verification.[39] When it comes to substantiating theological propositions, Sauter sees their justification/substantiation or rejection as a matter of dialogical control. He is concerned with the *reliability* of a statement that needs to be substantiated within a given context of "universal statements" *(Ist-Sätzen)*, which can be regarded *theologically* as promises, and from a philosophy-of-science point of view as hypotheses of infinite range.[40]

Sauter's context of justification embraces not only Christian tradi-

---

37. Sauter, in *Grundlagen*, 72ff.

38. For example, by regarding "peace" or "willingness to be reconciled" or "fellowship" as a final criterion of Christianity — one can only claim that these qualities emanate from a "truly Christian belief." See Sauter, *Wissenschaftstheoretische*, 266ff.

39. Compare the viewpoint of Gerhard Ebeling. Sauter, *Wissenschaftstheoretische*.

40. Sauter, *Wissenschaftstheoretische*, 260; see also *Grundlagen*, 56.

tion, Holy Scripture, or confession(s), but also intersubjectivity or *consensus* within the church as a sphere of communication — the latter in turn forms part of the broader context of current philosophical problem recognition.[41]

Hence the theologian cannot substantiate his or her propositions purely by "critical" comparison with those of certain theological traditions, or by means of a fundamentalistic biblicism. On the contrary, they must be justified by inquiry into their intersubjectivity within a recognized (Christian) problem-consciousness.

In this sense theological propositions can act as regulators of the dialogue of the church-rules or concentrates of dialogue indicating a specific area of theological discussion; hence, they are subject to a given theoretical context. This is what Sauter chooses to call a *context of justification*. Such a context is never snatched arbitrarily from thin air, but is constituted by the assent of those who speak the language of contemporary theology and that of the philosophy of science.

To Sauter's mind systematic theology can be a science if the problem of the incompleteness and the imperfection of its propositions does not represent an existential problem to theologians, but if they are prepared to content themselves with limited statements with due regard for the eschatological polarity between history and revelation. Sauter is trying to show that he is less concerned with a rational justification of faith than with elucidation of those aspects of faith that are not amenable to theory by applying the precision of questions from a philosophy-of-science point of view. This transition from an experience of faith to theoretical description is not a transition from irrationality to rationality, but rather implies that theoretical praxis in theology should be distinct from that which must remain antecedent and extrinsic to theory.[42] In the process, theology as such should become definable, since the inquiry into the objectivizing of theology does not lessen the search for its object, but actually enhances it.

---

41. See "Die Begründung theologischer Aussagen," 303.
42. Sauter, *Wissenschaftstheoretische*, 235; also *Grundlagen*, 56ff.

The Contribution of Wolfhart Pannenberg

Gerhard Sauter's inquiry into the essential nature of systematic theology is an attempt to show that this way of thinking on the part of the believer can qualify as scientific reasoning, capable of theory construction and controlled propositions. This ideal of Sauter's is closely linked with that of Wolfhart Pannenberg, although their theological designs have different emphases. Like Sauter, Pannenberg tries to show that theology can satisfy scientific criteria without forfeiting its identity. Hence both prefer an argumentative rather than a positional theology with its typically preconceived (untested) premises.[43] Pannenberg is particularly outspoken on the topic of theology as a "positive science," in which a specific view of revelation has acquired such authority that it precludes any substantiation or proof.

Moreover, he criticizes Sauter's contrast between theological propositions and the assertory language of faith, where the former need to be justified within a theological context of justification. Pannenberg finds this approach too limited since it still fails to transcend the limits of religious subjectivity.

To counter this he posits a design whereby theology is viewed as the *science of God,*[44] a theological program comprising two phases: (1) *a theology of religions* and (2) *the science of Christianity.* By thus defining theology as the science of God with God as its "object," Pannenberg denies that theology has a definite, demarcated field of study, because we have no direct knowledge of God as an object. The quest for God and for the basis of our experience of God takes us to the human experience of self. Not only does this forge an indissoluble link between

---

43. H. N. Janowski, "Wissenschaft von Gott und Religionskritik," in *Grundlagen,* 122. See also H. O. Jones, "Faith and Theology," *Theology,* no. 280 (March 1978): 102: "For them theology is a matter of argument and not of rhetoric, a grappling with problems rather than the statement of a position, a construction and critique of theories rather than a believing exposition of the Faith."

44. From Pannenberg's extensive publications on this subject we cite the following works: "Die Krise des Schriftprinzips," in *Grundfragen systematischer Theologie* (Göttingen, 1967), 11-22; "Wie wahr is das Reden von Gott?" in *Grundlagen,* 29-41; "Theologie als Wissenschaft. Ein Gespräch," in *Grundlagen,* 58-121; "A Theological Conversation with Wolfhart Pannenberg," *Dialog* 11 (1972): 287-95; and of course his *Wissenschaftstheorie und Theologie* (Frankfurt: Suhrkamp, 1973).

theological and anthropological inquiry, it also gives us human religious experience as the only clear basis of theology.[45]

If now from the outset theology should confine itself to a specific religion — say, Christianity — this could be justified only if we assume that Christianity is more fit than any other religion to integrate human experience into a meaningful conception of reality. However, in the present age, where the superiority of the Christian faith is no longer to be taken for granted, theological inquiry can no longer be confined exclusively to Christian revelation.

Any such claim on the part of Christianity cannot be upheld on an authoritarian basis, but needs to be referred to a theology of religions.[46] The latter must investigate and test historical religions and establish to what extent they express divine truth, that is, by what means a given religion manages to convey God as the power of the future. In fact, religion is *par excellence* the sphere where human experience of divine power can be related to the total experience of reality.[47]

As the science of God, Pannenberg's theology proceeds from the premise that God can never be experienced in a direct, immediate sense. However, people experience God indirectly through their total experience of finite reality, although the latter is not accessible as either an intact or a circumscribed entity. Instead it is in the throes of a historical process, and as such is incomplete and open to the future. For this reason humans can experience the fullness of meaning only in anticipatory snatches each time they experience meaning in its universality. The reality of God can be experienced in such subjective anticipation of total reality. The study of religions becomes theology only once it tries to establish to what extent the traditions of different religions have recorded the "self-revelation" of divine reality.[48]

As the science of God, theology can be a theology of religions only in a indirect way, since religion is preeminently the sphere of which

45. This theological angle of Pannenberg's is shared by Harry Kuitert. See his "Waarheid en Verificatie in de Dogmatiek," *Rondom het Woord* 14, no. 2 (1972): 97-131; and especially *Zonder geloof vaart niemand wel*, 15-23.

46. See for detail Pannenberg, *Wissenschaftstheorie und Theologie*, 316ff.

47. Pannenberg, *Wissenschaftstheorie und Theologie*, 330. Cf. Kuitert: With its narratives, myths, and rites, religion explains the problem of how those relate to the whole of perceived reality (*Zonder geloof vaart niemand wel*, 23).

48. Pannenberg, *Wissenschaftstheorie und Theologie*, 317.

divine reality forms the explicit theme. Since God is nowhere the direct object of human experience, all talk about God should be *problematic* rather than *dogmatic*.[49] To Pannenberg this in fact means that the *idea of God* is presented as a *hypothesis*, in a sense of a proposition or statement *about* something, as distinct from the person who makes that statement.

As a hypothesis the concept of God would have to be justifiable in some way, at least if theologians wish to take a credible part in a dialogue with the philosophy of science. However, since God is not experienced directly as an object, any proper test in the sense of verification or falsification is manifestly impossible.[50] But the idea of God can also be measured indirectly by its *implications* for our concept of the world.[51] If successful, this verification is not based on something alien or extrinsic to the concept of God, but on something that could be considered analogous to an ontological proof of God's existence. However, in view of the totally historical character of human reality and our very partial knowledge of it, the concept of God must remain hypothetical.[52]

Hence Pannenberg's approach to God as the object of theology tallies with the problematic nature of the concept of God in our age. As regards the theologian's role in a dialogue with philosophy of science, Pannenberg maintains that in theology (as the science of God) God can be the object in only a problematical rather than an axiomatic sense. As far as a dialogue with philosophy of science is concerned, the theologian must be content with a specific kind of language usage: theological statements are hypotheses based on hypotheses based on hypotheses.

Pannenberg's theoretical distinction between faith and theology must not summarily be dismissed as cold-blooded. Ultimately it is a matter of profound concern that theologians should posit hypotheses

49. Pannenberg, *Wissenschaftstheorie und Theologie*, 301ff.

50. Pannenberg is trying to get away from the demands for verification, and especially of falsification, of the Popper school. In this respect H. G. Gadamer's historical hermeneutics has had a decisive influence on Pannenberg's thinking.

51. Pannenberg, *Wissenschaftstheorie und Theologie*, 302.

52. "Es Tehört also zur Endlichkeit theologishen Erkennens, dass der Gottesgedanke auch in der theologie hypothetisch bleibt." Pannenberg, *Wissenschaftstheorie und Theologie*, 302.

that are related to faith and the life of faith but not dominated by any particular faith or viewpoint.[53]

It is in this sense that Pannenberg sees theology as a science, and argues that it complies with Heinrich Scholz's[54] minimum requirements for a dialogue with philosophy of science:

1. all theological propositions must be aimed, directly or indirectly, at a definite object;
2. theological propositions should be statements or hypotheses about a given object, hence should be cognitively valid; and
3. they should be testable in some way.

The latter links up with Pannenberg's insistence that theological propositions should be justifiable in terms of their logical consistency and ability to integrate human experience of reality.[55] Thereby he refutes any absolute demands for verification or falsification; instead he postulates as "context of justification" the biblical, theological, and philosophical tradition, both past and present, inasmuch as it is salient to current problems. This method of control applies not to theology alone (which would once more isolate it as a science with a difference) but to every science that deals with contingent historical events and human beings rather than with physical laws.[56]

Unlike Sauter, Pannenberg maintains that a theologian's personal faith functions only in the context of discovery (this being part of his or her life-world) of theological propositions and not in the context of their justification.[57] In fact, he feels that the two contexts are confused

53. Thus, quite rightly Jones, "Faith and Theology," 102ff.

54. H. Scholz, "Wie ist eine evangelische Theologie als Wissenschaft möglich?" in *Theologie als Wissenschaft* (München, 1971), 221-64.

55. H. M. Kuitert also cites the fact that Christian faith opens up the future as *an affirmation* of its adequate approach to human reality. H. M. Kuitert, "Gesprek met H. Ridderbos," *Kerkinformatie* (Feb./Mar. 1976): 24.

56. See Daecke, "Soll die Theologie," 22. See also the related viewpoint of H. O. Jones: "The theologian, who need not have the believer peering censoriously over his shoulder, makes normal academic decisions; he is like (say) the literary critic, the historian, the anthropologist and the philosopher in that he develops hypotheses and theories about a certain range of data, in his case, the life of faith" (103).

57. Pannenberg, *Wissenschaftstheorie und Theologie*, 323.

58. Pannenberg, *Wissenschaftstheorie und Theologie*, 326.

as soon as personal religious *conviction/viewpoint* becomes the premise of an argument that also lays claim to intersubjective validity. Hence the second phase of Pannenberg's theological program, namely *the science of Christianity,* is not merely a reversion to specifically Christian articles of faith. Confining theology to Christianity alone would only be justifiable if the "truth" or "universality" of Christian tradition were generally recognized by a specific society.

In an exclusively Christian tradition theology could therefore be restricted to a hermeneutics of Christian revelation, provided its assumed absoluteness remains open to argument, at least in principle, and is not protected a priori against critical reflection.[58] However, such a circumscribed theology of Christianity must have at least a fundamental theory of theology if only for the purpose of establishing the special nature of its own revelation. Only by isolating that which makes it *specifically Christian* can the reasoning of such a special theology become intelligible to non-Christians, and in that sense justifiable.

In this sense the inquiry into the history of Christianity, and hence the theoretical development that has molded both dogma and theology, relativizes the positiveness of its own origins to the problem of how these in turn fit into the broader history of humanity and religious experience. But such relativizing is not a sacrifice to historicism. The open-ended, incomplete nature of history points towards a future that can be known provisionally.[59] Even though any statement about God must inevitably be provisional, God is already manifest as the power of the future — the God of Christianity and the God of the Bible. In this way Pannenberg appeals to theologians especially to be modest and to recognize the incompleteness of their propositions.

He therefore states: "I use the term 'know,' but I have a rather modest interpretation of knowledge and of reason. There is hardly knowledge of any ultimate character. This is not even present in the natural sciences,

59. "I would rather like to use 'knowledge' as a rather open category, so we can say that we are aware in some sense of our human situation, of the incompleteness of our existence and therefore that we need a future fulfillment, and a directing of our lives toward the future destiny." "A Theological Conversation with Wolfhart Pannenberg," *Dialog* 11 (1972): 295.

60. Pannenberg in "A Theological Conversation with Wolfhart Pannenberg," 295.

much less in many other areas of existence." And finally: "I think we always have the truth in the present, but in a provisional way."[60]

Some Conclusions

Within the confines of this article it is impossible to give a full critical evaluation of the views of Sauter and Pannenberg. I trust that my high regard for their open-mindedness and critical approach towards the crucial premises of systematic theology is sufficiently evident from sections 1 and 2. Indeed, no systematic theologian can evade the issues surrounding the theories that must necessarily precede any theological propositions.

I would like to conclude with the following:

1. One could inquire of Sauter whether his attempt at argumentative theology is not largely neutralized by his endeavor to incorporate consensus within a particular (ecclesial) group in his "context of justification." Also, to what extent does the formation of theory predetermine the assertory nature of the language of faith?

2. Wolfhart Pannenberg would concede that systematic theology need not invariably be preceded by a more comprehensive "theology of religions." But when it is, one could ask whether personal faith — which operates in the "context of discovery" — can really be separated from the theoretical context of justification. Why not consciously allow for the accounting of this subjective element from the outset in one's method?

3. Reflection on the determinants of theory formation in the development of theological propositions is a prerequisite for any model in systematic theology. Any inquiry into the nature and basic methods of these propositions must also study the human context in which a meaningful discussion about God would be possible.

4. Personal faith cannot probe beyond itself for ultimate proof. On the other hand, if theological propositions are to have any validity

from a philosophy-of-science point of view, they cannot simply be proved in terms of such faith. This is directly linked with the fact that the essence of (personal) faith can be described adequately only in terms of its (eschatological) structure. This cannot be divorced from the *skandalon* nature of the Christian message, something that has posed a methodological problem for systematic theologians from the earliest times. Properly interpreted however, this need not result in a deterministically adamant methodological premise. In fact, it could lead to awareness of the hypothetical nature of all faith, as well as of confessional and theological statements. At the same time it makes one realize the plurality of current Christian awareness and expression.

5. When confessional doctrine or a given theological tradition becomes the exclusive context of justification for theological propositions, this context can do no more than *regulate* the teaching of the church. Such one-sided emphasis on consensus as an aspect of truth must inevitably breed excessive denominational conventionality, because the prevailing dogmas of the church ultimately form the basis of all theological statements.

A first step towards clarifying the relationship between theology and confession would be to realize that confessional denominationalism cannot serve as an unquestioned premise for systematic theology, thereby immunizing it against all criticism. By the very nature of its object, systematic theology is essentially ecumenical, hence it cannot proceed from the (confessional) differences between the Christian churches. Instead it should operate hermeneutically from the words and events of the Bible (as source documents of Christianity) and proceed from there to analyze Christian tradition and the problems this raises for our thinking today.

Chapter Seven

The Realism of the Text:
A Perspective on Biblical Authority

And my intellect's hunger was sated only when I saw the single horse that the monks were leading by the halter. Only then did I truly know that my previous reasoning had brought me close to the truth. And so the ideas, which I was using earlier to imagine a horse I had not seen, were pure signs, as the hoofprints in the snow were signs of the idea of "horse"; and signs and the signs of signs are used only when we are lacking things.

Umberto Eco, *The Name of the Rose*

W HEN I WAS FIRST TOLD THAT THE THEME FOR THIS PAPER WAS TO be the authority of the Bible, my initial response was one of slight surprise. This surprise was not at all caused by the fact that this theme might be regarded as rather strange or unusual. On the contrary, there is something so obvious about it: surely everybody must know that the Bible has always fulfilled — and today still fulfills — a central role in the Christian tradition. What did spark my interest, however, was the realization that precisely the so-called "authority" of the Bible has always managed to function as the *primary explanatory construct* of this tradition of faith. The rather astounding implications of this fact succeeded in confronting me with an unavoidable and exciting intellectual challenge. If the Bible really has some sort of "authority," surely these texts must then authorize us to make valid assertions about God and God's relation to our world? If this were true, it could indeed mean that the Bible should be seen as *the* classic model for understanding God and God's relationship to the world in the ongoing process of our theological reflection.

The real problem of course lies on a deeper level: How reliable is the knowledge we might gain from the Bible? How reliable, in other words, are the theological claims that seek to explain the Bible? Against this background, the question of the authority of the Bible, for the church and for theology, in reality becomes an inevitably *epistemological* problem.

The central question of this paper — "What do we really mean when we talk about the authority of the Bible?" — can now be rephrased in a much more accurate manner, namely: "What is the epistemological status of the Bible in theological reflection?"

If the role or function of the Bible in obtaining reliable knowledge becomes in this way an epistemological problem, systematic theology is immediately and inevitably drawn into the interdisciplinary context of contemporary philosophy of science. I am therefore convinced that there is no way that this question can be pursued in a private manner as an esoteric problem for the church only. This would invariably lead, even if presented in a sophisticated way, to a sectarian version of confessional theology that would destroy the very basic and valid epistemological perspective of the problem at hand. The problem of the authority of the Bible therefore confronts the systematic theologian with special demands and the need for high standards of reflection; as an epistemological problem it can never be regarded as a problem exclusive to, for example, Reformed theology or Anglican theology. It is in fact not even a Protestant or a Catholic problem. The problem of the authority of the Bible is a *transconfessional* problem. Systematic theology will have to deal with this issue responsibly by realizing that the epistemological nature of the problem will involve metatheological criteria.

Because of this, the quest for the epistemological status of the Bible in Christian thought is directly linked to the credibility of Christian faith as such. And the way we deal with this problem will to a great extent determine whether Christian faith is a curiosity to be tolerated, or whether it is an important dimension of intellectual life that may help us not only to construct adequate models of reality, but also to link that endeavor to our ultimate quest for meaning in life.[1] The epistemological question of the status of the Bible in the claims that theologians make for the reliability of their knowledge not only forms the obvious basis for all further contextual, methodological, and hermeneutical problems in theology, but also unites the theologian with all other scientists faced with the same problem. In the natural sciences and the humanities, scientists from different fields are also wrestling today with the fundamental problem of the validity and reliability of human knowledge.

This of course immediately raises the broader question as to the relationship between theology and science — a question that can, however, be answered only after we have examined the validity of the claims made by both theology and science. What is very important, at this stage, is to realize that both science and theology — the latter as reflection on the meaning and claims of Christian faith — have been profoundly affected by the epistemological theories of recent and current schools in the philosophy of science.

Science and theology also share another type of universality. In religion, we find one of the most characteristic features of all societies: humankind's long search for ultimate meaning and significance in a transcendent reality beyond this world. Christian theology is a very specific reflection on this universal quest. Just as universally, science today is a common factor pervading all cultures. Arthur Peacocke is therefore very much to the point when he states, "The relationship between these two claimants on mankind's loyalty is probably the most fundamental challenge that faces the mind and spirit of human beings today."[2]

In trying to come to terms with this complex issue, it could be very useful to start off by phrasing the common problem that confronts theology and the other sciences in the following way: What can be

---

1. See B. Waters, "Critical Realism within the Academy: A Response to Peacocke," *Religion and Intellectual Life* 2 (1985): 66.
2. A. Peacocke, *Intimations of Reality: Critical Realism in Science and Religion* (Notre Dame: University of Notre Dame Press, 1984), 13.

regarded as *real* for scientific thought? Or: What *realities* are scientists and theologians asserting when they theorize? And even more important: Are these realities really so important when it comes to assessing the reliability and validity of our knowledge?

The question of whether theology and science indeed inform us about something that might be *real out there* but also *real for us* is obviously extremely important for any Christian theology that consciously reflects from a commitment to a transcendent God as a reality out there. At this stage, however, I do want to stress that the way in which I am here relating theology and science to a common problem does not stem from any conviction that the natural sciences should necessarily always be regarded as *the* paradigm for what constitutes reliable knowledge. On the contrary, I am stressing what most of us might already know: in assessing their knowledge, in defining the important concepts of rationality and objectivity, and in exploring the important role of models and criteria for the validity of knowledge — whether about entities in nature or about God and God's revelation — both scientists and theologians have been profoundly influenced by the epistemological theories of recent and current schools of thought in philosophy of science. This should not be at all surprising, since philosophers of science are supposed to deal with the complex issue of the reliability of human knowledge. Redefining the problem of the authority of the Bible in theological reflection has thus brought us to the dynamic relationship between theology and the evolving models of rationality functioning in different epistemological theories of the philosophy of science. In my recent book[3] I analyzed this complex problem in detail and also focused on extraordinary revolutions that have taken place in the recent history of the philosophy of science, unfortunately largely unnoticed by the broader theological community. For all of us theologians, this has created a lamentable if not rather embarrassing situation: without even realizing it, our views on what constitute criteria for reliable knowledge in theology have been directly influenced by positivism, critical rationalism, Kuhn's revolutionary paradigm theory, and, lately, the emergence of scientific realism. For all the sciences, but especially

---

3. J. Wentzel van Huyssteen, *Theology and the Justification of Faith: The Construction of Theories in Systematic Theology* (Grand Rapids: Wm. B. Eerdmans, 1989).

for theology, this situation creates enormous challenges, but also problems. Positivism held sway from the 1920s to the 1970s and virtually forced theology into a retreat to an esoteric faith commitment and — as far as theological claims to reliable knowledge were concerned — into an intellectual commitment to theories that were equally esoteric and inaccessible for critical evaluation. Theology's intellectual stance and immunization tactics were to be severely criticized by critical rationalists.[4] Yet even today the standard positivist view of scientific knowledge still ruthlessly dominates many forms of theology in spite of their so-called "biblical" foundation.

Thomas Kuhn's historicist model caused a revolution in epistemological theories and today is still extremely influential.[5] The Kuhnian model necessitates that social factors are taken into account to explain theory acceptance and even existential commitment in a scientific community; as a result, the new problem of the underdetermination of theory by data, that is, the theory-ladenness of all data, has radically redefined the concepts of scientific objectivity, progress, and rationality. All this creates exciting new challenges for theology, but unfortunately also seemingly insurmountable problems concerning the problem of truth, as well as the possibility of theological propositions actually referring to a transparadigmatic reality.

The ongoing influence of Kuhn's perspective has led to socially contextualized views of scientific theories, resulting in a new emphasis on the sociological factors that influence the development of science. The sociology of knowledge has been specifically applied to the nature of scientific knowledge. For theology, in the light of the realization that scientific knowledge can apparently never be stable in meaning because it is never independent of social context, the status of its propositional truth-claims within the Kuhnian paradigm becomes more urgent than ever before. If it could indeed be finally asserted that scientific as well as theological assertions are socially created, it would seem highly likely that the ways of both science and theology to reality have been firmly barred. This in turn would create special problems for the truth-claims

4. See W. W. Bartley, *The Retreat to Commitment* (London: Chatto and Windus, 1964).

5. T. S. Kuhn, *The Structure of Scientific Revolutions*, 2nd ed. (Chicago: University of Chicago Press, 1970).

and the validity of all human knowledge, for if all scientific and thus also theological knowledge is purely social construct, there can be no way in which reference or reality depiction can be claimed for their theories. If neither science nor theology can claim some sort of valid knowledge about existing realities, what could prevent them from becoming merely social ideologies?

It is against this background that the very recent development of different forms of qualified scientific realism after decades of positivism, and the ensuing constant threat of a paradigmatic relativism, can definitely be seen as one of the most remarkable and welcome features of scientific thought in the twentieth century.[6] When it comes to reflecting on the reliability of scientific and theological knowledge, the concept *realism* could indeed be called the catchword of the 1980s.[7] As we will see, scientific realism is so called because it makes a proposal about the reliability of scientific knowledge as such, and is therefore basically a philosophical position. For all philosophers of science who advocate realism, it forms an important alternative to the Kuhnian critique of scientific progress. Without losing the validity of the fact that all human knowledge is socially contextualized, realists claim cognitive reference for their proposals.

Especially for those systematic theologians struggling to salvage the respectability of theological claims, epistemological realism therefore forms an important intellectual challenge. Personally I am convinced that no theologian who is trying to determine what the authority of the Bible might mean today, and to identify the epistemological status of the Bible in theological reflection, can avoid the important issues raised by some qualified forms of critical realism for theology. Burnham therefore very convincingly states:

> Now we are beginning to recognize that the common issue for both science and religion at this moment in time is not the origin of the universe, the validity of evolution or the existence of God, but the basic principles of epistemology: how do we human beings come to terms with "reality," that which is.[8]

6. See F. B. Burnham, "Response to Arthur Peacocke," *Religion and Intellectual Life* 2 (1985): 28.

7. See Peacocke, 11.

8. Burnham, 27.

One of the most basic philosophy-of-science questions of our time is, therefore, To what extent do scientific and theological terms *refer*? Or, To what extent do theology and science respectively describe reality, or certain domains of reality, in an epistemologically valid way?

When this question has been answered, I shall try to come to terms with the real issue at hand: the epistemological status of the Bible in theological reflection. To enable me to deal with this difficult problem, I will propose a modest or qualified form of critical realism combined with a very specific social understanding of cognitive reference.

Critical Realism in Theology

For some theologians the retrieval of a redefined postpositivist concept of rationality in order to claim validity and reliability for the process of theological thought has become a major issue. Closely related to this is the strong conviction that the quest for ultimate meaning in life cannot take place within a dichotomy between faith and knowledge, but only within their creative interaction. With this in mind, I think it is fairly obvious why some theologians during the past few years have begun to grasp the enormous potential of scientific realism for theology. During this time important works have been published by theologians like McFague, Peacocke, and Soskice on what has come to be known as *critical realism* in theology.[9]

I do think, however, that anyone considering the possibilities of scientific realism for theology should be extremely wary of an uncritical, superficial transferring of the realism of science to the domain of religious belief, and to theology as the reflection on the claims of this belief. I also think Hefner[10] quite correctly questions the somewhat doctrinaire sense in which the term *critical realism* is sometimes used in theology: it is indeed not yet quite an established theory of explanation, but rather

9. S. McFague, *Metaphorical Theology: Models of God in Religious Language* (London: SCM, 1983); Peacocke; J. M. Soskice, *Metaphor and Religious Language* (Oxford: Clarendon Press, 1985).

10. P. Hefner, "Just How Much Can We Intimate about Reality? A Response to Arthur Peacocke," *Religion and Intellectual Life* 2 (1985): 32.

a very promising and suggestive hypothesis, struggling for credibility while being at the center of discussion. At the basis of the reasons for using this term is the conviction that what we are provisionally conceptualizing in theology really exists. The basic assumption and the good reasons we have for it make it possible for theologians, like scientists, to believe they are theorizing in a valid, progressive, and therefore successful way.

The strength of the critical realist position certainly lies in its insistence that both the objects of science and the objects of religious belief lie beyond the range of literal description.[11] I personally think this eventually represents a major advance in our understanding of what not only science, but also theology, can achieve. To put it in Peacocke's words,[12] the scientific and theological enterprises share alike the tools of groping humanity — words, ideas, images that have been handed down, which we refashion in our own way for our own times in the light of present-day experience. Science and theology, for the Christian, can therefore be seen only as interacting and mutually illuminating approaches to reality. What exactly is meant by "reality" in this context will of course have to be carefully analyzed. I think Peacocke, as regards the issue of reality in science and theology, is correct in warning against a form of discrimination when we attribute "reality" as such. Indeed there is no sense in which subatomic particles are to be regarded as "more real" than a bacterial cell or a human person or, even, social facts or God.[13]

When Peacocke, however, proceeds to relate these realities to different levels of reality, it does become more problematical. It could imply that realism should then apply in a similar way to the fields of both science and theology, which, as we will see, would be highly problematical. I think McMullin pinpoints the problem by underlining the fact that there is no way that science and theology could deal with the same reality,[14] and rather than saying that there are different "levels" of reality, one should realize that science and theology for the most part deal with *different domains* of the same reality. He states it very clearly:

11. See E. McMullin, "Realism in Theology and Science: A Response to Peacocke," *Religion and Intellectual Life* 2 (1985): 47.

12. Peacocke, 51.

13. Peacocke, 36.

14. McMullin, "Realism," 39.

Science has no access to God in its explanations; theology has nothing to say about the specifics of the natural world.[15]

Where I do, however, think the two overlap, is on the level of reflection or human knowledge: each has something important to say about two very different but also very important domains of reality. For myself this is very important: it is on this level, the problem of the reliability of theological knowledge, that a theory of critical realism will have to be put to the test. A qualified form of critical realism, therefore, goes beyond the fruitless realist/antirealist debate of "proving" either that the reality theology is talking about really exists or that it is only a "useful fiction" for helping people to lead better lives. In this sense McMullin also sympathizes with the claim that both science and theology could be regarded as "realist," that is, as making reliable truth-claims about domains of reality that lie beyond our experience.[16]

Peacocke, when defining theology, underscores the important fact that theology is to be seen as the reflective and intellectual analysis of the religious experience of humankind, and in particular of the Christian experience.[17] Because believers regard themselves as making meaningful assertions about a reality that humans can and do encounter in faith experiences, religion and religious experience has always been and still is regarded as a "way to reality," that is, as referring to a reality beyond our experience.

While agreeing with this, the logical and important next question should now be, *What, within the context of the Christian faith, ultimately evokes genuine faith experiences?* It seems to me that this will bring us back to the central and basic role of the biblical text as the classical religious text of Christianity. Peacocke, however, unfortunately disregards this question and instead focuses on the following, but equally essential question: Can religious experience, which is so intimate and personally deep within the individual psyche, ever find a communicable language that could not only be socially effective but also manage to refer to God?[18] This is a valid and important question that will take us directly to questions regarding the

15. McMullin, "Realism," 40.
16. McMullin, "Realism," 39.
17. Peacocke, 37.
18. Peacocke, 39.

status of theoretical terms in theology, and thus also to an assessment of the role of models and metaphor in theology. For it is through the role of metaphors and models that the relationship between science and theology, on the one hand, and the different realities they are claiming in their respective assertions, on the other, becomes clear.

At this stage three important questions have now crystallized:

1. What ultimately evokes genuine faith *experiences* and how important are these experiences for theological propositions?
2. Is the *language of faith* structured in such a way that it can be socially and contextually effective as well as manage to refer to God in an epistemologically reliable way?
3. What is the role of models and metaphors in the relationship between *theological thought,* on the one hand, and the reality it is claiming in its statements, on the other?

I would like to argue that all three of these issues, that is, faith experiences, the language of faith, and the theoretical language of theological reflection, somehow presuppose an essential role of the biblical text and the interpretative tradition that presents this classical religious text of Christianity to us today. Or stated in a more direct way: The Bible plays a decisive role in the experience of Christian faith and in the structuring of the language of faith as well as the eventual nature of the theoretical structure of theological statements. The difficult question of course is, What exactly is the role of the Bible in Christian faith? Or in more traditional language, Does the Bible have any authority when it comes to experiencing faith, talking about faith, or reflecting theoretically about faith? The answer to these important questions will, in my opinion, not only determine the epistemological status of the Bible in theological reflection, but also be the final test for a theory of critical realism in theology.

Although Peacocke in his presentation of critical realism in theology never explicitly considers the Bible as being of direct importance to theology's eventual claims to reality, he does mention the problem that some Christians resort to the "pure Word of God" available through scriptures, with its inherent "divine authority."[19] To this widespread but

19. Peacocke, 39.

extremely problematical issue he adds an even more complex problem: How can we *know* that these scriptures are transmitting to us the genuine word of God? Peacocke never answers this question, but I hope to succeed in pointing out that for a convincing theory of critical realism in theology, the answer to this very legitimate problem is in fact essential.

For the critical realist science is always discovery and exploration as well as construction and invention.[20] Unlike the naive realist, and along with the instrumentalist, the critical realist model of rationality recognizes the importance of human imagination in the formation of theories. In this way the critical realist tries to acknowledge both the creativity of human thought and the existence of structures in reality not created by the human mind. Concerning the role of models in scientific theory, critical realism will be defending a position between literalism on the one hand and fictionalism on the other hand. In this sense theoretical models now become valid, but provisional and limited, ways of imagining what otherwise can never be truly observable.

The most fundamental claim of critical realism is therefore that while all theories and models are partial and inadequate, the scientist not only discovers as well as creates, but with good reasons also believes that his or her theories actually refer.[21] This of course now brings us to the central question: If all serious users of models believe that their models in some or other way refer to reality, *in what way do they refer?* [22] In the answer to this question the correspondence between models in science and in theology is indeed remarkable: models, as metaphorically based screens or "grids," indirectly redescribe reality. That means something new and valid is being said about reality, which the user of the model believes describes it better, more appropriately, than other competing views. Any realist position therefore rightly stresses the fact that there is no uninterpreted access to reality and that in the process of interpretation the role of metaphor is central.

In theology, critical realism will imply a model of rationality where theological concepts and models are indeed provisional, inadequate, and partial, but on the other hand, also necessary as the *only* way of referring

20. See I. Barbour, *Myths, Models and Paradigms: A Comparative Study in Science and Religion* (New York: Harper and Row, 1974), 37.

21. See Van Huyssteen, *Justification of Faith*, 143-46.

22. See McFague, 133.

to the reality that is God, and the reality of God's relation to humanity. In spite of important differences, which will be dealt with later, I do believe that in both science and theology our models actually refer and are as close as we can get to speaking accurately of reality. These models are therefore not literal pictures, but are also more than useful fictions.[23] The metaphorical language of the biblical text and the dominant models we have formed from it represent aspects of the reality of things Christians believe are in no way directly accessible to us.[24] As such they are to be taken seriously but not literally, for although they refer in an ontological or cognitive sense, they are always partial and inadequate. Not only for evaluating the possibilities of a critical realism in theology, but especially for determining the epistemological status of the Bible in theological thought, it is of fundamental importance to realize that the Bible — as the classical text of Christianity — has provided the Christian tradition with metaphors so basic to this faith that they are indeed indispensable. This will be the case not only for the models and theories they eventually generate for theology, but also for determining the status of the Bible.

Some of these well-known metaphors are the following: God is often described as Father, Creator, King, Shepherd, or Judge; Jesus is seen as the Christ, Messiah, Son of Man, Son of God, Redeemer, Saviour, Good Shepherd; and the third person of the Trinity as the Holy Spirit, Comforter, Sustainer. The Bible itself is of course seen as the "revealed" "Word of God" and as such as a very special and "inspired" book. Some of these metaphors have of course grown into dominant models that have generated theological theories that, although theoretical and conceptual, have never and can never lose their metaphorical roots. Peacocke therefore correctly states: these models are so deeply embedded in Christian language that it is extremely difficult to form theories and concepts entirely devoid of metaphor, for even abstract words like "transcendent" and "immanent" partake of spatial metaphors.[26]

Now, if metaphors always work by tentative suggestion and always imply assertions, it is only in an instrumentalist position that the prob-

23. See Peacocke, 42.
24. See Van Huyssteen, *Justification of Faith*, 125ff.
25. Peacocke, 41.
26. Soskice, 106.

lem of ontological reference can — and then only temporarily — be avoided. The most interesting metaphors in theoretical language are those that suggest an explanatory network and therefore are vital at the growing edges of the sciences and of theology. What could therefore never be consistent is the sort of hybrid position in which some theologians continue to speak of the *cognitive* use of metaphors and models in theological language when only implying the evoking of meaningful religious experience, and thus do not consider the problem of reference or reality depiction at all. Soskice is therefore correct in stating:

> The conclusion that theistic models are descriptive and representational, but what they describe and represent is the human condition, is not only disappointing when it comes at the end of a comparison of models in science and religion, but makes the whole comparison a nonsense.[27]

Realist assumptions have of course always been an essential part of Christian belief, and if there is to be any meaningful comparison between models in science and religion, it would have to be one that takes this realist assumption, and the faith commitment implied by it, seriously. It should be clear at this stage that for the realist, models in both science and theology are metaphorical, and as "candidates for reality" they are as close as we can get to speaking accurately of the respective domains with which science and theology are concerned. As such the formulation of models in both science and theology partakes of the nature of discovery and of increasing intelligibility.[28] In science it is the entities and structures of the natural world that are successfully discovered and rendered intelligible. In theology it is humankind's search for ultimate meaning in terms of Christian faith that is rendered intelligible.

As I have pointed out earlier, the importance of critical realism in theology could never be to provide "proof" for the existence of God. On the contrary, theological reflection — in the Christian sense of the word — takes place within the context of an ultimate faith commit-

---

27. Peacocke, 42.

28. Hefner, 33; see also R. J. Russell, "A Critical Appraisal of Peacocke's Thought on Religion and Science," *Religion and Intellectual Life* 2 (1985): 54.

ment to God as a personal but transcendent Creator. In this sense theology, and the domain of theology, differs profoundly from that of the other sciences: even an existential commitment to theories or to a certain paradigm of thought cannot be compared to the ultimate commitment evoked in the response of faith. This basic assumption, strengthened by the critical realist argument, makes it possible for theologians to believe they are theorizing in a valid and progressive way. This commitment is inevitably related to the referential power of the classic religious texts of Christianity. For my own understanding of critical realism in theology, this will eventually become a decisive factor.

What is important, however, is that on the level of theoretical theological reflection, this ultimate commitment does in reality function in the same way as realist assumptions in some of the other sciences. In this sense an ultimate religious commitment, like an existential commitment to the theories of scientific realism, becomes part of the realist argument and not an irrational retreat to commitment. Therefore, when Hefner wrestles with the difficult question,[29] Does the realist argument open up a way for us to know or assert confidently that the entities referred to in scientific concepts, or the God referred to by theologians, really exist, or do we have to take a "leap of faith" to assert that reality? we will have to answer by stating:

1. The critical realist argument opens up a way to *reliable and valid assertions* about the Reality to which we are ultimately committed[29] and which we have come to call "God."
2. We will also have to acknowledge the basic "need for faith" or the role of a faith commitment in the Christian theologian's attempt at the critical realist argument.

But in this attempt we will have to realize that we are not involved in "proving" the reality of God; instead, we are trying to give reasons why as theologians we reason and theorize in the way that we do, and to show that the "theological method" is not so different from what other scientists are doing. To the fact that even an ultimate faith commitment

29. See R. Trigg, *Reason and Commitment* (Cambridge: Cambridge University Press, 1973), 42.

is always already conceptualized and theorized, I shall return later. What is important at this stage is that whatever the difference between a religious commitment and an intellectual commitment to theories might be, *in practice* both function as already conceptualized background theories on the level of theoretical reflection.

In the case of the Christian faith a very definite view of the Bible always forms — at least in a tacit way — part of these background theories. Could it be that the Bible is after all not directly foundational for Christian arguments but instead is part of a much more comprehensive argument, which forms the *real* basis for a specific Christian viewpoint? This question, as we will shortly see, will become the most important issue that confronts critical realism in theology.

Theology thus basically reflects on religious experience and the ensuing religious language as ways to the Reality that is God. But these experiences, and their accompanying metaphorical language, can be reliably interpreted only on the basis of the classical texts of the Christian faith. In this sense the text of the Bible, as the ultimate "way" to the reality of God, and thus as Christianity's indispensable book of faith, in itself becomes a reality that functions epistemologically as a very exclusive access to the reality of God. This is what I mean when I talk about *the realism of the text.* The implications of this claim will now have to be analyzed. The same goes for the arguments that have crystallized — in direct relation to this central claim — in favor of a critical realism in theology:

1. As an historical fact, the Bible has survived as a religious text and as a book of faith in a long and remarkable interpretative tradition of an ongoing faith-context.

2. The text of the Bible has evoked, throughout centuries of belief in God, ongoing faith experiences; and the same text today still evokes Christian experiences. Theological reflection provides interpretation and reinterpretation of these experiences, of which God is believed to be the cause, on the basis of the biblical text. This allows us to refer to God, but without claiming to describe God.

3. The metaphorical structure of biblical language has creatively provided *the continuity of reference* to religious and theological language through the ages. This obviously presupposes a con-

tinuous language-using community[30] going back to the "initiating events" when these metaphorical terms were first introduced.

Determining the role of the Bible in obtaining knowledge of God will
provide us with an answer to the question as to the epistemological
status of the Bible. This, in turn, will determine what we should mean
when we talk about the authority of the Bible.

The Realism of the Text

In discussing the reliability of the claims made by theology in terms
of the Bible, we saw how the role of the Bible in theological thought
grew into a comprehensive epistemological problem. The problem of
the "authority of the Bible" was therefore rephrased as, What is the
epistemological status of the Bible in theological reflection? This
brought us face to face with the metatheological challenge of epistemological theories of present-day philosophy of science, and especially
the important issues raised by critical realism for the rationality of
theological reflection. The critical realist argument convincingly shows
that our only access to the reality for which the scientist is groping is
through the scientific concept. This is especially true of Christian
theology too; our only epistemic access to God is through the central
metaphoric concepts of the Christian tradition, which because of their
reference or reality depiction might be able to provide us provisionally
with reliable knowledge of a Reality that in fact lies beyond our intellectual grasp.

We also saw that the Bible — as the classical religious text of the
Christian faith — provides us with these metaphors. These metaphors
are so basic, so indispensable, that they play a central role in the evoking
of religious experiences as well as in the structuring of the language of
faith, and especially also in the theoretical language of theological reflection. In this sense the text of the Bible, as Christianity's indispensable
book of faith, proves itself to be a reality that functions epistemologically
as a very exclusive access to the Reality that is God.

30. See Peacocke, 47ff.

Seeing the Bible as a "very exclusive access" to God still sounds rather vague at this stage. But this basic fact, along with the metaphorical structure of biblical language, its reality depiction, and especially the *continuity of metaphorical reference this has creatively given to theological language through the ages*, finally prompted me to speak of the *realism of the biblical text*. What exactly this implies for the status of the Bible in obtaining reliable knowledge about God will now have to be pursued in detail.

1. The Status of the Biblical Text

When earlier I distinguished between an ultimate faith commitment and an intellectual commitment to theories, I briefly mentioned the fact that both — whatever their differences might be — function as already conceptualized background theories on the level of theoretical reflection. In the case of the Christian faith an implicit but very definite view of the Bible inevitably forms part of these background theories. This is so because speaking, reading, and therefore interpreting are human actions that always arise within very specific contexts.

Lundin can therefore persuasively argue that we all inevitably read as people who seek, belong, and act.[31] The sociology of knowledge, and the Kuhnian and post-Kuhnian philosophy of science, have of course underlined this idea. To this Lundin adds this important fact: because of the omnipresence of metaphor, there is no discourse, not even the discourse of the sciences, that can claim to be completely disinterested and untouched by the reality of human history.[32] Like texts themselves and those who seek to understand them, our interpretations are always part of history.

In an earlier publication I argued that our often very divergent views of the Bible, which as such are part of larger models of thought through which we approach the Bible, are always already and unconditionally part of our diverse theorized or conceptualized frameworks

---

31. R. Lundin, "Our Hermeneutical Inheritance," in R. Lundin, A. C. Thiselton, and C. Walhout, *The Responsibility of Hermeneutics* (Grand Rapids: Wm. B. Eerdmans, 1985), 27.

32. Lundin, 23.

of thought.[33] Whatever we might say later about the authority of the Bible is therefore directly related to this process of theorizing or the forming of opinions, which not only reflects our most basic and direct faith-experiences, but also our implicit intellectual decisions taken even *before* we approach the text. This also implies that a particular view of the Bible can never be the "true," "best," or "biblical" view just because it was presented to us by a reliable or even authoritative tradition. It could, of course, prove to be the most reliable view of the Bible — and thus also show progress in our theories about the Bible — but it will first of all have to prove itself to be appropriate to the text itself.

To the systematic theologian the question as to the status of the Bible in theological thought now becomes more problematic than ever. Not only has the problem of the authority of the Bible acquired a transconfessional and epistemological scope, but we now also know that no interpreter enters the process of interpretation without some prejudgments. And included in those prejudgments, through the very language we speak and write, is the history of the effects of the traditions forming that language.[34] The fact that we always seem to have a highly theorized and contextualized view of the Bible obviously implies that the Bible itself can never be the so-called objective, foundationalist, and "pure" basis for theological arguments it is so often taken to be, whether in the well-known Barthian sense or in the more traditionally Reformed sense of a direct resort to the text of the "pure Word of God." And once we take leave of these naive realist positions, it becomes obvious that the Bible — instead of being the presumed foundation of all our theological arguments — becomes in fact, epistemologically at least, a crucial *part* of our theological arguments.

This of course gives rise to a complicated new problem: If we always approach the Bible with a definite pretheorized background view about the Bible, and the Bible thus becomes part of our theological arguments, are there any criteria for determining good, better, or best ways to let the Bible function as a crucial part of our theological arguments? For

33. W. van Huyssteen, and B. Du Toit, *Geloof en Skrifgesag* (Pretoria: N. G. Kerkboekhandel, 1982), 1-10.

34. See D. Tracy, "Interpretation of the Bible and Interpretation Theory," in R. M. Grant, *A Short History of the Interpretation of the Bible* (London: SCM, 1984), 157.

an understanding of what eventually will be meant by the "authority" of the Bible, this is indeed a critical question. I hope to show that an argument that deals responsibly — both epistemologically and herme-neutically — with the *realism of the text*, will be able to supply these criteria and, in however provisional a way, lead to a redefinition of what might be called biblical authority. Only then will we be able to answer Kelsey's important questions: When a theologian takes biblical texts as authoritative for theology, what decisions does he or she make about these texts? What decisions does he or she make before even turning to the text at all?[35]

Since the Reformation and up to the present, Protestant theology has of course characteristically maintained the so-called scriptural principle. According to this *sola scriptura*–principle it is the Bible alone that is or ought to be the primary authority not only for the Christian faith, but also for Christian theology, as the reflective understanding of this faith. Apart from the "authority neurosis"[36] this created mainly among Reformed theologians, there is today a growing and understandable uncertainty among some theologians whether there is any sense at all in maintaining this principle. Ogden states as the two main reasons for this:

1. the growing dialogue between Protestant and Roman Catholic theology;
2. continuing developments in the historical-critical understanding of the Bible.[37]

To this I would like to add:

3. a rather violent reaction in Protestant theology against the epistemological primitivism[38] of all forms of fundamentalism, so often posing as "biblical" theologies in spite of the naive realist structure of this model of thought;

35. D. H. Kelsey, *The Uses of Scripture in Recent Theology* (London: SCM, 1975), ix.

36. See J. Barr, *The Bible in the Modern World* (London: SCM, 1973), 113.

37. S. Ogden, "The Authority of Scripture for Theology," *Inspiration* 30 (1976): 242.

38. See J. E. Barnhart, "Every Context has a Context," *SJTh* 33 (1980): 501.

4. the complex and challenging developments in modern literary criticism, especially reader-response theories and postmodern philosophies of deconstruction.

For the systematic theologian this poses a difficult double challenge: not only has the scripture principle always been so central to Protestant thought that he or she would be obliged to ask whether there is any sense at all in which it might today still be tenable, but also the scripture principle itself — even more so in the light of present-day developments in hermeneutics and literary criticism — apparently leads inevitably to relativist readings and interpretations of the Bible. Barr pinpoints this by saying:

> The Protestant insistence that doctrine must be compatible with scripture — and, especially, the specifically Calvinist insistence that doctrine must be not only *compatible* with scripture (as many Lutheran and Anglican reformers held) but must be positively *demonstrable* from scripture — only led to the demonstration . . . that scripture, if taken for what it actually said, could support a surprising variety of theological and ecclesiastical positions.[39]

This nicely illustrates what I would call the theological version of *the problem of the underdetermination of theories by data*. It also ties in directly with Kelsey's argument that theologians in fact *construct* what they call "the Bible,"[40] as well as with Deist's viewpoint that it is apparently impossible to fix a unique referent for the phrase "Word of God," because it is always relative to contemporary issues and therefore always relative to historical contexts.[41] Basic to this problem is of course the fact that theologians, thinking that they are theorizing on the basis of the Bible, are in fact using the Bible in the context of a more comprehensive argument. I regard the validity of this argument as beyond any doubt; theologians are using the Bible or selected biblical texts within the context of broader

39. J. Barr, *Holy Scripture: Canon, Authority, Criticism* (Oxford: Clarendon, 1983), 32f.
40. Kelsey, 2ff.
41. F. E. Deist, "The Bible — the Word of God or: Searching for the Pearl in the Oyster," in W. S. Vorster, ed., *Scripture and the Use of Scripture* (Pretoria: UNISA, 1979), 41ff.

arguments, in order to support some or other theory, opinion, or doctrine. It thus comes as no surprise that our arguments may, if closely scrutinized, reveal basic epistemological models of thought that finally and decisively legitimize the various ways in which the Bible might be "put to work" to authorize our preferred statements.

Although at this stage I have not as yet suggested what the "authority of the Bible" or the metaphor "Word of God" might eventually mean, precisely because their content is always decided by preceding epistemological models, there certainly are no valid or adequate reasons for declaring these crucial concepts meaningless. The real issue can now be restated: When using the Bible in an argument, what aspects of, or what patterns in the Bible are taken to be authoritative? It could of course be certain concepts, certain theological themes or doctrines, historical reports, symbols for evoking religious response, or a combination of any of these. Kelsey gives us an invaluable pointer — although to my mind he never really follows it through — when he states:

> The most basic decision a theologian makes is his answer to the question: "What is the essence of Christianity?"[42]

For me an answer to this question ties in directly with my earlier analysis of an ultimate faith commitment to God. In terms of biblical language the answer to this question points to what I regard as the root-metaphor of the Christian faith, that is, *redemption in Jesus Christ*. But now, when we regard the very many ways this root-metaphor could be interpreted, do we again face the problem that the underdetermination of theories in theology can lead only to a pluralism of interpretations and thus to relativism? I honestly do not think so. In our analysis of epistemological critical realism we saw that there can at times be a special class of entity whose entire warrant lies in the theory built around it. What is more, the critical realist argument convincingly showed that our only provisional access to the reality we are groping for is through the metaphorical concepts of science and of theology.

Therefore, unless the assertions made by the "authority" — in this case the Bible, not in a naive realist sense as foundational to the argument, but indeed as a *crucial part of the argument* — are themselves already epistemo-

42. Kelsey, 8.

logically authorized as valid, meaningful, and plausible by *some method other than* a direct and literal appeal to the biblical text as such, no statement derived from the Bible can, by that fact alone, be an authoritative statement.

This obviously calls for an analysis of the reception of the Bible by contemporary readers. But in the meantime, if the Bible and our quest for its authority in our postmodern world are seen as part of an argument based on the background theories of a theorized faith commitment, then this "some method" to me is the critical realist argument. The reasons for this are, as we shall shortly see, not only because it is appropriate to the complex hermeneutical interpretation and reception of the text, but also because it allows for provisionality, the evoking of religious experience, and a clear focus on the role of an ultimate commitment. Moreover, the text itself, as a religious text, forms the source for a long chain of continuous metaphorical reference to God and for faith in redemption in Jesus Christ. This irreversible thrust towards the future is, again, what I in an epistemological sense have called *the realism of the text.* I do believe that the realism of this text, as a crucial part of the critical realist argument in theology, not only gives credibility to the argument, but is especially appropriate to the central metaphorical concepts of the text itself.

The Bible as such — had it existed in such a positivistic way — could therefore never be a sufficient authorization for the meaning or truth of theological propositions. The adequacy and provisional truth of theological propositions eventually depend on a more comprehensive argument, a broader framework of criteria.[43] This still does not finally solve the problem of the theory-ladenness of data in theology: biblical texts and religious experiences are "data" that, because of the hermeneutical problem in theology, are as theory-laden as can be. This of course becomes very obvious from the fact that each different theology has its own criteria for justifying its claims.

I think that one will have to acknowledge that the whole problem of theory-assessment and theory-choice in theology in a very specific way differs from that of the other sciences. McMullin recently showed that in the natural sciences the criteria for deciding between alternative theories, though complex, are reasonably specific.[44] Normally scientists have consensus on what should count in favor of a theory: predictive

43. See van Huyssteen, *Justification of Faith,* 169-214.
44. McMullin, "Realism," 41ff.

accuracy, internal consistency, coherence with other accepted theories, absence of unexplained "coincidence," long-term fertility in suggesting more detailed specification of the associated model, and so on. For scientific realism it is the application of criteria like these that allows science to progress and to get an even better grasp on reality. What enables this realism to be a critical one is the quality of the evidence available and the broadly agreed-upon character of theory-assessment.

Against this background one would have to grant McMullin the fact that the notions of evidence in theology are very different from those prevailing in science.[45] Obviously in theology any evidence will count *as* evidence for only a *limited group;* but to call any group in theology "those for whom the revelation is given"[46] can be dangerously misleading. In trying to come to grips with the problem of the pluriformity of interpretations in theology, I would rather start with the epistemological access given to us by the realism of this classical text.

Theologians, as we know, use different models to explain the specific religious domain of reality they are tentatively reaching for. But in theology all models are interpretatively used in association with the basic biblical text. The Bible, although interpreted differently by different groups, has its own inner hermeneutical limits, as we shall shortly see. The reality of the text, and the reality of the process of reception of this text by contemporary readers, will eventually assist us in solving the problem of the underdetermination of theories in theology, even if only in a provisional way.

What I do find problematical, however, is that McMullin can state:[47]

On certain understandings of the authority of scripture, it ought in principle certify itself *as* revelation to any unbiased person.

And:

All . . . attempts to present a special revelation from God as evidence to people other than those who first received it, run into problems that have no analogue in natural science.

45. McMullin, "Realism," 42.
46. McMullin, "Realism," 42.
47. McMullin, "Realism," 42f.

I think this could be said only of a naive realist position where the metaphoric structure of the concept "revelation" is ignored, and where the Bible itself starts to function as an unquestionable and foundationalist basis for "theological" arguments. This is not at all the case, however, for a position where the Bible functions as part of a qualified argument for a modest form of critical realism in theology. In such a critical realist theology, the hermeneutical factor becomes central, and so does the possibility of a meaningful plurality in interpretations of the biblical text — which is not at all the same as committing the text to the relativism of an infinite number of possible interpretations.

2. Understanding the Biblical Text

Systematic theologians have unfortunately become notorious for so often ignoring the fact that the text of the Bible can also be seen as literature and as such is fully open to the literary critical analysis of all the various new schools. But equally important is the fact that these same literary texts are also and always *religious texts* responding to explicitly religious questions.[48] Whatever important bearing present-day literary theory might have on issues concerning biblical interpretation, biblical hermeneutics also inevitably raises additional theological questions of its own.[49]

Central to these questions is certainly the disturbing possibility of the relativism that would be created by an infinite number of readings and interpretations of the biblical text. The interpreter must therefore somehow be prevented from finding in the text only what he or she is already hoping to find there. A responsible hermeneutics[50] will do much to prevent a shallow skimming from the text of the interpreter's preformed viewpoints, so often deceptively and dangerously clothed in the so-called authority of the biblical text. This obviously makes it clear how important the role of the reader has become in biblical hermeneu-

---

48. See D. Tracy, "Theological Interpretation of the Bible Today," in Grant, 167.
49. See A. Thiselton, "Reader-Response Hermeneutics, Action Models, and the Parables of Jesus," in Lundin, Thiselton, and Walhout, 79.
50. See Thiselton, 80.

tics. The role of the reader can, however, never be pressed in such a way as to imply an infinite relativism on the part of the text or its authors.

In biblical hermeneutics, until quite recently, the main emphasis of research on the theory of textual interpretation was on text-production and text-transmission, that is, on the source and the message of the text. This historical approach was mainly interested, in spite of all its many variations, in the origin and source of the text, believing that it held the key to understanding the text. Structuralists, again, concentrated on the text itself — the text as "work" — analyzing its structure on various levels.[51] Contemporary research on what this text is has forced theologians, however, to rethink the approach to the whole process of reading as such.[52] As a result we have come to realize that in written communication the text not only mediates the "conversation" between writer and reader, but becomes *a reality in its own right*. As such the text — as a reality — therefore now becomes the object of two activities, namely *writing* and *reading*. A text, once written, therefore becomes a reality in itself — whatever the "exact" intention of the original author might have been.

This does of course mean that the text itself now lives only *in relation to a reader*. In fact, it comes to life through the reader.[53] The reader, in this relational way, thus revives the text and gives new meaning to it. Calling the biblical text a reality could therefore never mean a "closed" reality, with a meaning that the historical writer has put there *once and for all*. Reading and interpreting the biblical text in an interactionist and relational way is therefore a creative and imaginative experience in which the text will permit several readings, but definitely also resist others because it has its own inner patterns or limits. Vogels phrases it well: reading is therefore giving new life to a text while respecting it.[54]

The writing and the reading (interpretation) of the text are therefore both directly related to the reality of the biblical text. This text, as original "witness" to the events and Person of our faith, in a very specific

51. See B. Lategan, "Reference: Reception, Redescription and Reality," in W. S. Vorster and B. Lategan, *Text and Reality: Aspects of Reference in Biblical Texts* (Philadelphia: Fortress, 1985), 67.

52. See W. Vogels, "Inspiration in a Linguistic Mode," *Biblical Theology Bulletin* 15 (1985): 87.

53. Vogels, 87.

54. Vogels, 88.

sense, *is all we have*. The metaphorical reference of its central concepts remains our only epistemic access to the God we believe in. Because of the importance of this fact, we can talk on an epistemological level about the *realism of the text*. At this stage one can therefore already sense how the problem of the underdetermination of theories in theology changes when translated into a hermeneutical problem: a theory of interpretation, which focuses primarily on the response of the reader to the biblical text, not only allows, but encourages, what Tracy calls a responsible pluralism of readings based on the relationship between text and reader(s).[55] For Tracy this pluralism also denies the imperialistic way some hermeneutical methods claim to be "the only" method and thereby get twisted into an ideology.

Different models of interpretation each in their own creative way probe the "inner limits," or to use Ricoeur's striking metaphor, the *itineraries of meaning*[56] contained within the text itself. For the critical realist in theology this would obviously be basic to the way in which the text itself — in spite of various enriching models of interpretation — refers. For this very reason, incidently, I do not think that deconstruction as such could easily be treated as just another enriching model of interpretation, as Tracy apparently treats it.[57] If one should want to discuss the important issue of deconstruction, one would have to realize that what is at stake is not just another enriching model, but the radical challenge of a whole new paradigm of thought.

Tracy is however completely to the point when he — because of a critical and responsible plurality of readings — emphasizes the reception by the reader of the biblical text.[58] Ricoeur also opposed the idea that the Bible is a "closed" book with a fixed meaning and as such opposed to imaginative reading, maintaining instead that this reading is a creative and constructive process.[59] For Ricoeur the act of reading is a dynamic activity and as such is not confined to an endless, static repetition of the text. Reading the Bible, on the contrary, prolongs what

55. D. Tracy, *The Analogical Imagination: Christian Theology and the Culture of Pluralism* (New York: Crossroad, 1981), 124.

56. P. Ricoeur, "The Bible and the Imagination," in G. Ebeling, J Barr, and P. Ricoeur, *The Bible as a Document of the University* (Chico, Calif.: Scholars Press, 1981), 50.

57. Tracy, *Analogical Imagination*, 118.

58. Tracy, *Analogical Imagination*, 118.

59. Ricoeur, 49.

Ricoeur calls the *itineraries of meaning*, the inner patterns or limits of the text opened up by the creative process of interpretation. As such, reading and interpreting is in a sense rule-governed and is in fact guided by a productive imagination at work in the text itself.

Of great importance, however, to the problem of reference and the central place it occupies in the critical realist argument, as well as to solving the problem of underdetermination in its hermeneutical form, is the fact, which Ricoeur notes,[60] that the act of reading should be seen as the meeting point of the itineraries of meaning, or offered by the text and the imaginative power of the reader in redescribing reality. This application of inherent biblical patterns of thought to life today happens through the process of *metaphorization*, a process that is contained in the text itself by virtue of its literary form.[61] The so-called itineraries of meaning, or (as I would phrase it) root-metaphors, contained in the text are metaphorized through an act of creative, imaginative interpretation in the direction of a basic overall theme that governs the whole process of interpretation beyond the specific text.

These basic themes or overarching ideas can be any central perspective creatively reconstructed from the Bible, like *redemption in Christ* or *the kingdom of God*. These central biblical metaphors are the result of a process of metaphorization working in the text itself, which, although directly involving the imaginative interpretation of the reader, at the same time also restricts interpretation to the itineraries of meaning found in the biblical text itself. The process of metaphorization, as a form of reader-response to the biblical text, gains even more in meaning when Ricoeur links it to intertextuality, as a process through which one text in referring to another both displaces this other text and at the same time receives from it an extension of meaning.[62]

For the critical realist this is extremely important. The Bible is not simply an arsenal of important metaphors that evoke religious experience because they refer realistically. Even before the origin of what we have since come to know as the written Bible, the "Word" of God, these metaphors generated a dynamic process of metaphorization that not only has made it possible for Christians through the ages to interpret

60. Ricoeur, 51.
61. Ricoeur, 52.
62. Ricoeur, 53.

these ancient texts creatively, but also has provided *in the metaphors themselves a continuity of reference, in spite of the so often divergent interpretations of the biblical text.*

As we will see shortly when we discuss central biblical metaphors like "Word of God," "Holy Spirit," and also "inspiration," this process of metaphorization not only supports the qualified critical realist argument in theology, but through the continuity of its reference also provides an answer to the very specific hermeneutical nature of the problem of underdetermination in theology. Also for the systematic theologian what eventually is called for is a hermeneutics of the text's referential intentionality.

Recently, especially in reader-response theories — not necessarily as comprehensive hermeneutical models but as valid hermeneutical perspectives[63] — a whole new emphasis on the reader's reception of the text has emerged. With this has come the realization that an adequate theory of textual communication must be able to give an account of the process of reception.

Reader-response criticism therefore focuses attention on the reader's imaginative and creative actions involved in responding to a text.[64] In reader-response criticism an examination of the text, as such, is replaced by a discussion of the reading process and thus of the interaction of reader and text. What should interest the systematic theologian is precisely the reader's actions involved in responding to the biblical text: this text (1) evokes religious experiences, (2) implies ontological commitment, and (3) provides, through the metaphorical nature of the central concepts of biblical language, a striking continuity of reference in the history of Christian thought. The biblical text is directly involved in all three of these factors, and as such now becomes, also from a hermeneutical point of view, the epistemologically crucial part of the critical realist argument in theology.

Reader-response criticism therefore gives a more active role to the reader than other modes of biblical criticism; meaning here is the product of the interaction between text and reader, but in the end the meaning always represents the text's intention.[65] Although there may

---

63. See Thiselton, 106.

64. See J. Resseguie, "Reader-Response Criticism and the Synoptic Gospels," *Journal of the American Academy of Religion* 52 (1984): 307.

65. Resseguie, 322.

be several realizations of a specific text, they are always implied, circumscribed, and restricted by the text itself.

And *the realism of the text*, epistemologically so important for a critical realist theology, therefore implies hermeneutically that the reader is in a sense inscribed or encoded in the text, and as such forms part of the text's meaning. The epistemological status of the Bible in critical realism therefore corresponds with, and in fact forms the basic epistemological presupposition for, reader-response theories; *vice versa*, reader-response theories in an important way provisionally justify the claims made to reliable knowledge by critical realism in theology.

Critical realism in theology therefore reclaims the importance of reference as well as the continuity of what is being referred to, in spite of important historical and sociological shifts in the creative development of our theological knowledge. Walhout therefore sharply observes:

> The denial of referentiality stems from the desire to avoid the philosophical positions on which theories of reference seem to depend.[66]

Understanding the biblical text in terms of reader-response theories not only points to a way in which the problem of the underdetermination of theories in theology might be solved, but also has important implications for the issue of reference as such:[67]

1. The communication of the biblical text — also epistemologically as part of the realist argument — is not complete until it has reached its final destination: the *reception* of the text by the reader.
2. Because reading is not merely a reproductive but also a productive activity, *reference cannot be analyzed merely in terms of the world of the text, but must also be analyzed in terms of the world of the reader as presupposed by the text.*
3. Just as the intention of the author can be determined only in terms of the reality of the text, so the text constitutes the basis for analyzing the reader's anticipated reception.

66. C. Walhout, "Texts and Actions," in Lundin, Thiselton, and Walhout, 52.
67. See Lategan, 68f.

Lategan puts it very well:

> Reference inwards to the world of the text presupposes reference
> outwards to the reception by the reader.[68]

This brings us back to the realism of the biblical text: the real or implied authors of these ancient religious texts were ultimately committed to a Reality; and their faith in this Reality, which we have come to call God, in fact preceded the text itself. It is to this Reality that the text ultimately keeps on referring, and this continuous reference is the essence of what we have come to call the realism of the text.

3. The Authority of the Biblical Text

At the beginning of this paper I redefined the problem of the authority of the Bible as the problem of the epistemological status of the Bible in the process of theological reflection. I therefore find it of special importance that Barr can say that the effectiveness of the Bible, as a document for the believing Christian community, is directly related to the extent to which the study of it is shared by the believing community with the academic world.[69]

For me this implies that reflection on the biblical text can never be permanently caught up in the enclosed confessional realm of the church. The mere ability of the Bible to evoke response as a religious text on a theological level becomes intelligible only through metatheological epistemological criteria, and of course through the insight that the Bible itself forms a crucial part of the critical realist argument. The realism of the text in this sense points to metatheological criteria that can be epistemologically valid, but also to hermeneutical criteria that are appropriate to the text itself. I think, therefore, that a theologian — as this paper has tried to show — can provide a *theological* interpretation of an academic problem like the status of the Bible in theology, as long as the religious dimension of these biblical texts is consistently taken into

---

68. Lategan, 69.

69. J. Barr, *The Scope and Authority of the Bible*, Explorations in Theology 7 (London: SCM, 1980), 123.

consideration. I have therefore always rejected a type of confessional theology that at the beginning already sets forth some sort of antecedent and foundationalist criterion of authority. And if this criterion happens to be the Bible as the sole and primary epistemological authority for Christian theology, the Bible obviously becomes the sole authorization for the claim that certain theological statements or doctrines are not only meaningful, but also indisputably true. The naive realism of this thought-model has been discussed at length, and fundamentalism, as the intellectual sect that necessarily accompanies it, has been even more thoroughly scrutinized in Barr's well-known publications.[70]

In the concluding part of this paper I would like to argue that the realism of the biblical text, which epistemologically as well as herme-neutically implies a faith commitment while referring to a Reality we have come in biblical terms to call God, ultimately and metaphorically refers to the reality of redemption in Christ. And only in relation to this root-model of our faith can the problem of biblical authority for faith, and the status of the Bible in theological reflection, eventually — although provisionally — be resolved.

If the biblical texts refer to God, and if this reference ultimately refers to what we have metaphorically come to know and accept as redemption in Christ, then Jesus Christ alone authorizes the Bible. In this sense the Bible has an *authorized authority*,[71] and as a text that primarily evokes religious response and faith commitment, it has what we may call a redemptive or Christological authority for life in faith, and thus also for life in the church. But on the level of theological reflection, as we have seen, this problem is transformed to that of the epistemological status of the Bible as a crucial part of theological argu-mentation.

What is important is that we have come to speak, when referring to the biblical texts, of the "whole" or the "unity" of these texts as a canon, thereby acknowledging the authoritativeness that this specific collection of religious texts has acquired for faith and for life in faith.

---

70. J. Barr, *Comparative Philology and the Text of the Old Testament* (Oxford: Claren-don, 1968); J. Barr, *Biblical Words for Time*, 2nd ed. (London: SCM, 1969), 2; Barr, *Bible in Modern World*; Barr, *Scope and Authority*; J. Barr, *Fundamentalism*, 2nd ed. (London: SCM, 1981), 2; see also J. Verburg, *Canon of Credo?* (Kampen: Kok, 1983), 119f.

71. See Ogden, 247.

The faith of the first Christians and the essential substance of what eventually was to form specifically the New Testament, was of course much earlier: primarily oral traditions, later tending towards a more or less fixed form.[72] Obviously, if tradition acquires such a definite form and is finally standardized, writing it down, eventually, would in principle scarcely add anything new to the referential power of the tradition itself.[73] What is, however, of tremendous importance for understanding the status of the Bible in the Christian tradition, as well as for its epistemological status in theological reflection, can be summed up as follows:[74]

1. the fact of the church's eventual historical decision to constitute these classical texts as the Bible;
2. the congruence of this fact with the fundamental structure of the preceding Christian faith.

Both of these, each in its own way, support the arguments for a qualified form of critical realism in theology:

1. The fact of the decision to constitute the biblical texts as canon, however difficult it might be to reconstruct or even provisionally understand, not only directly ties in with what we earlier analyzed as the process of metaphorization and intertextuality, but essentially represents a fundamental decision to recognize these texts as the *classic model for understanding God.* The reality of this text and its ongoing process of metaphorization through the reception thereof by present-day readers, as well as the authority and status it might have for us, refers back to the referential basis of this complex and historical decision.
2. Acknowledging the decision to constitute the biblical texts as an authoritative canon certainly reveals a sensitivity for the inherent "religious logic" or "theological consistency"[75] of these texts. This, I think, can only be traced back to the *referential and pro-*

72. See Barr, *Scope and Authority,* 111f.
73. See Ogden, 249.
74. See Barr, *Bible in Modern World,* 117.
75. See Barr, *Biblical Words,* 282.

leptic structure of the living Christian faith that preceded these texts
— at least those of the New Testament. The historic decision of
the ancient church therefore makes profound sense; the basic
nature of the "original" faith in Christ structured these texts and
the way in which they ontologically refer. All later expressions of
faith were *Christian* only because they could relate to the classic
models of faith as expressed in the biblical texts. Christian faith
is therefore Christian faith because it directly refers to Jesus of
Nazareth and the God of Israel. And the collection of religious
texts we call the Bible is our only and exclusive epistemological
and spiritual access to this reality.

The fact that Jesus of Nazareth came into a world where there was
already — and in a very important sense — a religiously authoritative
collection of texts, and a community within which this was interpreted,
was indeed of great significance.[76] The Old Testament in fact provided
what we could call the "religious paradigm" for the New, because it
provided so much of the essential conceptuality of the New Testament.
The writings of the Old Testament contain the most fundamental presuppositions, and in this sense provide all the main concepts, symbols,
and metaphors, of the Jesus-kerygma of the earliest church.[77]

   Logically speaking one could therefore certainly say that the relation of the Old Testament to the earliest Christian witness is like that
of the necessary presuppositions of an assertion to the assertion itself.[78] But Ricoeur's theory of metaphorization might even take us a
step further: Ricoeur's theory of intertextuality in fact reveals the
power of metaphor in the interaction between texts and the extension
of meaning that takes place in the process of metaphorization.[79] The
text of the Bible, as a living unity, consists of texts, smaller units, and
sequences of texts written down, eventually encompassing both Old
and New Testaments and growing into *one* classic text. This unity,
although not a fundamentalist "closed unity" but a historically grown
unity, is the living Bible believers all over the world live by from day

76. See Barr, *Holy Scripture*, 11.
77. See Ogden, 260.
78. See Ogden, 260.
79. Ricoeur, 67.

to day; and as this unity it forms the epistemological structure and basis of the realism of the text.

Both on the level of the pretheoretical individual living faith, and on the level of the communal faith of the church, there is no reason not to retain the canon of the biblical texts, even if not interpreted in the traditional sense. On the level of theological reflection, however, the realism of the text gives us exciting reasons for retaining the unity of these texts — again, however, even if not interpreted in the traditional sense.

When McMullin therefore, in discussing the role of biblical texts or passages as "evidence" for theological arguments, states, ". . . what warrants them for the believer is not primarily their explanatory power, but their incorporation in scripture,"[80] this could not be applied to the sense in which theological explanation and hermeneutics were discussed earlier. This could be valid only for a naive realist theology where the "incorporation in scripture" will refer to a closed biblical text, which as such is not a crucial part of the theological argument, but the "infallible" and fundamentalist epistemological base for all theological knowledge.

Finally, no perspective on the authority of the Bible — especially if offered by a systematic theologian! — will be complete if the metaphor *inspiration* is not briefly considered.

The intention behind this metaphor has always been very obvious, which is also the reason why it has grown into one of Christianity's premier metaphors: to set the Bible — as a religious text — apart from other "ordinary" and very human literary texts. Inspiration is also very closely related to another central biblical metaphor, *revelation*. In a critical realist argument the concept revelation could eventually be used as a metaphorical depiction of the reality of the originating process of the Bible and of certain experiences of faith in the biblical texts, which in their referring to a reality beyond our intellectual grasp became a disclosure of the reality of the presence of God.

The metaphor revelation must certainly not be violated and interpreted literally to form a seemingly "unbiased" and authoritative starting point for a foundationalist or fundamentalist theology. The same type of epistemological naive realism should be avoided when interpreting the metaphor inspiration. This happens whenever inspiration is ex-

80. McMullin, "Realism," 45.

plained in terms of the so-called prophetic model,[81] and is thus supposed to mediate the uninterpreted, "direct" Word of God in the text of the Bible. Every explanation of the metaphor inspiration that relates it exclusively to the authors of the text, or the process of production of the text, interprets this concept exclusively in terms of the origin of the text. In terms of what was said earlier about a responsible, hermeneutical understanding and reception of the text, it should be obvious that this position in theology can lead only to naive realism and the fundamentalism of all the well-known "theories" of inspiration, whether seen in its most primitive form as "verbal" or "mechanical" inspiration, or in a more sophisticated version, as "organic" inspiration.

In a critical realist perspective, where I indeed think the retention and reinterpretation of this central and indispensable metaphor should be seriously considered, inspiration should predominantly be seen as a *quality* of the biblical text. We have seen what the unique qualities of this religious text are. What is very important, however, is that for the Christian these qualities are not only the result of the writing of the text, but are indeed related to the two creative activities that are both equally and essentially important for the reality and the interpretation of the text, namely *the writing and the reading of the biblical text.* [82]

Therefore, to limit the concept of inspiration to either the writing or the reading of the text (not to mention constructing a "theory" for it) would obviously be too narrow. The real reason for this lies in what I have come to call the *realism of the text.* Through all its different forms, all the narratives, prophecies, legends, and parables, the written text of the Bible — as it is being read and interpreted — refers to God and the reality of God's relationship to humankind,[83] to its creation and salvation. This made it possible for me to develop a critical realist theory of reference that could demonstrate a continuity of reference in the central biblical metaphors as used through the ages.

The reality for which all biblical metaphors, and our theological interpretations of these metaphors, are indirectly and provisionally groping is of course, theologically speaking, the reality of the presence of the living God in our midst. For the reality of this presence, the Bible

---

81. See Vogels, 89.
82. See Vogels, 89.
83. See Peacocke, 42.

itself presents us with one of its most original and basic root-metaphors, namely the Holy Spirit. By referring to the presence of God as the Spirit, one of the most central biblical themes is taken up; the Spirit is, through a process of metaphorization, consistently — in both Old and New Testaments — depicted as the origin and the giver of life (and not as the origin of "supernatural knowledge"[84]).

So, in the end we are confronted by a double metaphor: the biblical text is *inspired* by the *Holy Spirit*. And if the Spirit is in reality the creative, life-giving presence of God, then inspiration could never be attributed only to the text as a final product. It does, however, form the basis of the ontological reference of the written text, and of what we have called its redemptive authority. God, through this Spirit, was present with God's people in the formation, the transmission, the writing down, and the completion of this process in its final fixation as scripture.[85] Because of the continuity of metaphorical reference in the process of this long history, we can now also attribute to this text another of its own central metaphors, namely the Bible as the *Word of God*, whatever the different and often divergent interpretations of this creative and fertile metaphor might be.

The biblical text has a quality of inspiration because, apart from the long process of its origin, there has been, and still is today, a community of readers who can — in the presence of God, or "under the guidance of his Spirit" — respond to the referential power of the text. This community has always been and still is a faith-community, a community for whom the text refers to a reality that is therefore metaphorically and powerfully revealed by the text.

Seeing inspiration as a quality that the text has on account of God's presence means that the same Spirit who was at work in the community that created the text is also present in the community that recreates the text by reading and interpreting it for today.[86] Recalling what Ricoeur said about itineraries of meaning in the text, it is eventually only the inspired community that can find the inner limits of the inspired text,

---

84. W. Pannenberg, *The Apostles' Creed in the Light of Today's Questions* (London: SCM, 1972).

85. See Barr, *Scope and Authority,* 63.

86. See Vogels, 89.

the meanings that the text rejects, as well as the meanings that the text allows us to develop creatively for today.

The Bible, with its special relational qualities of inspiration and reference, is in a critical realist sense *the way to God*, for the text that was produced by an inspired community is today still capable of inspiring faith in God. Therefore, it makes no sense to ask whether inspiration was a quality only of the original Hebrew or Greek text, or to succumb to naive realism by asking whether the original texts might have been infallible. When one realizes that the reading process is as essential to inspiration as the text itself, it becomes clear that only a specific believing community can recognize the text of the Bible as inspired. To regard only the ancient Hebrew or Greek texts as "inspired" is obviously to fall back on some sort of bibliolatry.[87]

A translation of the biblical texts is therefore never only a translation; if God was somehow present through the different stages of the production of the original text, surely the same God must be referred to in, and thus revealed through, the many translations of the Bible. This, incidently, gives the translator a great responsibility, but also a unique position: in him or her the communities of faith — those preceding the text, those writing the text, and those reading the text — hermeneutically meet one another.[88] The Bible and the realism of its text is, therefore, in a sense not only a bridge between humans and God, but also a bridge between the producing community and the reading community, in which the same Spirit was and still is at work. I do think, therefore, that the central Christian metaphor "inspiration" can be retrieved and revitalized — not, however, as a formal theological blueprint to generate new "theories of inspiration," but as an invaluable metaphorical reference to the unique spiritual quality of the text.

In conclusion: I think James Barr challenges theologians in a very special and subtle way when he states:

> . . . it seems to me that in the future we shall judge theologies not by their antecedent criterion but by their output, their results.[89]

87. See Vogels, 91.
88. See Vogels, 91.
89. Barr, *Bible in Modern World*, 51.

In this endeavor the classic biblical text remains the central and decisive factor. The progressive development of theological thought in terms of reliable epistemological and appropriate hermeneutical criteria provides us with guidelines to speak modestly and tentatively of that Reality that is God. As Peacocke so aptly reminds us, our theologies can never be infallible, but some of them will certainly be surer.[90]

90. Peacocke, 47.

Chapter Eight

Experience and Explanation: The Justification of Cognitive Claims in Theology

It is a significant feature of our times that neither scientists nor theologians exude the kind of assurance today that once gave rise to the familiar stereotypes of cocksure empiricist and dogmatic prelate. One lasting benefit of this changed climate might be the recognition, across disciplinary fences, that the grass on the other side is not that much greener after all.

Frederick Ferré[1]

CRITICAL THEOLOGIANS, IN AN ATTEMPT TO TRANSCEND THE INTEL-lectual coma of fideism and dogmatism, have to face a very special kind of challenge: the truth-claims of religious assertions. Religious beliefs are normally held to be true, not merely useful, and their assertions about reality are universal in intent. This also raises the questions of the possible role of explanatory justification in theology: What do religious beliefs explain, and can their cognitive claims be justified in any way?

1. Frederick Ferré, "Science, Religion and Experience," in Eugene T. Long, ed., *Experience, Reason and God* (Washington: Catholic Univ. of America Press, 1980), 97.

162

The theologian of course has to realize that the questions raised by reflecting on religion are not those raised by science. Accepting that different kinds of knowledge are involved in the practices of science and theology and that neither can provide the content of the other's knowledge does not mean that they do not inform the context within which their respective knowledge is to be constructed.[2] This epistemological problem reveals the common adherence of theology and all the sciences to the problem of rationality, as we shall soon see. It also challenges us to evaluate the role of justification and explanation in both theology and science.

The relationship between *explanatory power* and *truth* has always been a central issue in the understanding of science, and is even more problematical today.[3] Philosophers of science have also convincingly pointed out that there can be no undisputed and monolithic notions of reality or of explanation in science: the objects of our interest dictate not only different strategies but also different views on what could be regarded as adequate forms of explanation. Yet the central question remains: Does theology exhibit a rationality comparable to the rationality of science, and how plausible can an explanatory justification of the cognitive claims of theology be?

In this paper I would like to show that the rationality of science and theology is in each case determined by specific goals and criteria, that is, by particular epistemic values. In both theology and science, whatever their other differences might be, the supreme value that determines rationality is *intelligibility.* What is real for theology and for science is not the observable but the intelligible,[4] and in both theology and science beliefs and practices are attempts to understand at the deepest level, where understanding can be construed as seeking the best explanation.[5] What is at stake, therefore, is not only the general epistemic status of religious belief, but especially the implications this will have for the epistemic and thus rational

2. See Eileen Barker, "Science as Theology: The Theological Functioning of Western Science," in *The Sciences and Theology in the Twentieth Century* (Notre Dame: Univ. of Notre Dame Press, 1981), 276.

3. See Ernan McMullin, "Explanatory Success and the Truth of Theory," in Nicholas Rescher, ed., *Scientific Inquiry in Philosophical Perspective,* (New York: Lanham, 1986), 52.

4. See Ian G. Barbour, *Issues of Science and Religion* (New York: Harper & Row, 1971)), 170.

5. See Wayne Proudfoot, *Religious Experience* (Berkeley: Univ. of California Press, 1985), 43.

integrity of theological discourse as such. At the same time the high degree of personal involvement in religion will present a very special challenge to any theory of rationality in theology. Because of this, and because of the contextuality of religious experience and the cognitive claims that arise from this, I shall argue for a theory of rationality in theology that encompasses both *experiential adequacy* and *epistemological adequacy*.

Rationality in Theology and Science

Constructing a model of rationality that can deal adequately with a theology that claims cognitivity and reality-depiction for its central statements will certainly not be an easy task. Not only is rationality a word protean in its meanings,[6] but the lasting influence of positivism and the prestige of the natural sciences is a direct challenge not only to our view of the sciences,[7] but also to our concept of rationality. Post-Kuhnian philosophy of science has shown us that there can be no sharp line of demarcation between scientific rationality and all other forms of rationality.[8] In fact rationality in science relates to the reasonableness or a more basic kind of rationality that informs all goal-directed human action. In this sense one might have a richer theory of rationality that includes not only empirical adequacy but also compatibility with metaphysical or philosophical theories.[9]

In spite of some important differences between theology and the other sciences, I would identify rationality as an epistemological issue that ties in directly with the overall goals of theology and science, that is, intelligibility as an understanding at the deepest possible level. In this sense rationality would imply a reliance on argument and explanation and

6. See Edward J. Echeverria, "Rationality and the Theory of Rationality," *Christian Scholar's Review* 15, no. 4 (1986): 372.

7. See Edward L. Schoen, *Religious Explanations: A Model from the Sciences* (Durham, N.C.: Duke Univ. Press, 1985), vii.

8. See Wentzel van Huyssteen, *Teologie as Kritiese Geloofsverantwoording* (Pretoria: RGN, 1986), 63-75; also published as *Theology and the Justification of Faith* (Grand Rapids: Wm. B. Eerdmans, 1989).

9. See W. H. Newton-Smith, *The Rationality of Science* (Boston: Routledge & Kegan Paul, 1981), 7.

an acceptance of those models that appear to be the most effective problem solvers in terms of certain criteria of rationality. These criteria could be seen as rules specifying what would count as reasons for believing something. In this sense they function as epistemic values that directly tie in with the goals of our theorizing. Rationality in theology and science is therefore directly related to these goals, and if the goals change or more important ways of realizing these goals are found, rationality itself will change.[10] If science and theology are complex intellectual activities of specific communities of inquirers, there is no way to prescribe a certain type of rationality for that activity without looking at its actual practice.

With this in mind, it is important to reflect on the fact that Ian Barbour has already identified a critical realist model of rationality that accommodates the interaction of experience and interpretation, the use of models and analogies, and the role of a community of inquiry in both theology and science.[11] Barbour's argument that personal involvement in science and in religion differ only in degree and that the knowing subject always makes an important contribution to all knowledge not only will have to be developed further, but also will have profound implications for the problem of rationality in theology.

In theology we seek as secure a knowledge as we can achieve, a knowledge that will allow us to understand and where possible to construct theories as better explanations. This goal of theology not only determines the rationality of theology, but very much depends on the way we deal with the problem of the justification of cognitive claims in theology. If in both theology and science we want to understand and explain, then surely the rationality of science is directly relevant to that of theology.

Critical Realism in Theology

In any analysis of the development of theories of rationality in contemporary philosophy of science, the very recent development of different

---

10. See Ernan McMullin, "The Shaping of Scientific Rationality: Construction and Constraint," in McMullin, ed., *Construction and Constraint: The Shaping of Scientific Rationality* (Notre Dame: Univ. of Notre Dame Press, 1988), 22ff.

11. Barbour.

forms of qualified scientific realism after decades of positivism and the ensuing constant threat of a paradigmatic relativism can definitely be seen as one of the most remarkable and welcome features of the scientific thought of our time.[12] The fact that the concept of *realism* can in an epistemological sense be called the catchword of the 1980s[13] and that there seem to be almost as many scientific realisms as there are scientific realists was discussed at length in my *Theology and the Justification of Faith* and *The Realism of the Text*.[14] What is of importance for this essay is that in scientific realism the notion of explanatory success is central, as is the view that there is good reason to believe in the existence of entities substantially like those postulated by theories that have been successful over a long period of time.

Ernan McMullin, who opts for this kind of restricted realism, also qualifies this definition in some important ways:

1. Realism commits one to saying that there are "good reasons," but not that there are compelling grounds; the logical possibility that even a highly successful theory might be false should be held open.
2. Any theory may therefore develop further and can in principle be revised and sharpened.
3. Only theories that have already shown a considerable degree of explanatory power would qualify as having reliable ontological implications.
4. The success of a theory *suggests* truth and never implies truth.[15]

The success of a theory in a scientific realism does not therefore warrant the claim that something exactly corresponding to this construct exists. The success of a theory can at best warrant a claim that an entity exists that possesses *among others* the properties attributed to it by the theory. This not only accounts for the notion of *approximate truth* in realism

12. See F. B. Burnham, "Response to Arthur Peacocke," *Religion and Intellectual Life* 2 (1985): 28.

13. See Arthur Peacocke, *Intimations of Reality: Critical Realism in Science and Religion* (Notre Dame: Univ. of Notre Dame Press, 1984), 11.

14. See n. 8; Wentzel van Huyssteen, *The Realism of the Text* (Pretoria: UNISA, 1987).

15. McMullin, "Explanatory Success," 57.

but also for the central role of *metaphors* in scientific theorizing.[16] Theories — and their metaphors — thus provide epistemic access to entities that could not have been known otherwise.

For a theologian, realism as an epistemological theory of rationality is of course very appealing because it is rather obvious that Christians have traditionally been realists one way or the other.[17] The problem is, however, whether this position can be philosophically defended, and if so, what form of realism would be appropriate for theology? Even more important, what specific problem should realism in theology address? I will eventually argue for a qualified and weak form of critical realism in theology: a realism that does not offer a strong defense of theism but deals with the cognitive claims of religious language and theological reflection. In order to counter the claims of the instrumentalist that religious language provides a useful system of symbols that can be action guiding and meaningful for the believer without being ontologically referential or reality-depicting, the critical realist in theology will have to attempt to say *how religious language can claim to be about God at all.*

I therefore am convinced that anyone considering the possibilities of scientific realism for theology should be extremely wary of an uncritical, superficial transferring of the realism of science to the domain of religious belief, and to theology as the reflection on the claims of this belief. I also think Philip Hefner quite correctly questions the somewhat doctrinaire sense in which the term *critical realism* is sometimes used in theology;[18] it is indeed not yet quite an established theory of explanation, but rather a very promising and suggestive hypothesis, struggling for credibility while being at the center of discussion. The reasons for using this term are based on the conviction that what we are provisionally conceptualizing in theology really exists. This basic assumption and the good reasons we have for it make it possible for theologians, like scientists, to believe they are theorizing in a valid, progressive, and therefore successful way.

16. See Ernan McMullin, "A Case for Scientific Realism," in Jarrett Leplin, ed., *Scientific Realism* (Berkeley: Univ. of California Press, 1984), 30-32.

17. See Janet M. Soskice, "Theological Realism," in W. J. Abraham and S. W. Holzer, eds., *The Rationality of Religious Belief: Essays in Honour of Basil Mitchell* (Oxford: Clarendon Press, 1987), 109.

18. Philip Hefner, "Just How Much Can We Intimate about Reality? A Response to Arthur Peacocke," *Religion and Intellectual Life* 2 (1985): 32.

The strength of the critical realism position certainly lies in its insistence that both the objects of science and the objects of religious belief lie beyond the range of literal description.[19] I personally think that this will eventually represent a major advance in our understanding of what not only science but also theology can achieve. To state it in Arthur Peacocke's words: "The scientific and theological enterprises share alike the tools of groping humanity: words, ideas, images that have been handed down, which we refashion in our own way for our own times in the light of present-day experience."[20] Science and theology, for the Christian, can therefore be seen only as interacting and mutually illuminating approaches to reality. What exactly is meant by *reality* in this context will of course have to be carefully analyzed. Regarding the issue of reality in science and theology, I think Peacocke is correct in warning against a form of discrimination when we attribute reality as such. Indeed there is no sense in which subatomic particles are to be regarded as more real than a bacterial cell or a human person, or even social facts, or God.[21]

When Peacocke, however, proceeds to relate these realities to different levels of reality, a cut through the totality of reality, it does become more problematical. It could imply that realism should then apply in a *similar* way to the fields of both science and theology, which would be highly problematical. I think McMullin pinpoints the problem by underlining the fact that there is no way that science and theology could deal with the *same* reality, and rather than saying that there are different levels of reality, one should realize that science and theology for the most part deal with *different domains* of the same reality.[22] He states it very clearly: "Science has no access to God in its explanations: theology has nothing to say about the specifics of the natural world."[23]

Where I do, however, think the two overlap, is on the epistemological level of reflection or human knowledge: each has something important to say about the two very different but also very important domains

19. See Ernan McMullin, "Realism in Theology and Science: A Response to Peacocke," *Religion and Intellectual Life* 2 (1985): 47.
20. Peacocke, 51.
21. See Peacocke, 36.
22. McMullin, "Realism in Theology and Science," 39.
23. McMullin, "Realism in Theology and Science," 40.

of reality. To me this is crucial. It is on this level, the problem of the reliability of theological knowledge and the justification of its cognitive claims, that a theory of critical realism will have to be put to the test, and not at all in the sense of "proving" that the Reality about which theology converses really exists or showing that it could be only a "useful fiction" for helping people to lead better lives. In this sense McMullin also sympathizes with the claim that both science and theology could be regarded as "realist," that is, as making *reliable* truth-claims about domains of reality that lie beyond our experience.[24]

Rationality and Reference

The problem of the justification of the cognitive claims of theological statements has now been rephrased as the question of how religious and theological statements can claim to be about God at all. This question not only has surfaced as the central problem for any qualified form of critical realism in theology, but also implies further problems, such as: How do we know that religious and theological language manage to refer and can be regarded as reality-depicting? How is reference fixed in religious and theological language, and is it fixed in such a way that the cognitive claims of theology can be justified in one way or another? The answer to these questions will prove to be directly related to the way *metaphor* functions in religious language. It will also determine the epistemological adequacy of critical realism as a model of rationality for theology, and because of the experiential grounding of metaphorical concepts, will provide a key to *experiential adequacy* in theological theorizing.[25]

The high degree of personal involvement in theological theorizing not only reveals the relational character of our being-in-the-world, but epistemologically implies the mediated and interpretative character of all religious experience. In a sense one's concept of experience will

24. McMullin, "Realism in Theology and Science," 39.

25. See Elaine Botha, "Metaphorical Models and Scientific Realism," in *Proceedings of Philosophy of Science Association* 1 (1986), 360; George Lakoff and Mark Johnson, *Metaphors We Live By* (Chicago: Univ. of Chicago Press, 1980), 19-22.

therefore entail one's concept of meaning, which in turn will determine one's concept of knowledge.[26] According to this view religious experience, and the way we define it, serves as a matrix out of which meaning and knowledge as a basis for theological theorizing arise. Yet religious language is the way in which alleged religious experiences are expressed, and in this sense no religious experience can be seen as prelinguistic or uninterpreted. The theory-ladenness of all data in the sciences thus parallels the interpreted nature of all religious experience. The underdetermination of theories by data is therefore epistemologically as important in theology as in the sciences.[27]

The important fact that all religious experience is interpreted experience implies that religious language is constitutive of experience as much as it is expressive of it. Because of the mediated structure of the religious dimension of all experience, other experiences provide the context for religious awareness. Even more important: If religious experience is mediated and intentional, then the most appropriate language form for this type of experience would be *metaphorical language*. In fact the use of metaphors and models in religious cognition — a use that parallels that in scientific cognition — also argues for the claim that the structure of religious cognition is that of interpreted experience.[28]

The basic question now emerging from all this is how are the alleged cognitive claims and referential value of religious language (and eventually also of theological language) affected if all religious experience is interpreted experience and thus articulated in theory-laden terms emerging from a particular tradition of faith? This question can also be phrased in a different way: How can metaphorical language be referential and reality-depicting *prior to and without definite knowledge of the referent*?[29] In other words, how can we know that religious language, and the theological theories that are creatively constructed in terms of this language, *refers* if that to which it refers is still unknown to us?

26. See Jerry H. Gill, *On Knowing God* (Philadelphia: Westminster Press, 1981), 19.
27. See van Huyssteen, *Realism of Text*, 32-36.
28. See William A. Rottschaefer, "Religious Cognition as Interpreted Experience: An Examination of Ian Barbour's Comparison of the Epistemic Structures of Science and Religion," *Zygon: Journal of Religion and Science* 20 (1985): 269.
29. See Soskice, "Theological Realism," 111.

Regarding this important problem and its direct relevance for the problem of justification of the cognitive claims of theological statements, important studies by Saul Kripke[30] and Hilary Putnam[31] argue that reference can indeed take place independent of the possession or availability of any definite description or definite prior understanding of the referent. The reason for the referential character of religious metaphorical language will therefore not so much be any prior or "given" knowledge of what is being referred to, but the fact that a speaker is a member of a linguistic community that has *passed on* the information, going back to the person or event itself.[32] The notion of reference in this case is obviously an epistemic one. The issue at stake concerning this reference is the role of a concept or metaphor in making possible socially coordinated epistemic access to the referent.[33]

According to this view reference therefore depends on a chain of historical and contextual communication, and this chain of communication is there by virtue of the membership of a community that passes on a name or the meaning of an event from link to link. What is important is not first of all how the speaker got the reference, but the actual chain of communication.[34] This obviously does not mean that every sort of causal chain reaching us will warrant reference. We refer to someone or something by virtue of our connection with other speakers in a community, going back to the referent itself. In some way the referent must be historically, or we might even say causally, connected to the speech act.[35]

From this we can conclude that if reference or reality-depiction in theology depends on both context and content and can be regarded as a statement-dependent notion,[36] then theological statements derive

30. Saul A. Kripke, "Naming and Necessity," in Donald Davidson and Gilbert Harman, eds., *Semantics of Natural Language* (Dordrecht: D. Reidl, 1972), 253-355.

31. Hilary Putnam, "Mind, Language and Reality," *Philosophical Papers* 2 (1975): 190-205.

32. See Kripke, 295.

33. See Richard Boyd, "Metaphor and Theory Change: What is 'Metaphor' a Metaphor for?" in Andrew Ortony, ed., *Metaphor and Thought* (Cambridge: Cambridge University Press, 1980), 358.

34. See Kripke, 300.

35. See Keith S. Donnellan, "Proper Names and Identifying Descriptions," in Davidson and Harman, 377.

36. See Soskice, "Theological Realism," 112.

from interpreted religious experience. In this sense the context as well as the content — that which has been passed on in tradition and is now being referred to — determines the meaning and cognitive claim of the referent. It now not only becomes possible, through the provisional constructs of theological theories, to fix reference prior to and apart from any definitive knowledge, but in the terms of a critical realist interpretation of theory, it is the metaphorical concepts that provide an epistemic access to the referent.

The function of metaphor and model in religious and theological language thus becomes crucial for a weak form of critical realism that is not set on presenting a strong defense of theism, but rather a justification of the cognitive claims of theological reflection: why theological statements can claim to be about God at all. Theological theories and their flexible and open-ended networks of metaphorical concepts, while not necessarily directly or exhaustively descriptive in a positivist or naive realist way, can nevertheless claim to be referential or reality-depicting. This not only justifies the use of metaphor in theory construction in theology and science, but also strengthens the case for a qualified form of critical realism in theology.

All language, but especially metaphorical language, is therefore contextual language embedded in certain traditions of conviction, reflection, and investigation, which in their turn determine the interpretative character of experience. This is also true of theological language, which basically reflects on religious experience, and the ensuing religious language, as ways to the Reality that Christians believe is God. However, these experiences can be reliably interpreted only in terms of the hermeneutical tradition of a linguistic community that has passed on the root metaphors of the Christian faith through a long historical and interpretive tradition going back to the classical texts of this tradition of faith. In this sense — and *not* in any fundamentalistic sense — the referential nature of the central metaphors of the Bible fixes the referent hermeneutically as a very exclusive access to the Reality that is God. In this sense this classic text is the ultimate way to the reality claimed by theology, an epistemological claim that might be defined as *the realism of the text*.[37]

In a very important way reference, or reality-depiction, as well as

---

37. See van Huyssteen, *Realism of Text*, 30.

critical realism in theology, is therefore supported in the following ways. First, the Bible, as classic text of the Christian faith, has survived as a religious text and as a book of faith in a long and remarkable interpretative tradition of an ongoing faith context. Second, it is supported by the reality of ongoing faith experiences that this text has evoked through centuries of belief in God, and the way in which the same text today still appeals to Christian experience. Of these experiences, of which God is believed to be the cause, theological theorizing provides interpretation and reinterpretation on the basis of the central metaphors of this text. This allows us to refer to God without describing him in terms of any definite prior knowledge or understanding. A third factor contributing to critical realism is the metaphorical structure of biblical language, and the continuity of references this has creatively given to religious and theological language through the ages. This obviously presupposes a language-using community going back to the initiating events when these metaphorical terms were first introduced and the referent fixed.[38]

Reference in theology is therefore not determined by any prior knowledge of the referent but by the history of religious experience as contextual and relational, interpreted and mediated, experience. Reference or reality-depiction thus directly relates to the fact that the speaker is a member of a community of speakers who, through a tradition of historical links, speak in a certain way, a way that implies certain "baptismal events" as well as a corresponding commitment to an ultimate commitment, that is, to finding maximal meaning in life. It is not words that refer but speakers using words who refer.[39]

A critical realist argument in theology thus becomes possible if we dispense with the empiricist dogma that reference is fixed only by unrevisable description or not at all.[40] What is more: the case for critical realism in theology can therefore never be argued only in terms of some form of explanatory success analogous to that of the natural sciences, but in an important way becomes plausible in terms of metaphorical reference. What is offered is no strong form of defense of theism, but an attempt to argue how and why religious language and the theories

---

38. See Peacocke, 47.

39. See Janet M. Soskice, *Metaphor and Religious Language* (Oxford: Clarendon Press, 1985), 136.

40. See Soskice, *Metaphor,* 151.

of theology can claim to be about God at all. This also answers the question whether and to what extent an individual's religious experience could provide a proper basis or a justification of religious belief.[41]

The difference between realism in science and critical realism in theology is obviously directly related to the difference in degree of a personal involvement in theology and science respectively. Not only can religious experiences not be repeated under controlled circumstances, but using them to fix reference involves commitment to the validity of the experience, as reported by the experiencer.[42] Theology, in its attempt to obtain maximum intelligibility, thus makes claims based on religious experience. And as in science, this experience, although different from the kind on which scientific statements are based, is understood as a context of shared assumptions interpreted within the wider framework of a continuity of metaphorical reference. In both religion and science claims are made within a context of inquiry, but this does not deprive them of their referential value and therefore is not a relativist position. Those metaphoric and interpreted expressions around which the language of the Christian religion clusters can in this sense be said to have justified themselves as meaningful and referential to vast numbers of people throughout the centuries and across cultures. It is this kind of experiential adequacy, and not a justified certainty, that makes a belief a responsible belief. A model of rationality that can accommodate this is already justifying its claim to epistemological adequacy.

Experience and Explanation

The justification of cognitive claims in theology through the grounding of reference in religious experience is supported by the fact that scientists and philosophers of science have turned, although not as easily as literary critics and some theologians, to noncognitivist views of metaphor. The most interesting metaphors in both theology and science are those that suggest an explanatory network and are vital

---

41. See J. Runzo and C. K. Ihara, eds., *Religious Experience and Religious Belief: Essays in the Epistemology of Religion* (New York: Univ. Press of America, 1986), xi.
42. See Soskice, "Theological Realism," 138.

at the growing edges of our reflection.[43] The crucial issue is: What do theological theories explain, and will a form of explanatory justification in theology have implications for the cognitive claims of theological theories? I would like to argue that although there might be no epistemological shortcut possible from the explanatory success in science to progress and problem solving in theological theorizing, this explanatory progress elucidates religious experience and theological reflection in such a way that theology can indeed claim a form of truth approximation.

The belief that religious statements (and through implication also theological theories) can never be seen as truly explanatory remains extraordinarily pervasive.[44] Misconceptions as to the nature of science usually underlie those arguments that would want to object to any analogies between religious and scientific belief. However, the way contemporary philosophers of science deal with the problem of rationality in scientific reflection has done much to challenge this widely held prejudice. Over against Thomas S. Kuhn's inability to account for the resolution of theoretical disagreements, and for the success of science, realism claims that many of the current theories of science are probably approximately true and that this assumption provides the best explanation for the success of science. The realist argument therefore in a very important way reveals the importance of inference to the best explanation for science.[45]

The type of critical realism that I would like to develop as a model of rationality for theology would maintain that the same style of argument — in conjunction with metaphorical reference and epistemic access to the referent of theological theorizing — has a significant role to play in the justification of the cognitive claims of theology. This again, in spite of the admittedly different tasks of realism in theology and science, implies a strong analogy between religious and scientific belief. The notion that religious belief and the cognitive claims of theological reflection can be given some sort of explanatory justification rests on the supposition that these beliefs indeed function as explanations in

43. See Soskice, *Metaphor,* 101-4.
44. See Schoen, 24.
45. See Michael C. Banner, *The Justification of Science and Rationality of Religious Belief* (Oxford: Oxford University Press, 1986), ii.

theological argument. If this is indeed so, Anthony O'Hear's conviction that the interpretation of religious experience is quite deficient in explanatory power will not qualify as a better explanation for the nature of theological theorizing.[46]

Because of the referential nature and resulting reality-depiction of theological statements, not only religious beliefs and practices, but also and especially theological theorizing, are attempts to understand, where understanding can be construed as seeking the best explanation.[47] Of course there are important differences between the interpretation of religious experiences, the hermeneutical interpretation of religious texts, and methods of explanation in the mature sciences. Yet the interpretation of experience or texts does not preclude the further step of seeking the best explanation for a belief. Finding better and more valid interpretations for experiential or conceptual problems in theology[48] will imply an inference to the best explanation in theological theorizing. The approximate but tentative truth-claim implied by this is what a weak form of critical realism is about.

Representatives of the hermeneutical tradition and those of the natural sciences often see this interpretative tradition and inferential procedures as mutually exclusive. In theology, however, both these tasks (though different) are required to reach maximal intelligibility as the overall goal of theological theorizing. All contextual, experiential, and hermeneutical issues in theological theorizing presuppose an epistemological model of rationality. The rationality of a critical realist theology is directly determined by the goals, that is, by the epistemic values of theological theorizing. In theology these epistemic values or criteria are:

1. *the reality depiction of theological statements,* in both an ontological and a contextual sense;
2. *the ability to critically identify and solve problems,* in this case experiential and conceptual problems; and
3. *the constructive and progressive nature of theological theorizing.*

---

46. Anthony O'Hear, *Experience, Explanation and Faith: An Introduction to the Philosophy of Religion* (Boston: Routledge & Kegan Paul, 1984), 44-50.

47. See Proudfoot, 43.

48. See van Huyssteen, *Teologie as Kritiese,* 206-10.

In the construction of theories in theology it thus becomes possible, in terms of epistemological and experiential adequacy, to identify, eliminate, or at least reduce experiential and conceptual problems. Although no strong claim for convergent truth can be shown to be plausible for theological theorizing, the arguments for explanatory progress and metaphorical reference do make it possible to claim truth approximation. In critical realism the only means open to us for judging the provisional or approximate truth of a theory is therefore through an assessment of its explanatory progress.

Explanatory progress in theology thus shows itself to be a form of inference to the best explanation. The approximate truth or likelihood of a theory depends on the degree of explanatory progress the theory enjoys. In theology a better explanation or hypothesis is one that solves experiential problems as well as reduces conceptual problems arising from interpreted, mediated religious experience. This leads one to infer that such a theory is true in the sense of highly likely, and can therefore claim approximate truth. To infer in this sense is strictly speaking to *conjecture*, and where inference comes in is in concluding that a specific theory is in fact the best available explanation. Ernan McMullin formulates it as follows: "We do not infer to the best explanation; we infer that a given explanation is the best available explanation."[49] In this sense, also in theology, we do not infer to the best explanation, but *from* the claim that a given theory is the best explanation *to* the conclusion that this explanatory hypothesis is highly likely.

Inference from the best explanation, or rather from explanatory progress, commits the critical realist in theology to saying that there are good argumentative reasons for holding on to a theory, but not that there are compelling grounds. The logical possibility that even a highly progressive theory might be false should thus in principle be held open. Any theory in theology may therefore be developed further and can in principle be revised and sharpened. The problem-solving and progressive nature of a theory in theological theorizing can therefore provisionally *suggest* truth approximation, but can never claim truth in a direct sense. In terms of overall goal of intelligibility in theology, rationality in theology implies the acceptance of those models that are the most effective problem solvers.

49. McMullin, "Explanatory Success," 65.

Because of the metaphorical roots of these models and the epistemic notion or reference they imply, explanatory models in theology should indeed be taken seriously but not literally. The metaphors of our explanatory models and theories indeed refer, but because we have no (and need no) prior knowledge of that which is being referred to, this metaphorical reference and the resulting explanatory progress in theory construction can never be literal. They do, however, provide exciting epistemic access in the difficult process of theorizing in theology. The cognitive function of models in theological theorizing is therefore primary and forms the basis for all affective, hermeneutical, and contextual claims in theology.

In theology, as in science, models are used as explanatory, and such models are indispensable in both. Although the basis from which a model may claim to depict reality differs between religious and scientific ones, their application as explanatory is not as different as is so often suggested.[50]

Rationality and Commitment

The central role of experience and explanation in the justification of the cognitive claims of theology finally implies that the important distinction between *commitments, an ultimate commitment, beliefs,* and *religious faith* should always be maintained. I am also convinced that no strong form of justification is possible for a commitment to an ultimate commitment (i.e., the search for maximal meaning in life) outside the way of life of which it forms part. This is no retreat to irrationalism, because experiential and epistemological adequacy, and not justified certainty, makes a commitment and its resulting beliefs and propositions responsible. This also implies that the beliefs that are implied in a commitment (whether to realism, to the Christian faith, or to critical realism in theology) should in principle always be open to criticism. From a perspective of religious experience this does not go against what could be called the certainty of faith. It does, however, imply a highly critical sensitivity towards the construction of theories in theology and certainly prevents any form of dogmatism in theological theorizing.

50. See Soskice, *Metaphor,* 112.

In a critical realist model the beliefs implied in a commitment to an ultimate commitment could never be justified by any foundationalist doctrine of justification, but it might indeed be possible to provide good or adequate reasons for *not* giving up a commitment and its implied propositional beliefs. Beliefs are therefore never just the "frills on a commitment,"[51] but can in a process of explanatory progress offer good reasons why it would make more sense (i.e., be more rational) to be committed to a certain way of life than not to be committed to it. In this sense there is no contrast between scientific and religious beliefs, nor between a commitment to realism in science and a commitment to critical realism in theology.

We could therefore say that all commitments must involve beliefs (are propositional) that might eventually turn out to be true or false. According to this view (which is also my own) it is therefore not enough to maintain that beliefs have a truth that is relative only to a group, a society, or a conceptual system. Obviously a conceptual framework or paradigm could involve beliefs that are true only within this context, but eventually we are of course confronted with the meaningfulness or provisional truth of the paradigm as such, as well as being committed to a certain set of beliefs. Such a commitment should be based on beliefs that are themselves external to the system. This is what I have tried to indicate throughout as *epistemological adequacy:* beliefs that function as criteria for rationality or epistemic values in a critical realist approach to theorizing in theology.

Basic to all this is the conviction that there is an undeniable religious dimension to human existence and that this dimension would be unintelligible without reference to God or a transcendent being. Religious experience and theological explanations thus open up the way for a tentative, provisional justification of the cognitive claims of theology, and for the claim of theological statements to be about God at all. This weak form of critical realism therefore argues for the credibility of a commitment to the Christian faith. In this sense theology and its explanations might differ from the other sciences, but it certainly is not less rational.

51. R. Trigg, *Reason and Commitment* (Cambridge: Cambridge Univ. Press, 1977), 36.

Chapter Nine

Narrative Theology: An Adequate Paradigm for Theological Reflection?

IN A RECENT ARTICLE ENTITLED "TWO TYPES OF NARRATIVE THEOL-
ogy," Gary L. Comstock defines narrative theology as a reflection on the religious claims embedded in stories and regards this significant approach to theology as one of the most viable and important alternatives for doing theology today.[1] As a paradigm for postmodern theology, narrative theology grows directly from the deep conviction that temporal narrativity constitutes the substance of personal human identity; as such it is aimed at the ultimate interpretation of the "story of our lives." This basic narrative condition of what it means to be human can also be described as the ontological condition for human stories of any kind: without it there could be no literature, no history, no philosophy, and certainly no religion.[2] Narrative theology takes this basic narrativity seriously in order to think through the nature of specifically religious knowledge.

Taking into account important German and British contributions, narrative theology still might be regarded as mainly an American contribution to postmodern antifoundational theological thought. The historical starting point of narrative theology could most likely be linked

1. G. L. Comstock, "Two Types of Narrative Theology," *Journal of the American Academy of Religion* 55, no. 4 (1987): 687.
2. See P. Brockelman, "Narrative Knowledge, Religious Truth and Pluralism" (paper read at the Annual Meeting of the American Academy of Religion, Chicago, November 1988), 2.

to H. Richard Niebuhr's 1941 essay entitled "The Story of Our Lives."[3] It is, however, especially since the 1970s that this theme has become increasingly dominant. Today prominent although diverse theologians are associated with narrative theology: Paul Ricoeur, Hans Frei, David Tracy, George Lindbeck, Stanley Hauerwas, Sallie McFague, Johann Baptist Metz, Michael Goldberg, James H. Cone, Ronald F. Thiemann, Carol Christ, David Burell, Harvey Cox, and James McClendon, to mention but a few.

Despite the rapid growth of narrative theology, it would appear that a definite tension has set in, dividing narrative theologians into two distinct groups, each with a more or less definable set of theological presuppositions and methodology. For the sake of analysis these two groups of narrative theologians can be identified as "pure narrativists" and "impure narrativists."[4] Pure narrativists can be described as antifoundational, cultural-linguistic, Wittgensteinian-inspired descriptivists. For theologians like Frei, Lindbeck, Hauerwas, and David Kelsey narrative as an autonomous literary form is particularly suited to theological reflection. Narrative here has a special status in the construction of theological statements, while abstract reasoning and philosophical categories do not belong to the essential task of what it means to do theology. Christian faith here is best understood by grasping the grammatical rules and concepts of its texts and practices.

Impure narrative theologians, on the other hand, find their inspiration in the circle of revisionist, hermeneutical, Gadamerian-inspired correlationists.[5] Theologians Tracy, McFague, and Ricoeur, while agreeing with pure narrativists about the central role of narrative in the communication of the Christian story, deny it any exclusive autonomous theological function in theological theorizing. For them narrative exhibits philosophical, historical, and psychological claims, and these need to be examined with the methods of those particular disciplines. In addition, pure narrative theologians very consciously construct a

3. See G. Comstock, "Telling the Whole Story? American Narrative Theology after H. Richard Niebuhr," in P. Frese, ed., *Religion and Philosophy in the United States of America* (Essen: Verlag Die Blaue Eule, 1987), 125.

4. See Comstock, "Two Types," 688ff.

5. See Comstock, "Two Types," 688.

postmodern paradigm for theology, while impure narrativists creatively revise the paradigms of language, reason, and practice of the liberal tradition in diverse attempts to justify the cognitive claims of theological reflection.

The explicit tension in the ranks of narrative theology is already implicit in the work of H. Richard Niebuhr, who — as "father" of contemporary narrative theology — made an important and far-reaching distinction between "internal" and "external" history. Gary Comstock supplies us with an illuminating analysis of this distinction: internal history has to do with the self-description of the Christian community in terms of their present experiences of the divine revelation; external history, on the other hand, is past history understood from the perspective of the observer — "objective" history that could as such be subjected to the queries of scientific investigation.[6]

For Niebuhr the very real tension between these two types of history had to be maintained; Christians must begin with their own present experiences of Christ, but should not isolate this from the criticism and correction of "external" or scientific history. For Niebuhr Christians had to tell both stories, the internal history of our experiences with Christ as well as the external story of our experience with nature, history, and science. Gary Comstock correctly states that present-day narrativists have been unable to tell "the whole story" by opting for either internal or external history, giving rise to a new and improper tension between pure and impure narrativists.[7] A way out of this impasse might be to find a way to reinterpret Christianity so as to be faithful to the biblical narratives, while at the same time remaining open to the philosophical and hermeneutical claims that result from the interpretation and explanation of these narratives.

Within the family of narrative theologians three common features or resemblances are shared: description, explanation, and justification. When, however, one examines the different ways in which narrativists describe, explain, and justify the Christian story, serious differences between the so-called pure and impure narrative theologians appear.[8] All narrativists agree that acceptable description should be conducted

6. Comstock, "Telling Whole Story."
7. Comstock, "Telling Whole Story," 143f.
8. See Comstock, "Two Types," 690ff.

in terms of Scripture's own narratives and autobiographies and not in categories alien to the Biblical stories. An adequate explanation of the Christian story should be arrived at in terms of the internal rules and procedures of the Bible's own language game, and not in terms of imported philosophical theories or social-scientific laws. Justification of Christianity should take the form of pragmatic demonstration that this tradition entails a liberating and authentic form of life: a form of life and thought that does not need justification by means of philosophical criteria for rationality and logic.[9]

It is, however, precisely on this point that serious differences between pure and impure narrativists appear: while, for example, purists do not reject critical thinking, they are wary of speculative reason and any attempt at a foundationalist epistemology. Because theology is fundamentally descriptive and regulative, it should not step outside the boundaries of the confessing community as the biblical narrative determines what can be said and done in theology. While purists have little or no room for the apologetic task of theology, impure narrativists like David Tracy — while not discounting the centrality and power of the biblical narratives — nevertheless deny absolute independence to narrative as such and argue that narratives contain all kinds of historical, psychological, and metaphysical claims and therefore invite the critical inquiry of historians, feminists, and philosophers.

A second deep rift between purists and impurists appears on the level of explanation. For a purist like George Lindbeck the Christian story posits a kind of language game sui generis, having its own unique procedures and rules. In this model, doctrines are regulative rules for a confessing community and as such make no factual or ontological claims. While for this purist position it would be improper to explain the Christian story in terms of some other language game, for impure narrativists the Christian language game is in continual public conversation with other language games and should therefore be critically correlated with the insights of contemporary philosophers, ethicists, and social scientists.

9. See H. Pieterse, "Gary Comstock's Two Types of Narrative Theology: An Evaluation" (paper read at the UPE Symposium on "Narrative and Interpretation," February 17, 1989), 2f.

A third point of contention between purists and impurists centers around the justification of the Christian story. Pure narrative theologians want to bring theology to a complete halt once it has narratively described (and therefore explained) Christianity. Justification of the truth-claims of the Christian faith is therefore of a pragmatic nature. On this impurists obviously disagree: according to them the truth-claims of Christianity demand metaphysical inquiry in order to determine whether Christian beliefs are rationally acceptable and whether there are ontological and/or epistemological grounds on which they can be justified.[10]

These important differences between pure and impure narrative theology now highlight what I would see as two central problems for any contemporary theology:

the *epistemological* problem of determining criteria for assessing the truth-claims and cognitive status of theological statements;
hermeneutical criteria for distinguishing between good or bad receptions of Christianity's classic text, and thus for assessing the validity of different interpretations of this text.

As reflection on the religious claims embedded in stories, narrative theology indeed touches the nerve of theology: What is the epistemological status of theological theories if they are based on discourse that is fundamentally narrative and metaphorical? With this in mind it is important to realize that in our age postmodern thought has highlighted the limits of human knowledge as well as a new understanding of the paradigmatic value of truth.[11] It is therefore perfectly understandable that a pure narrativist like Ronald Thiemann can caution theology not to formulate a specific theory for understanding faith, because all such theories obscure both the diversity and the mystery of human response to the gospel: to acknowledge the biblical narrative as God's promise is to believe that the crucified Jesus lives.[12] In this sense a postmodern

---

10. See Comstock, "Two Types," 703ff.

11. See H. Glanville, " 'What is Bongaloo, Daddy?' On Narrative Knowledge, Religious Truth and Pluralism" (paper read at the UPE Symposium on "Narrative and Interpretation," February 17, 1989), 3.

12. R. F. Thiemann, "Radiance and Obscurity in Biblical Narrative," in G. Green, ed., *Scriptural Authority and Narrative Interpretation* (Philadelphia: Fortress, 1987), 38.

pure narrative theology can even be seen as a call for a "new Reformation": to free Scripture once again, but this time from the papacy of the scholar.[13]

This specific kind of postmodern viewpoint, I have argued elsewhere,[14] eventually reduces theological reflection to a form of Wittgensteinian fideism while at the same time abandoning all truth-claims as well as any plausible notion of explanatory progress for theological reflection. The hermeneutical and epistemological problems created by the divergent trends in contemporary narrative theology is especially highlighted by Thiemann's pure form of narrative theology when the irrational inclusion of God as the hard core of a theological paradigm reveals a retreat to an esoteric commitment that firmly bars theology's way to the reality about which it proposes to make statements. This is especially prominent in Thiemann's recent work, where he argues that the category of "narrated promise" offers a nonfoundational way of reconceptualizing Christian theology.[15] This model for doing narrative theology becomes extra problematic when Thiemann contrasts narrative theology as descriptive theology with all forms of explanation, which for him always implies a foundationalist epistemology.

To counter this problem it is important to realize that biblical narratives are already interpretations, and biblical concepts in themselves are minitheories that reveal the way in which the classic text of the Bible was received and interpreted through the ages.

The biblical narratives as we have them are therefore already interpretations, already seen through the eyes of faith. In this sense Janet Martin Soskice can correctly state: to narrate is to explain.[16] With this statement Soskice rightly exposes the fine division between narrative and discursive forms of theology as a naive and even potentially danger-

13. M. Wiles, "Scriptural Authority and Theological Construction: The Limitations of Narrative," in Green, 44.

14. W. van Huyssteen, "Inference to the Best Explanation? On Narrative and the Shaping of Rationality in Theological Reflection" (paper read at the Annual Meeting of the American Academy of Religion, Chicago, November 1988), 12.

15. R. F. Thiemann, *Revelation and Theology: The Gospel as Narrated Promise* (Notre Dame: University of Notre Dame Press, 1987).

16. J. M. Soskice, "Myths, Metaphors and Narrative Theology," in *Proceedings: 7th European Conference on Philosophy of Religion* (Utrecht University, 1988), 130.

ous illusion.[17] Although narrative is an essential genre for communicating the Christian gospel, no form of pure narrative theology will be able to solve the epistemological problems of contemporary theology. A nonfoundationalist pure narrative theology, with its concern for a descriptive justification internal to the Christian framework, eventually reveals a peculiar brand of neo-Wittgensteinian fideism. On this view religious beliefs have no need for explanatory support and in the end can hardly be seen as more than a groundless language game. In fact, these kinds of beliefs become a species of belief whose truth is discovered by means of criteria internal to the language game itself.[18] The consequences of a so-called pure narrative theology therefore become clear: pure narrative theology leads not only to a relativistic understanding of justification, truth, and knowledge, but also to an epistemological relativism that would be fatal for the cognitive claims of theological statements.

It is, however, of great importance to realize that the rationality of Christian theology is distinctively shaped by the fact that myths and metaphor are intrinsic to our knowing and naming of God, and that narrative is the very essence of the Christian faith. The essential narrativity of the Christian faith, as we have seen, does have a special appeal for postmodern theological reflection.

Any discussion of the merits of either pure or impure narrative theology will therefore have to include a careful analysis of what is meant by "postmodern" as opposed to "modern." An analysis of the postmodern mentality as opposed to modernity is important not only because the rift within the family of narrative theologians can be largely reduced to this important conceptual problem, but also because it directly addresses the problem of fideism and foundationalism in contemporary theology. An analysis of these epistemological problems will eventually lead to an analysis of the hermeneutical problems implicit in all overt contextual theological models.

Furthermore, if postmodernism really is a departure from modernism and not merely a reaction to it, it could mean that the epistemological

17. See W. Jeanrond, "Response to Janet Martin Soskice," *Proceedings: 7th European Conference on Philosophy of Religion* (Utrecht University, 1988), 158.

18. See A. D. Steuer, "The Epistemic Status of Theistic Belief," *Journal of the American Academy of Religion* 5, no. 2 (1987): 241.

and hermeneutical problems connected with a modern paradigm are at best irrelevant to the postmodern approach.[19] This could mean that the so-called resemblances identified by Gary Comstock between pure and impure narrative theology — namely description, explanation, and justification — could well designate a far greater incommensurability between the two approaches to doing theology than initially conceived.

Narrative theology — in all its pure and impure forms — can in the end be fully understood only within the broader framework of postmodern thought. Postmodernism itself is more of an attitude than a specific demonstrable trend or paradigm.[20] Typical of postmodernism is its skepticism concerning the central role assigned to reason and rational thought. Over against indubitable truth-claims, an overconfident faith in science, and a metaphysical way of reasoning, the interrelatedness of truth-perspectives, ethical pluralism, and cultural relativism is typical of the postmodern perspective.

Over against a literal and empirical understanding of knowledge and truth, postmodernism emphasizes the linguistic dimension of human nature as well as the deep conviction that temporal narrativity constitutes the substance of what it means to be human. Within this postmodern framework literal language is replaced by an awareness of the metaphoricity and relationality of all language, but especially of religious language. Religious narrative thus seeks to make life's ultimate hermeneutical goal known: through narrative, past events become "graspable" and create an awareness of a transcendental reality "beyond" this world.[21] It is through myth and metaphor that this "beyond" is actualized in our experience and understanding. Religious narrative leads us to see "through the window" of metaphor, to the way we ought to believe. Epistemic access through metaphor is therefore neither empirically deductive, nor literally true, nor subjective illusion.

For this reason Janet Martin Soskice, in answer to the question, "What would the epistemological status of theological concepts be if they were not based on a discourse that is fundamentally narrative and metaphorical?" can correctly claim: whatever they would be, they would

---

19. See Pieterse, 5.

20. See C. Du Toit, "Aspekte van die postmodernistiese idioom in die teologie," in *Theologia Evangelica* 21, no. 3 (1988): 36-50.

21. Glanville, 5.

not be Christian.[22] For the same reason a pure narrative theology that consciously brackets the question of truth and validity can be seen only as a kind of sectarian instrumentalism: a narrative theology that achieves a meaningful Christian story at the cost of detaching this story from any dialogue with other Christians and with the secular world.

When the problems of justification of the cognitive claims of theological statements are considered, the central role of metaphor now becomes crucial. The reason why it becomes so important to single out the role of metaphorical language in religious texts is precisely because of the function of these metaphors. Metaphors certainly do not function only to "name" something; on the contrary, they provide epistemic access to that which is being referred to. As such they function to catch great strands of association, conscious and perhaps unconscious, for readers of a certain religious tradition.[23] This does not mean that what metaphor gives epistemic access to, and "catches" as meaningful, is not real; what the metaphor catches or opens up is closely connected to the overall narrative construction of the texts involved.

In this sense theology basically reflects on religious experience and the ensuing religious language as ways to the reality we call God. But these experiences, and their accompanying metaphorical language, can be reliably interpreted only on the basis of the classic texts of the Christian faith. In this sense the text of the Bible, as the ultimate "way" to the reality that is God, in itself becomes a reality that epistemologically functions as a very exclusive access to the reality of God. To this I have previously referred as the realism of the text.[24]

Within the context of this biblical text, narrative can be seen as a particular kind of textual structure characterized by its sequential, storylike qualities.[25] From this logically flows that not all biblical genres can be regarded as narrative, and certainly not all biblical metaphors are parts of narrative structures. This eventually will imply that theological reflection can never be exclusively defined in terms of only one biblical genre, however important it may be.

Narratives, as first-order accounts, histories, or stories, in a sense

---

22. Soskice, 131.
23. See Soskice, 134.
24. W. van Huyssteen, *The Realism of the Text* (Pretoria: UNISA, 1987), 30.
25. See Soskice, 135.

are even opposed to theology as a second-order reflection on the classic texts and Christian experience. The popularity of a narrative theology — especially a pure form of narrative theology — certainly is also concerned with reconfirming the place of the Bible in Christian life and thought. But, as Janet Martin Soskice has recently pointed out: one reason for the popularity of the narrative theology paradigm is that it effectively brackets the question of truth.[26] This obviously also is the reason why many postmodern theologians feel comfortable with the narrative theology paradigm: both accurate historical reports and pure fiction can be narratives, and epistemological truth-claims — however provisional — are sacrificed to the supremacy of narrative meaning. And when in this way a narrative interpretation becomes a narrative theology, at least a few epistemological eyebrows should be raised,[27] because narrative in this mode is a retreat into the ghetto of a world created rather than illuminated by the scriptural text.[28]

Narrative, then, although an essential genre for communicating the Christian faith, by itself will not solve the epistemological problem of the shaping of rationality in contemporary theology.

A pure narrative theology that brackets the problem of the justification of the cognitive claims of theological statements in the end ignores the question of truth and the problem of the shaping of rationality in theological reflection. It also bypasses the problem of reference or reality-depiction, as pure narrativists see the problem of justification in religious faith as entirely an internal, pragmatic matter. The cognitive claims of the Christian faith should be justified not only by their pragmatic effect and transformative power, but also by other epistemic values like reality depiction, contextuality, problem solving, and explanatory progress. A theology that takes these implicit philosophical and epistemological claims seriously could well be called an "impure narrative theology." From a contemporary philosophy-of-science point of view, a weak form of critical realism can provide epistemic warrants for the rationality of such an impure narrative theology — an antifideist and nonfoundational theology that still has a valid place within the postmodern paradigm. Such a theology not only takes the problem of the shaping of theological ratio-

---

26. Soskice, 139.
27. See Soskice, 139.
28. See Wiles, 49.

nality seriously, it also takes seriously the inescapable relation of theology to religious experience, to metaphor, and to story.

Against this background it would be rather naive to think that narrative as a biblical genre is precritical, preinterpretative, and thus always preferable to interpretation, justification, and argumentation.[29] All forms of theological communication contain interpretative elements, take sides, reveal particular perspectives, and therefore need critical assessment. It now also seems that the question of an adequate theory of reference in theological theory formation must remain on the agenda of all forms of narrative theology.

Our discussion has shown that even in a postmodern paradigm it seems to be impossible to bracket the epistemological problems of validity, credibility, and truthfulness when dealing with religious narratives. For this reason systematic theology will have to deal responsibly with a valid theory of metaphorical reference as a logical result of the basic realist assumptions and commitments of Christian theology.

With this in mind, it becomes doubtful whether Gary Comstock's assertion that the Jewish theologian Max Kadushin's system of value-concepts does in fact provide an answer to the present dispute between pure and impure narrativists can be regarded as epistemologically convincing.[30] Kadushin analyzes the interpretative role of value-concepts or control beliefs that provide us with a picture of the text/reader relationship. Value-concepts from the Torah, like charity, kingship, holiness, and prayer, cannot be pinned down by objective description but nevertheless have great pragmatic weight. These value-concepts guide behavior and express the self-identity of successive generations of God's people. Comstock uses this approach as a resource for understanding Christian narrative and its appeal to the quality of one's entire life before God. It is, however, not clear how Comstock hopes to transcend the pragmatic criterion of pure narrative theology by appealing to value-concepts when interpreting central Christian narratives. I am not convinced that he has succeeded in resolving the epistemological and hermeneutical problems referred to above.

29. See Jeanrond, 151.

30. "Everything depends on the type of concepts that the interpretation is made to convey." G. L. Comstock, "Max Kadushin among the Narrative Theologians," *Modern Theology* 5 (1989): 169ff.

In conclusion: the realist choice implied by a nonfoundational impure narrative theology is justified only by uncovering the basis of Christian narrative in history. It has already become clear that the only way we can manage to say anything about God at all is through our extended concepts, that is, through analogies and metaphors. The important and final question that now arises, is, Do we have good enough reasons to believe that these extended concepts are managing to do what we think they are doing, that is, managing to refer, to "get ahold of reality?"

To ask this is to ask for adequate epistemological reasons for a weak form of critical realism in theology. I have suggested that the following could count toward a critical realist theory of metaphorical reference in Christian theology:

> the fact that the Bible, as the classic text of the Christian faith, has survived as a religious text and as a book of faith in a long and remarkable interpretative tradition of a still ongoing faith-context;
>
> the reality of ongoing faith experiences that this text has evoked through centuries of belief in God;
>
> the metaphorical nature of biblical language and the continuity of reference this has creatively given to religious and theological language through the ages. This presupposes a continuous language-using community going back to the "initiating events," when these metaphorical terms were first introduced and their references fixed.

I think one could safely say that the very reason narrative achieved such preeminence in Christianity is because of this religion's concern to show that God acts in the human world and its history: narrative becomes important for Christians and for Christian readings of the Old Testament because of the life of Jesus. In this sense one can rightfully claim that all forms of narrative theology grow from Christology.[32] Epistemologically then, this realist choice and the fixing of metaphorical reference is justified by uncovering the basis of Christian narrative in history.

31. Van Huyssteen, *Realism of Text*, 31.
32. See Soskice, 150.

And as to the events in the life and death of Jesus: one can only generalize from parable to myth and from myth to fiction if it can be shown that historical questions are irrelevant to a full and proper religious understanding of the gospel narratives.

Part Three

Theology and Science

Chapter Ten

Evolution, Knowledge, and Faith: Gerd Theissen and the Credibility of Theology

I. An Evolutionary Interpretation of Christian Faith

Gerd Theissen's recent *Biblical Faith: An Evolutionary Approach*[1] is an excellent example of the fact that the credibility of theology is invariably linked to the problem of the credibility of Christian faith as such. To be able to fully appreciate his important perspective on this problem, I think this book should be read against the background of his earlier *On Having a Critical Faith* .[2]

From both these books emerge what can surely be seen as the most basic problems for any critical contemporary theologian:

why he/she still continues to identify consciously and openly with the Christian tradition;

the problem of truth in theology, which as such poses the unavoidable epistemological quest for rationality in theological thought.

The basic theses of both Theissen's books can be summed up as follows:

1. G. Theissen, *Biblical Faith: An Evolutionary Approach* (London: SCM, 1984).
2. G. Theissen, *On Having a Critical Faith* (London: SCM, 1979).

1. There are good reasons for being a Christian and for constructing Christian theology in a scientifically credible way;
2. However, this does not mean that Christianity can be defended in its traditional form;
3. If good theology, and therefore what I would prefer to call the quest for epistemological credibility, has to be retained, Christian faith will have to (and should be able to) change.

Theissen explicitly wants to point out that Christian faith can stand up to relativist, empiricist, and ideological critique, and what is even more important, the Christian theologian can offer unconditional personal commitment and renounce any absolutist claims for theological statements at the same time. This intention of his will have far-reaching consequences when in *Biblical Faith: An Evolutionary Approach* he specifically follows Karl Popper and opts for a critical rationalist paradigm of thought. Already in the first of the two books Theissen — to my mind correctly — states that "truth" in theology could never be a limited number of established propositions but instead functions as a normative idea that constantly puts all our theological statements to the test.[3] What Theissen really means by this will of course have to be assessed very carefully.

Theissen rightly warns that theologians should avoid the intellectual coma[4] of positivism in theology[5] at all costs. This means that traditional Christian religious statements should be reformulated in such a way that they could be shown to be expressions of possible religious experience. Here Theissen is very much to the point: relating theological statements, as the intellectual reflection on religious statements, to religious experience as such could be the only way of countering that suspicion that religious statements may be projective, illusionary, and thus antirealistic by nature.[6] This is probably the most important reason why I would typify Theissen's work as a *quest for realism in theology*, although he unfortunately never identifies this all-important problem

3. Theissen, *Critical Faith*, 2ff.
4. Theissen, *Critical Faith*, 6.
5. See W. van Huyssteen, *Teologie as kritiese geloofsverantwoording. Teorievorming in die sistematiese teologie* (Pretoria: RGN, 1986), 23ff.
6. See van Huyssteen, *Teologie as kritiese*, 169ff.

from a contemporary philosophy-of-science point of view. My main objections to the way in which he eventually opts for the evolutionary paradigm will be directly related to what I would prefer to call an epistemological blurring of paradigms, and thus of models of rationality, in Theissen's otherwise excellent work.

I would therefore like to show that it is not so much Theissen's underlying realist position that I personally find problematical, but much rather the epistemological model of thought and the type of assumptions he works from to arrive at this position.

A central theme of both books is therefore to be found in the profound statement that an ontological gulf permeates reality.[7] For Gerd Theissen this is the basic (epistemological) reason why the objects of religious experience transcend the ordinary everyday world. He consequently speaks of a "more than life," a "search for a reality which has yet to be disclosed,"[8] and an "adaptation to a reality which extends beyond humanity."[9] From a philosophy-of-science point of view this obviously reveals a theoretical commitment to some form of realism in theology. But in neither of the two books is this basic assumption ever put to discussion. What could have become the most exciting and creative basis for Theissen's argument, for this very reason unfortunately becomes the most problematical.

I can otherwise fully identify with Theissen's basic and central question, Will religion eventually and irreversibly be dissolved in the process of secularization, or does it in fact preserve an attitude to reality that will never be out of date?[10] Obviously religion is tied up with the quest for meaning in human life, but the central question remains: Do religious experiences indeed have a *real content*,[11] or as I would prefer to phrase it, do religious experiences and our theological statements about these experiences really refer?

Theissen in fact specifically raises this question (although to my mind he never answers it in a satisfactory way): Are there any reasons why religious conceptions should be grounded in an objective reality,

---

7. Theissen, *Critical Faith*, 12.
8. Theissen, *Critical Faith*, 13.
9. Theissen, *Biblical Faith*, 15.
10. Theissen, *Critical Faith*, 20.
11. Theissen, *Critical Faith*, 26.

or are they based on dogmatic confessions of faith?[12] To this question he provides a very ambiguous answer, which I think is directly related to a very problematical reception of the Popperian model of thought, or what I earlier called a "blurring" of paradigms, in his own theorizing:

> On the one hand Theissen clearly states that it is as impossible to show some of our contemporaries that religion involves a fundamental relationship to reality (and is not just a reaction to frustration or an unconscious piece of self-realization) as it is to show colors to a blind man.[13]
> On the other hand Theissen claims that we must look for an "empirical" basis for religious statements, on the basis of the fact that statements can be tested only if the reality to which they relate can be compared with the reality that we experience.[14]

I fully sympathize with the fact that in the long run religious experience should be seen as the only real origin of statements of faith and thus also of theological statements. But if this empirical basis should imply a correspondence theory of truth, where the reality of religious experiences should be "tested" against the reality to which these experiences relate, this of course becomes highly problematical. Theissen explicitly states:

> The anthropomorphic reality which religious statements seek to express must be compared with the reality which we experience; this is the only way of testing its truth-content.[15]

This not only implies an epistemological retreat to a positivist paradigm as far as a model of rationality for theology goes, but also goes directly against Theissen's own Popperian or critical rationalist idea of a normative truth.

In theology any access to the reality to which believers relate in

12. Theissen, *Critical Faith,* 28f.
13. Theissen, *Critical Faith,* 23.
14. Theissen, *Critical Faith,* 29.
15. Theissen, *Critical Faith,* 32.

terms of a corresponding theory of truth is obviously impossible. But quite apart from the problems positivism has created and still creates for theology, access to the reality to which believers relate is possible only through the metaphorical concepts of the Christian faith. And this becomes epistemologically credible only within a critical realist model of rationality. And as I have tried to point out earlier, it is only within this type of rationality model that the Christian theologian can offer unconditional personal commitment and at the same time critically renounce all absolutist claims for theological knowledge. And this, I think, is precisely what Theissen wants to achieve.

Against this background I find it tremendously important that Theissen can explicitly state that religious conceptions have a symbolic character and that in these conceptions "the familiar is projected on to the unfamiliar, and earthly images serve as metaphors for 'divine mysteries.'"[16] My critical question here would be — especially when he eventually uses metaphors from the theory of evolution — whether Theissen really follows through the creative possibilities of this line of thought, and whether he indeed grasps the full epistemological and methodological implications of this implied theological realism for the scientific credibility of theology.

The constructive choice in Theissen's thought for a form of realism in theology seems very obvious when he asks, "Are there structural affinities between non-human and human reality? Only if this is so, can there be a justifiable foundation for the anthropomorphism of religious imagery."[17] What really is meant by "structural affinity" will eventually be all-important for an evaluation of Theissen's choice for an evolutionary explanation of Christian faith. It will obviously also be basic to any credible form of realism in theology, and will therefore have to be defined carefully.

Furthermore, what is very important for understanding Theissen's version of realism in theology is that he can — and correctly so — state: "Whatever we may understand by 'God,' he cannot be conceived of without his being related to the whole universe, the most distant galaxies and the tiniest atomic elements."[18] And to this he adds the profound

16. Theissen, *Critical Faith*, 30.
17. Theissen, *Critical Faith*, 32.
18. Theissen, *Critical Faith*, 33.

statement: "Religion seeks to relate man [sic] to the whole of reality, not only to our fellowman, even if our neighbor may concern us more than anyone else."

Theissen eventually chooses a comprehensive concept that covers both relationships between human beings and experiences of the holy other than in human relationships, and this he calls *the experience of resonance*.[19] This concept implies not only structural affinities that are objectively present, but also their subjective effects: on the one hand, humans show a longing for resonance with reality. On the other, humans are powerfully affected by the structures in reality that are capable of resonance and adopt a responsive attitude towards them.[20]

What is more: Since religious experiences are concerned with meaning, every experience of resonance stands out from the background of possible absurdity. For Theissen religion is the sensitivity towards the resonance and absurdity of reality.[21] And the credibility of religion would therefore depend on whether there is an experience of the holy that is capable of moving life to the very depths and that at the same time can withstand critical examination.

After having discussed the amazing structural affinity between the constructs of science and what he calls "objective reality,"[22] Theissen proceeds and develops his argument for what would eventually become (in his 1984 work) an evolutionary interpretation of the essentials of the Christian faith, by specifically stating:

> It could well be that the similarity between nature and the structures created by our understanding requires the hypothesis of an objective spirit, a creative understanding or an intrinsic purpose within the universe.[23]

Why Theissen specifically chooses the theory of evolution to try to deal with the credibility of Christian belief from the perspective of scientific thought is never really made quite clear — except for the fact that the

---

19. Theissen, *Critical Faith*, 33; Theissen, *Biblical Faith*, 19f.
20. Theissen, *Critical Faith*, 33.
21. Theissen, *Critical Faith*, 34.
22. Theissen, *Critical Faith*, 35f.
23. Theissen, *Critical Faith*, 35.

evolutionary paradigm is regarded as the most comprehensive scientific framework that we can use in our time.[24] His choice for the theory of evolution might perhaps best be explained by the following statement:

> It is possible to interpret the whole of evolution from aqueous matter to the most complicated organisms as a heightening of life. In that case, man's [sic] own life appears as the echo of an all embracing tendency of life towards something more than life.[25]

This quotation highlights — to my mind — the two most important factors in Theissen's theological model, and also the basic reasons for his choice for the paradigm of evolution as an explanatory model for Christian faith:

1. his decision for a very definite form of realism in theology;
2. his basic and ultimate decision for Christianity.

An evaluation of Theissen's exciting thought will therefore have to deal not only with his interpretative adaption of evolutionary categories for theological thought, but also very specifically with the realist implications of his basic argument and with the difficult question as to whether his ultimate commitment to the Christian faith is indeed compatible with his apparent choice for what he calls the "evolutionary epistemology" of Karl Popper's critical rationalism.[26]

In his recent book Theissen very clearly outlines his objectives: he wants to analyze and interpret biblical faith with the help of evolutionary categories, seeing the theory of evolution as one of the most fascinating constructions of human reason, which as such can generate an explanation of the explanation that determines our life.

Theissen therefore clearly handles the theory of evolution as an explanatory structure by which our knowledge can — as he specifically states[28] — adapt to reality. Obviously the theory of evolution itself has

24. Theissen, *Biblical Faith*, xi.
25. Theissen, *Critical Faith*, 48.
26. Theissen, *Biblical Faith*, xii.
27. Theissen, *Biblical Faith*, xi.
28. Theissen, *Biblical Faith*, xi.

undergone evolution, can never be absolutized, and as such has limited validity. But what is even more important is that Theissen also explicitly rejects any form of biologism, that is, a naive transference of biology to human culture.[29] In fact he interprets human history (including the history of biblical faith) by means of a theory that analogously derives from biology and therefore does not claim an unbroken continuity between biological evolution and human history.

When Theissen eventually analyses and interprets biblical history, he therefore never sees straight lines of development from the beginnings of Israel to primitive Christianity. On the contrary, he consistently stresses discontinuity, the break in history, the new beginning: thus monotheism in Israel and Jesus of Nazareth, his proclamation and ministry, are not interpreted as a result of an "evolution," understood as continuous development.[30] Both of these are instead to be viewed as revolutions in the history of religion.

In outlining the analogies between biological and cultural evolution, Theissen uses the theory of evolution as an explanatory model for dealing with the complex and problematical relationship between faith and knowledge. Eventually he tries to demonstrate that with the aid of evolutionary categories like *adaption, selection,* and *mutation,* faith and knowledge can be shown to have much more in common than the so-called "contradictions" between scientific thought and religious faith would seem to suggest.[31]

The fact that Theissen contrasts scientific thought and faith in the first chapter of his book seems to be rather obvious and unproblematical. However, his attempt to pinpoint the knowledge-faith problem by identifying three contradictions between scientific thought and faith I find highly problematical. I think that not so much the so-called contradictions between scientific thought and faith should be discussed, but much rather — and much more appropriate — the problematical relationship between scientific thought, on the one hand, and theological reflection on faith, on the other.

Later in the book — unfortunately after having discussed the three contradictions between scientific thought and faith — Theissen does in

29. Theissen, *Biblical Faith,* xii.
30. Theissen, *Biblical Faith,* 43ff., 83-128.
31. Theissen, *Biblical Faith,* 3-8.

fact refine this problem in a way and suggests a parallel development or co-evolution of knowledge and faith, or science and theology.[32] He in fact typifies science and theology both as thought-through and therefore systematized forms of belief. It is indeed not so much the relationship between science and faith, but instead the relationship between science and theology — as critical reflection on faith — that is the real problem here.

I also think that this refined and more accurate distinction would have rather profoundly influenced the way Theissen identifies "contradictions" between science and faith. Religious faith would be in opposition to science only within a positivist paradigm, and of course also in a critical rationalist one. Within a critical rationalist model of rationality, faith could of course be meaningful and even true.[33] Faith, and statements about faith, could, however, never form part of the so-called scientific context of justification and therefore of the scientific process itself. The fact that Theissen consciously chooses for a Popperian and thus critical rationalist epistemology will obviously be of direct relevance for the way in which he deals with the relationship between religious faith and knowledge. Whether Theissen in fact remains true to the Popperian line of thought remains to be seen.

I am convinced that in the end Theissen's choice for the theory of evolution as an attempt to integrate human knowledge is motivated not so much by the critical rationalist ideas of verisimilitude, corroboration, and falsification, but by the realist assumptions and the eventual realist implications of this model for theology. From the point of view of the philosophy of science it would therefore have been more consistent as well as more fruitful to opt for a realist position in scientific as well as theological thought. This would have enabled him to retain his arguments for the credibility of theological thought, but then with a much more convincing and stronger epistemological basis.

---

32. Theissen, *Biblical Faith*, 37.
33. See van Huyssteen, *Teologie as kritiese*, 44.

III. The Three Contradictions between Scientific Thought and Faith

Eventually Theissen correctly sees knowledge and faith as complementary expressions of life.[34] His attempt to integrate faith and knowledge now makes it necessary to take a closer look not only at the way he identifies three contradictions between scientific thought and faith, but also at the way each of these contradictions is in the end "revitalized" by Theissen. The three contradictions and Theissen's revised and improved interpretations of these "standard problems" are outlined as follows.

1. Scientific statements are hypothetical, while statements of faith are apodeictic.[35]

Over against this Theissen states:

Hypothetical scientific thought and apodeictic faith are different forms of adapting to an unknown reality.[36]

The way in which Theissen's choice for a critical rationalist model of rationality determines both these formulations has already been briefly pointed out. From a realist position, where the real problem has been identified as the problematical relationship between scientific thought and theological thought, it would suffice to say: *Both* scientific and theological thought are provisional, and therefore each in its own way hypothetical, and as such forms of "adapting" to different dimensions of an unknown reality. What is more, this does not in any way contradict the "apodeictic" character of living faith and the ultimate religious commitment that grounds this faith. I am therefore convinced that the character of the act of faith, and the ultimate religious commitment that always precedes it, should in no way be confused with the nature of statements of faith, which in their own way are as hypothetical as any other scientific statements.

What I therefore find lacking in Theissen's otherwise excellent work is

---

34. Theissen, *Biblical Faith*, 18ff.
35. Theissen, *Biblical Faith*, 4.
36. Theissen, *Biblical Faith*, 18.

a clear distinction between the role and functions of an *ultimate religious commitment* and that of a *theoretical commitment* to a specific paradigm of thought. And should he — with good reasons — still prefer to opt for the explanatory possibilities of the evolutionary model, to move away from the often tacit limitations of positivism that still haunt the rationality model of critical rationalism, to the much more creative epistemological possibilities of current scientific realism, that should have been argued more clearly.

What makes this so important is that Theissen, although apparently following Popper in his choice for an evolutionary epistemology, does not seem to realize the implications of this choice for the credibility of theological thought: from a critical rationalist viewpoint not only faith and an ultimate religious commitment are bracketed out of the scientific "level" of the so-called context of justification, but also the analogous interpretation of cultural evolution as a higher form of biological evolution is — when it comes to the history of Christian faith — in no way open to falsification in the true sense of the word. The acceptance of an evolutionary epistemology and certain basic concepts from critical rationalism in this way therefore leads to the "blurring" of paradigms of which I spoke earlier. The answer to this problem is, I think, to be found in the transcending of this thought model and in an exploration of the very obvious quest for realism that so clearly typifies Theissen's work.

2. Scientific thought is subject to falsification; faith goes against the facts.[37]

In contrast to this Theissen claims:

> Science controlled by falsification and faith which goes against the facts are different forms of coping with the pressure of selection exercised by reality.[38]

I think this statement of Theissen can be applied only to religious faith as a lived deed (*fides qua*), but never to theological reflection and therefore to theological statements about faith as such. Of course, in most

---

37. Theissen, *Biblical Faith*, 4.
38. Theissen, *Biblical Faith*, 4.

of the (natural) sciences progress is monitored in terms of success and therefore in terms of the elimination of errors. In theology this process of justifiability by experimental or empirical falsification is obviously not possible. I am, however, convinced that within a critical realist paradigm theological theories can be shown to be problem-solving and progressive, but then in terms of hermeneutical, philosophy-of-science, historical, literary, and linguistic criteria.

In this case the constructs of both science and theology give us our only access to the different domains of reality we are groping for, and as such are always provisional and hypothetical. The real problem therefore is not so much falsification by facts or going against facts, but:

> that scientific and theological thought can both function only within the framework of a very definite theoretical commitment to specific models of rationality, and
>
> that theological thought is apparently always preceded by a very definite ultimate (religious) commitment.

3. Scientific thought delights in dissension; faith is based on consensus.[40]

This "contradiction" is now rephrased by Theissen to read:

> Science which delights in dissent and faith which depends on consensus are different forms of the openness of our spiritual life to mutations.[41]

Again, this might be true, but the problem surrounding the credibility of theological thought from a philosophy-of-science point of view has still not been addressed at all.

Indeed faith as such, as lived by believers in the church, tends toward consensus. Theissen is also correct in pointing out that the early church developed three social controls to protect this consensus: the canon, the

39. Theissen, *Biblical Faith*, 18.
40. Theissen, *Biblical Faith*, 4-8.
41. Theissen, *Biblical Faith*, 30ff.

regula fidei as a confession to what was seen as the essence of Christian faith, and the episcopacy. This indeed in a sense obligates the church and its believers to tradition,[42] to consensus,[43] and to authority.[44]

None of these, however, can be said to be true of an epistemologically (and thus scientifically) credible, constructive theology where the weight of rational argument is as important as in any scientific progress of theorizing. Moreover, the classical text of the Christian tradition not so much controls consensus in an authoritarian way but should hermeneutically function within a critical realist problem-solving model where text and tradition are to be constantly reinterpreted.[45] As far as church office and the authority that goes with it are concerned, this to my mind may function in a meaningful way in the church itself, but is as such totally irrelevant for a constructive theology.

I therefore think that Theissen obscures not only the very valid distinction between faith and statements about faith, but also that between community faith[46] and theology as such. This obviously can leave no room for a transconfessional, more broadly conceptualized constructive theology, but can lead only to a very restricted form of "church" or "confessional theology."

To contrast, therefore, the originality of science with community faith's fidelity to tradition can within this context never be accepted. In theological thought, originality and creative construction (within a valid and thought-through realist paradigm) can form the essence of theological theorizing.[47] What is more, Thomas S. Kuhn convincingly showed that also scientific communities — in periods of "normal science" — display an enormous fidelity to tradition.[48]

---

42. Theissen, *Biblical Faith*, 33.

43. Theissen, *Biblical Faith*, 34.

44. Theissen, *Biblical Faith*, 45.

45. W. van Huyssteen, *Theology and the Justification of Faith: Constructing Theories in Systematic Theology* (Grand Rapids: Eerdmans, 1989), and *The Realism of the Text* (Pretoria: UNISA, January 1987).

46. Theissen, *Biblical Faith*, 4.

47. van Huyssteen, *Theology and Justification of Faith*, 206ff.

48. T. S. Kuhn, *The Structure of Scientific Revolutions* (Chicago: University of Chicago Press, 1970), 180f.; "Logic of Discovery or Psychology of Research," in I. Lakatos and A. Musgrave, eds., *Criticism and the Growth of Knowledge* (Cambridge: Cambridge University Press, 1970), 253.

Theissen's argument can now be summed up as follows:

1. Just as in biological evolution life has developed through mutation and selection towards constantly new forms of adaptation
   to reality, so too culture has developed different forms of
   adapting to the basic conditions of reality; and of these science,
   art, and religion are the most important. And only when these
   complement one another do they do justice to the richness of
   reality. Each of these should in fact be seen as an independent
   way of coming to grips with reality.
2. In this process of coming to grips with reality, forms can be
   established that are analogous to those in the processes of mutation
   and selection. In this sense features common to knowledge and
   faith can be established in the light of the basic categories of the
   theory of evolution, namely adaption, selection, and mutation.[49]
3. Theissen therefore assumes a continuity between biological and
   cultural evolution (which leads to the analogies between them)
   but says that cultural evolution is not simply the continuation of
   biological evolution but a higher form of it. In both areas development presupposes (i) the appearance of variation; (ii) a selection from the variants; and (iii) their preservation. The paradigm
   of evolution therefore reveals two phases of evolution, biological
   and cultural (i.e., science, art, and religion), which are as such
   different forms of coming to grips with reality. And it is precisely
   Theissen's consistent referring to an adaption to reality that to
   me reveals his implicit realist position.
4. Theissen eventually proceeds and views knowledge and faith as
   two different patterns of behavior in cultural evolution.[50] For
   this the analogies between biological and cultural evolution are
   obviously very important:
   a. For Theissen every cultural innovation can be seen as a kind
      of "mutation": while it takes over traditional elements by com-
      bining them in a new way, it also creates something that has
      not been there before. This may be any new theory or innova-
      tive event in art or ethics, etc. Theissen thus uses the concept

49. Theissen, *Biblical Faith*, 8f.
50. Theissen, *Biblical Faith*, 18ff.

"mutation" *metaphorically,* leaving behind its literal reference to genetic changes. Cultural innovations therefore perform the same function in cultural evolution that mutations do in biological evolution by providing a choice of variants.[51] These mutations, as cultural innovations, are therefore creative responses to a particular problem and can happen in language, writing, and imagery.[52]

b. Implied in the metaphor "mutation" is that of "selection": human beings select the most effective cultural patterns of behavior by learning processes, that is, by trial and error, imaginative learning, and problem solving.[53] This process of cultural selection then leads to an adaption to a reality *"which extends beyond humanity."*[54]

c. In biological evolution, mutation and selection lead towards increasingly differentiated organisms only if improvements which have once been achieved are not lost again, and are protected from chance deteriorations. In nature, of course, there are remarkable processes that ensure the reduplication of forms of life.[55] For Theissen it is obvious that cultural evolution works with analogous processes: it substitutes tradition for genetic transmission, and cultural identity for separation.[56] Tradition in this sense is therefore seen as the transference of nongenetic information from one generation to the next.

IV. Concluding Statements

1. On Critical Realism in Theology

Theissen's remark that "the only reason for identifying oneself with a particular religious tradition is the conviction that it does in fact present

51. Theissen, *Biblical Faith,* 178.
52. Theissen, *Biblical Faith,* 11.
53. Theissen, *Biblical Faith,* 11f.
54. Theissen, *Biblical Faith,* 15.
55. Theissen, *Biblical Faith,* 15.
56. Theissen, *Biblical Faith,* 15ff.

an appropriate solution to religious problems" is not only revealing but also very relevant for the problem of credibility in theological thought.[57]

In an attempt to interpret the epistemological implications of this statement for theological thought, I would like to claim that not Theissen's critical rationalist attempt at an evolutionary epistemology, but critical realism offers us what Theissen is rightly searching for, that is, a credible integration of knowledge and faith. I have also (already) tried to indicate that this position is in fact implied in Theissen's arguments.

When Theissen therefore states that knowledge should be seen as the adaption of cognitive structures to reality, this is already an outspoken realist viewpoint.[58] And faith is not a structure that has become obsolete, but in fact struggles at the limits of human consciousness.[59] As such faith can also be seen as an anticipation of future possibilities of evolution, which have not yet reached the level of our consciousness. While Theissen then proceeds and views knowledge and faith as two different patterns of behavior in cultural evolution,[60] I would add that not only scientific knowledge but indeed also theological reflection could be viewed as "forms of adaption" to reality. In both science and theology our constructs and theories give us some provisional insight into the different domains of the reality of that which is being studied. In this sense the critical realist in theology is convinced that there is a "fit,"[61] however provisional, between the structure of his theories and the structure of the reality he is groping for: not an assurance that comes from a comparison between them — he has no independent access to this reality in terms of naive realist correspondence theory — but an assurance that comes from the inner logic of the realist argument itself. In this way the realist argument shows that our access to the reality on which the scientist (and thus also the theologian) focus, *is through the scientific concept.*

In this sense I could agree with Theissen that we are enabled through scientific (and theological) knowledge to have the experiences of "res-

---

57. Theissen, *Critical Faith,* 77.

58. Theissen, *Biblical Faith,* 19.

59. Theissen, *Biblical Faith,* 17.

60. Theissen, *Biblical Faith,* 16ff.

61. E. McMullin, "The Motive for Metaphor," *Infinity* 55 (1982): 32; "A Case for Scientific Realism," in J. Leplin, ed., *Scientific Realism* (Berkeley: University of California Press, 1984), 35.

onance" that he so often discusses in both his books. Precisely through what we provisionally know can we have intimations of a central reality that determines and conditions everything.[62]

When therefore regarded from a much more credible epistemological critical realist basis, Theissen could indeed with good reasons state: "thus evolutionary epistemology confirms a first basic experience of any religion, namely that behind the familiar human world a mysterious other world opens up which appears only indirectly, brokenly and symbolically in the world that we experience and interpret."[63]

2. On the Function of an Ultimate Religious Commitment in Theological Reflection

When Theissen sees faith and knowledge as attempts to understand the whole of life as a response to an ultimate reality,[64] it becomes very obvious that his thought requires an epistemological model of rationality that would be able to accommodate an ultimate faith commitment. Within the Popperian or critical rationalist paradigm this could never be possible, whereas critical realism in theology opens up a way to acknowledge the fundamental role played by commitment — both theoretical and ultimate religious commitments — in scientific and theological reflection.

Theissen's decision for Christian faith forms a consistent theme in his own thought, and statements like the following would indeed require a definite account-rendering of his own commitment to Christianity:

> But what is that mysterious ultimate reality towards which our organic, intellectual and religious structures develop attempts at adaptation? Religious tradition knows only one appropriate term for it: God. . . . Compared with this name, all other terms like "central reality" and "ultimate reality" are only counsels of desperation.[65]

62. Theissen, *Biblical Faith*, 19.
63. Theissen, *Biblical Faith*, 20.
64. Theissen, *Biblical Faith*, 26.
65. Theissen, *Biblical Faith*, 25, 30.

3. On the Role of Metaphors in Theological Reflection

Theissen acknowledges that images of God from evolutionary theory might show us a way of overcoming the hermeneutical conflict between New Testament Christology and modern consciousness.[66] He also correctly states that the use of metaphors leads us into the obscure intermediate area between poetry and reality, and between creative imagination and reality. Metaphors therefore transcend boundaries that are set by strict reflection and are therefore indispensable for theological reflection.[67]

This of course — as we saw earlier — is true of all scientific thought, and that is why the criterion of fertility is directly linked to the use of models and metaphors in a critical realist paradigm.[68] This is also why it should be obvious that new metaphors in theology should be creatively developed with material from the experience of our time.

The way in which metaphors are thus linked to the very center of scientific thought is of the utmost importance, not only for understanding scientific realism, but also for evaluating critical realism in theology. The direct implication of this important fact is that the language of the scientist is not so direct and "literal" as it was once thought to be. Not only are even the most literal-sounding terms "theory-laden," but since they are always to a certain extent provisional, they must be regarded as metaphoric.[69] To regard certain concepts as metaphorical is not to say that they are not precise, or that they are always ambiguous. On the contrary, McMullin states it well: metaphors are not normally ambiguous, yet at crucial moments in the continuing development of science, they do generate ambiguity, just the sort of fruitful ambiguity that permits a theory to be extended, reshaped, rethought, and so on.[70] Therefore:

> The metaphor is helping to illuminate something that is not well understood in advance, perhaps, some aspect of human life that

---

66. Theissen, *Biblical Faith*, 87.
67. Theissen, *Biblical Faith*, 87.
68. See McMullin, "Case for Scientific Realism," 30ff.
69. See McMullin, "Motive for Metaphor," 37.
70. See McMullin, "Case for Scientific Realism," 37.

we find genuinely puzzling or frightening or mysterious. The manner in which such metaphors work is by tentative suggestion.[71]

The role of metaphor in scientific thought is also the scientific realist's answer to Kuhn's well-known thesis of the *incommensurability* between paradigms, and therefore often also between theories, in science. As regards the problem of continuity when the scientist moves from a rejected theory to a new theory, what provides the continuity is the underlying metaphor or metaphors of successive theories. Thus one may find that in scientific thought one aspect of an original or older theory may eventually be dropped, while others are thought through again and creatively retained. Even in a total "paradigm switch" it will be only metaphor(s) that constitute the continuity.

In our understanding of the world (including scientific and theological understanding) metaphors therefore play a significant if not central role. In fact the explanatory power or success of a theory depends on the effective metaphors it can call upon. For this reason I would call the epistemological model that scientific realism offers us a *relational model*. The scientist as subject, the metaphor-maker is now recognized as an inseparable part of the scientific endeavor.[72] Of this McMullin says:

> Yet this in no way lessens the *realism* of science, the thrust of the scientist to grasp the "irreducible X" before him. It is, indeed, precisely the quality of a scientific theory as fruitful metaphor, in lending itself to further development, that most commends it as *good science*.[73]

For the critical realist the theoretical language of theological reflection is therefore theoretical explanation of a special sort. It is metaphorical, and thus open-ended and ever capable of further development. The precise metaphorical basis of all scientific language gives this language resources of suggestion that are the most immediate testimony of its ontological worth.

71. McMullin, "Case for Scientific Realism," 31.
72. McMullin, "Motive for Metaphor," 37.
73. McMullin, "Motive for Metaphor," 37.

Against this background it should now be clear why scientific realism has developed into one of the most important positions in the current philosophy-of-science debate: it not only highlights the role of metaphorical reference in scientific theory-formation while honoring the provisionality and socio-historical nature of all knowledge, but it also enables us to retain the ideals of truth, objectivity, rationality, and scientific progress in an exciting and reinterpreted way. It is therefore not at all surprising that the realist challenge has at present been taken on in the humanities, especially the social sciences and also in theology. I am fully convinced that, because of the important relational analysis and the accompanying interpretative and thus hermeneutical dimension of all knowledge in the realist paradigm, this venture can in no valid way be seen as a return to the positivist ideal of the uniformity of all scientific knowledge. On the contrary, it opens up creative and exciting possibilities — also and especially for theology.

Chapter Eleven

Theology and Science:
The Quest for a New Apologetics

FOR THOSE WHO ARE SERIOUS ABOUT LIVING THE CHRISTIAN FAITH
in the context of our contemporary postmodern world, the task
of doing theology in a way that might really make a difference presents
itself as a daunting and even confusing challenge. Deeply affected by
contemporary cultural and political issues, by the successes of the
natural sciences and technology and the pervasive presence of especially the psychological and social sciences in our daily lives, this
challenge translates as follows: Do we still have good reasons to stay
convinced that the heart of the Christian message does indeed provide
the most adequate interpretation of our experience with our world,
our culture(s), and ourselves? Put in a different way, does the postmodern world, with its radical religious and cultural pluralism, its
spectacular technology, and its values that also force us to confront
the realities of environmental destruction and political, economic,
racial, and sexual injustice, still ultimately make sense in the light of
Sinai and Calvary?

Our world has, of course, been fundamentally changed by an
all-pervasive scientific culture that shapes the rationality of the way
we live our daily lives. The advent of modern thought has in fact led
to an unparalleled transformation in the way we as human beings
have come to regard the natural world and our relation to it. In a way
it could even be argued that, in the history of Western thought, the

advent of scientific culture outshines everything since the rise of Christianity.[1]

Today theologians and scientists, whether they agree or not, and whether they even talk or not, are together in their awe for the way the powers of human reason and imagination manage to far exceed our demands for biological survival, and for the extraordinary ability of the human mind to represent aspects of the world that are inaccessible to our ordinary senses. But scientists are also teaching theologians something today about the baffling and puzzling incompleteness of all our attempts at finding meaning and intelligibility in our world. Our knowledge of the natural world stretches out in two directions: to the basic constituents of physical reality on the one hand, and to the higher levels of biological complexity on the other.[2] We should indeed be in awe in the face of the amazing and inventive creativity of the world in which we have evolved: the elusive and unpicturable basic subatomic entities out of which everything is made, including ourselves, have potentialities unknown and undescribable in terms of the physics that discovers and the mathematics that symbolizes them. Therefore, at both the extremes of our comprehension — the subatomic and the personal — we face such baffling depths that even scientists today speak of the mystery of the universe.

Arthur Peacocke has recently convincingly argued for the merging of this search for intelligibility with the search for ultimate meaning in life[3]: science today forces us to contemplate the future of our planet since we have to reckon with its certain disappearance. The energy of our sun, which sustains life on earth, is finite: the sun is about halfway through its life, and the time left for the existence of the earth is about the same as the length of time it has already existed. Thus, the demise of all life on earth, including our lives as humans, is really quite certain. Science today therefore forces us to ask, What is the meaning of this universe and of our presence in it? These are the ultimate questions that bring theology and science closer together, for they are questions that cannot be answered through the resources of science alone. Thus the scientifically observed and understood character of the natural world,

1. See Arthur Peacocke, *Theology for a Scientific Age* (Oxford: Basil Blackwell, 1990), 27.

2. See Peacocke, *Theology for Scientific Age*, 82.

3. Peacocke, *Theology for Scientific Age*, 83ff.

including our existence as human beings, is today of immense theological importance. For what nature is like, what the meaning of human life is, what God is like, indeed whether or not God exists, have become questions that are so interlocked that they cannot be considered in isolation anymore.

For theology today, an all-important focus of its dialogue with our contemporary culture is therefore not only the tremendous problems that would arise if theology should choose to retreat to the insular comfort of an exclusivist theological confessionalism, but also and precisely its uneasy relationship with the sciences. In fact, as theologians we find ourselves confronted with a special challenge: first, we have to try our best to keep together, in a meaningful whole, a very specific sense of continuity with the Christian tradition and a respect for religious and cultural pluralism, as well as a resisting of any form of political or confessional authoritarianism.[4] Second, postmodern thought also challenges us again to explore the presupposed continuity between Christian theology and the general human enterprise of understanding the world rationally.

In trying to do this, however, we soon discover that not only theology, but also the sciences have been profoundly influenced by our postmodern contemporary culture. This gives an unexpected and complicating twist to the centuries-old theology and science problem: not only theology, but also postmodern science and philosophy of science have moved away quite dramatically from positivist and technocentric conceptions of scientific rationality, with its closely aligned beliefs in linear progress, guaranteed success, deterministic predictability, absolute truths, and some uniform, standardized form of knowledge. Some contemporary philosophers of science now argue for a postmodern philosophy of science that, along with feminist interpretations of science, focuses on trust in local scientific practice while, at the same time, all global interpretations of science are rejected.[5] This kind of postmodernism in science not only sharply deconstructs and rejects the autonomy and cultural dominance of especially the natural sciences in

4. See Mark Kline Taylor, *Remembering Esperanza: A Cultural-Political Theology for North American Praxis* (New York: Orbis Books, 1990), 31ff.

5. Joseph Rouse, "The Politics of Postmodern Philosophy of Science," *Philosophy of Science* 58 (1991).

our time, but seriously challenges any attempt to develop a meaningful and intelligible relationship between science and Christian theology today.

In certain significant ways postmodernism, with its clear-cut option for pluralism and diversity,[6] seems therefore to leave both theology and science fragmented. And this seems to be the perplexing challenge we have to deal with: is it at all possible to somehow meaningfully relate the fragmented, specialized world of contemporary science to the equally fragmented intellectual world of contemporary theology? In spite of its postmodern guise, the "theology and science" problem has of course been with the Christian church for centuries. In his important recent publication, *Creation and the History of Science*, Christopher Kaiser argues that the problem of the God-and-science relationship in the Judeo-Christian context goes back at least as far as the second century B.C.[7] This essentially grew into the enduring question, Can Christians reconcile their faith in God with their scientific work in the laboratory?

In addition to this, it is well known that theology has been fundamentally influenced by both the philosophical cosmology of the ancient world and the scientific discoveries of our time. In addition, however, the natural sciences have been seriously influenced by theological presuppositions throughout their long history: from the days of the early church, through the revival of Aristotelian thought in the Middle Ages and the beginning of modern science in the Renaissance and the Enlightenment, up to post-Newtonian mechanics in the nineteenth century, ultimately concluding with the theological implications of the thoughts of the founders of twentieth-century physics, Niels Bohr and Albert Einstein. From the beginning of the Christian era to the late eighteenth century, an operational faith in God as Creator was an essential factor in the development of all branches of science. This created a kind of matrix in which theologians and scientists could coexist in a way that we can only dream about today.

The nineteenth century, with the triumph of individualism in religion and professionalism in science, obviously changed all that when

6. See David Harvey, *The Condition of Postmodernity: An Enquiry into the Origins of Cultural Change* (Oxford: Basil Blackwell, 1989), 9ff.

7. Christopher Kaiser, *Creation and the History of Science* (Grand Rapids: Wm. B. Eerdmans, 1991).

science, under the surge of Darwinism, moved away from theology rather dramatically. Even in our complex world today, however, Christian theologians who are looking for ways to meaningfully interpret the idea of creation still hang on to some very basic commitments: the idea that nature is intelligible; that nature is relatively autonomous; and that reality, as created by God, has some intrinsic unity as God's creation. For many in the contemporary theology-and-science debate, especially with the abandonment very often of the traditional idea of a Creator God, this has become a driving force behind all their reflection; even if the origin of the cosmos may ultimately be unintelligible, nature itself is eminently intelligible and reflects the same rationality as the human mind. Human intelligence in the end seems to go hand in hand with an intelligible universe. In fact, an act of faith is always necessary for the scientist too: a commitment to the metaphysical belief that the world is intelligible and open to rational exploration.[8]

A fundamental commitment to this kind of intelligibility has no doubt been the impetus behind an intense revival of worldwide academic interest in the troubled relationship between theology and science, especially during the past decade. In the United States, such institutions as the Center of Theology and the Natural Sciences in Berkeley, the Institute for Religion in an Age of Science, the Chicago Center for Religion and Science, and, in Princeton, the Center of Theological Inquiry have certainly become leaders in the task of nurturing the emerging discipline, and also in introducing it in the podiums of the American Academy of Religion and the American Association for the Advancement of Science. Princeton Theological Seminary followed suit by establishing the first, and at this time the only, tenured chair in theology and science in the world. In all of these instances, the groundbreaking work of American and British scholars like Ian Barbour, Arthur Peacocke, John Polkinghorne, and Thomas Torrance is being carefully analyzed and built upon by a host of younger scholars in fields as diverse as philosophical theology, philosophy of science, cosmology, evolutionary biology, neurobiology, genetics, physics, astrophysics, quantum physics, ecology, biochemistry, anthropology, technology, and the cognitive and social sciences.

8. See John Polkinghorne, *Reason and Reality* (Philadelphia: Trinity Press International, 1991), 49.

The Quest for Intelligibility

In spite of this tremendous diversity, the theology-and-science debate today is dominated and held together by an inspiring quest for intelligibility. The inspiration for this is found in a similar quest for intelligibility in religion. Most of us would agree that God transcends our final grasp, and that encounters with God obviously involve deeper levels than that of the rational, enquiring mind alone. But, as many scientists and theologians today will acknowledge, the quest for intelligibility, or the search for understanding at the deepest possible level, will be incomplete if it does not include within itself the religious quest for ultimate meaning, purpose, and significance.

This mutual quest for intelligibility has not only created exciting new areas of discussion between theology and science, but also again brought theology and science closer together. In this mutual quest for intelligibility and consonance, scientists, philosophers, and theologians in the field increasingly realize that both theology and science are responses to the way things are: both appeal to the coherent intelligibility that each achieves through its insights. Each can be seen as an attempt to understand our world of experience and in the light of this experience to establish possible points of contact and also possible points of conflict. In this sense theology and science can indeed be seen as mutually illuminating approaches to one and the same reality. For this reason the current debate between theology and science converges on the understanding of the human person as a psychosomatic unity in both science and religion and on the integration of evolutionary-biological ideas with a sense of God as a transcendent but also an immanent, ever-working Creator. Roger Trigg recently argued that it is no more a miracle that the human mind can understand the world than that the human eye can see it: evolution in a sense explains both, and also demonstrates why we are so at home in the world and why superior intelligence corresponds with a highly intelligible world.[9] For the same reason so much of the current debate is focusing on relating the origins of our cosmos, in the light of contemporary astrophysics and cosmology, to the Judeo-Christian doctrine of creation. Not just questions such as,

9. Roger Trigg, *Reality at Risk: A Defense of Realism in Philosophy and the Sciences* (New York: Harvester Wheatsheaf, 1989), 212.

What is the theological significance of the Big Bang theory? but also the implications of the novel features of quantum physics and relativity are now part of the daily and ongoing discussion of those who are working in theology and science.

The current theology-and-science discussion thus very much presents itself as contemporary apologetics for the Christian faith, and as such it will fundamentally shape our expression of the Christian experience of God. It also shapes our intellectual expression of the Christian faith and cautions us to greater epistemological and methodological sophistication. Theologians, however, will have to be careful to protect the integrity and unique character of theological reflection in this important discussion. And, maybe more importantly, theologians will have to be extra careful not to create the impression that while science appears to be very rational and open to correction, theology seems always to be ready to play the trump card of unquestionable and self-authenticating revelation.[10] Indeed, in the case of the natural sciences we are offered knowledge of what the physical world might really be like: science here imposes conditions or constraints that theologians should respect when they give accounts of what is regarded as God's relationship to this world.

Theology, Science, and Epistemology

The question how theology and science should relate to one another is, of course, neither a theological nor a scientific issue. It is, rather, an *epistemological* issue, that is, an issue about how two very different claims to knowledge are to be related.[11] What is at stake here is basically the nature of knowledge and the way it presents itself in the often very divergent claims resulting from religious and scientific worldviews. Our conviction that our world is highly intelligible, however, at least partly motivates us to search for some form of unified theory. There is no way

10. See Polkinghorne, 49ff.

11. See E. McMullin, "How Should Cosmology Relate to Theology?" in A. R. Peacocke, ed., *The Sciences and Theology in the Twentieth Century* (Notre Dame: University of Notre Dame Press, 1981), 26.

that we could be content with a plurality of unrelated languages if they are in fact languages about the same world — especially if we are seeking a coherent interpretation of all experience.[12] In our attempt to integrate a single worldview that would incorporate both theology and science, the obvious question is therefore going to be, What is the status of scientific claims about our cosmos, and what sort of knowledge-claims, if any, do we make in theology? If, furthermore, any form of "revelation" is to be seen as the basis of religious knowledge-claims, what kind of knowledge do we have here? What is more, is it at all possible — or even desirable — that our theological perspectives may be able to assist us, for instance, in choosing between different scientific theories that may be more or less compatible with biblical worldviews?

The complexity of these issues is very well illustrated when, for a moment, we briefly look at the history of the relationship between scientific cosmology and the Christian doctrine of creation. At the beginning of the early medieval period Jews, Christians, and Moslems were agreed on at least one theological "given": the universe had a beginning in time. This, of course, was based on the Genesis story of the creation; and Augustine, who in principle was willing to take the road of metaphor to avoid any conflict with "demonstrated truths," was keen to show that there was no conflict here: creation was seen as a single timeless act through which time itself came to be.[13]

The rediscovery of Aristotle, however, first in Islam and then in the Latin West, introduced a new challenge to the doctrine of creation: Aristotle argued strongly that neither matter nor time could have a beginning. This led to a serious confrontation between a "pagan" cosmology and Christian theology that, as Ernan McMullin convincingly argues, brought about the most serious intellectual crises the church had faced in almost a thousand years.[14] In 1215 the Fourth Lateran Council attacked the Aristotelian position and defined it as a doctrine of faith that the universe had a beginning in time. Later, Aquinas would show that neither side of the debate could be demonstrated philosophically. With the coming of the "new science" in the seventeenth century, however, the

---

12. See Ian Barbour, *Religion in an Age of Science*, The Gifford Lectures Volume One (San Francisco: Harper and Row, 1990), 16.

13. See McMullin, "How Should Cosmology Relate," 28.

14. McMullin, "How Should Cosmology Relate," 29f.

terms of the debate changed when Newton's mechanics appeared to allow for a compromise position: the absolutes of space and time were without beginning, but also without content. Creation meant that God brought matter to be within the confines of space at a finite time in the past.

However, the numerous traces of historical development on the earth's surface (eventually followed by the establishment of geology as a new science at the University of Cambridge in 1870) and the discovery later of the second law of thermodynamics made the Aristotelian notion of a unchanging, eternal cosmos seem quite implausible.[15] Even later Einstein's general theory of relativity, combined with Hubble's 1929 discovery of the galactic red-shift, led to the widely acclaimed postulate of an expanding universe, or the so-called Big Bang theory, according to which a singularity is postulated about 15 billion years ago from which the expansion of our universe began. The importance of the Big Bang theory is easily recognized: for the first time physics was led by its own resources to something that sounded like a beginning of time.[16] This was followed by theological responses that ranged from positions like that of Pope Pius XII, who hailed the theory as unqualified support for the Christian idea of creation, to rejection because either it looked too much like creation or it conflicted with the fundamentalist or literalist notion of a creation a few thousand years ago. It is clear, however, that none of these positions take the complexities of the relationship between scientific and theological epistemology into consideration at all. The Big Bang cannot automatically be assumed to be the beginning of either time or the universe, nor can it be taken for granted that the lapse of time since the so-called Big Bang is necessarily the age of the universe.[17] The Big Bang theory, and scientific cosmology in general — as Willem Drees has recently convincingly pointed out — is not in the first place about the origin of the universe, but rather about its subsequent evolution. Stephen Hawking's question, "Did the universe have a beginning, and what is the nature of time?" thus has to be very carefully defined both scientifically and theologically.[18] But in the same careful

15. See McMullin, "How Should Cosmology Relate," 30.

16. See Willem B. Drees, *Beyond The Big Bang: Quantum Cosmologies and God* (Chicago: Open Court, 1990), 17ff., 211ff.

17. See McMullin, "How Should Cosmology Relate," 35.

18. Stephen Hawking, *A Brief History of Time* (New York: Bantam Books, 1990), 1.

way we have to realize that the intent of, for instance, the Genesis passages is to underline the dependence of an intelligible and contingent universe on a Creator, and not to necessarily specify a first moment in time, at least in the technical sense of contemporary cosmology. This example from the history of Western thought alerts us to the epistemological fallacy of directly inferring from contemporary science to theological doctrine. It would be a serious category mistake to infer directly from, for example, the Big Bang to creation, from field theory to the Spirit of God, from chance to providence, from entropy to evil, or from the anthropic principle to design. The Big Bang model, for instance, does not entitle us to infer — theologically or scientifically — an absolute beginning in time. On the other hand, there's nothing scientifically or philosophically inadmissible about the idea that an absolute beginning might have occurred. And if it did occur, it could look something like the horizon event described by the Big Bang theory. But to eventually describe this horizon event as "the Creation" is to explain it in terms of a cause that would not be scientific anymore.

What could a theologian then rightly infer from this highly successful theory? It would be possible to say, theologically, that if our universe had a beginning in time through the unique act of a creator, from *our* point of view it would look something like the Big Bang cosmologists are talking about. What one cannot say is that the doctrine of creation "supports" the Big Bang model, or that the Big Bang "supports" the Christian doctrine of creation.[19] As Christians we should therefore take very seriously the theories of physics and biology — not to exploit or to try to change them, but to try to find interpretations that would suggest consonance with the Christian viewpoint. Theology can, therefore, never claim to be capable of scientific theory–appraisal, but should rather be seen as one element in the constructing of a broader cultural worldview.[20] The Christian can never separate his or her science from her or his theology, but she or he should also learn to distrust epistemological short cuts from the one to the other. One way to do this would be to find a paradigm that would yield fine-tuned epistemological consonance.

Thus are revealed the philosophical and epistemological complexi-

19. See McMullin, "How Should Cosmology Relate," 39.
20. See McMullin, "How Should Cosmology Relate," 51.

ties involved in trying to relate theology and science today. In fact, I think that it is safe to say that until fairly recently, theological discussions, especially on the relationship between theological and scientific epistemology, have been notoriously vague, imprecise, and even confused. Since the Enlightenment and the days of Immanuel Kant, right through to the thought of D. F. Strauss, Feuerbach, Freud, and Marx, science was seen to be in conflict with religion, in fact to be the great alternative to religion. This inevitably led, as is well-known, to the stark opposition of a foundationalist empiricist/positivist conception of science to an equally foundationalist conception of biblical literalism. This also reveals that genuine conflicts between science and theology are exceedingly difficult to detect and accurately specify. In retrospect many of these serious clashes turn out to be not between religion and science, but between incompatible, even incommensurable worldviews or philosophies.[21]

The current focus on the relationship between theology and science — some prefer to talk of the emerging discipline of theology and science — suggests, however, a fall from epistemological innocence regarding this complex and fascinating issue. For the philosophical theologian this presents a challenge to his or her personal commitments and beliefs: a challenge that also implies a quest for a plausible model of theological contextuality, because it thrusts to the front questions about the status of religious claims to knowledge and about the rationality of belief in God.

Currently, however, the relationship of theology and science is indeed still as vague and confusing as ever: some see them as fundamentally in conflict with one another; others as independent of one another; others as in creative dialogue and consonance with one another, while still other thinkers want to integrate theology and science in terms of either a theology of nature or some form of natural theology.

21. See Nicholas Lash, "Production and Prospect: Reflections on Christian Hope and Original Sin," in E. McMullin, ed., *Evolution and Creation* (Notre Dame: University of Notre Dame Press, 1985), 277.

Foundationalism in Theology and Science

What we are certain about, today at least, is that in any contemporary evaluation of the relationship between theology and science, a foundationalist view of either science or theology would be epistemologically fatal. Foundationalism holds that, in the process of justifying our knowledge-claims, the chain of justifying evidence cannot go on ad infinitum if we are ever to be in a position to claim that we have justified our knowledge.[22] Thus, foundationalists specify what they take to be the ultimate foundations on which the evidential support-systems for various beliefs are constructed. The sort of features most frequently mentioned are self-evidence, incorrigibility, being evident to the senses, indubitability, and being self-authenticating and properly basic, that is, foundational.

Foundationalism, as the thesis that our beliefs can be warranted or justified by appealing to some item of knowledge that is self-evident or beyond doubt, certainly eliminates any possibility of discovering a meaningful epistemological link between theology and the other sciences. To claim that knowledge rests on foundations is to claim that there is a privileged class of beliefs that are intrinsically credible and that are able, therefore, to serve as ultimate terminating points for chains of justification. These "givens" could be anything from sense data to universals, essences, experience, and God's revelation. In this sense the "doctrine of the given" can indeed be called the comrade-in-arms of all foundationalism.[23] In the natural sciences, foundationalism implies a positivist empiricism or scientific materialism that per definition renders all religion, and certainly all theology and theological reflection, meaningless.[24] In theology, foundationalism implies biblical literalism, or on a much more sophisticated level, a self-authenticating "positivism of revelation" that isolates theology because it denies the crucial role of interpreted religious experience in all theological reflection: here the theologian is left speaking a language whose conceptuality might be internally coherent but which at the same time is powerless to com-

---

22. See Axel D. Steuer, "The Epistemic Status of Theistic Belief," *Journal of the American Academy of Religion* 55, no. 2 (1987): 237.

23. See Nancy Frankenberry, *Religion and Radical Empiricism* (Albany: SUNY, 1987), 6.

24. See Barbour, 4.

municate its content because it is unrelated to all nontheological discourse.[25]

Philosophers like Ludwig Wittgenstein, Thomas S. Kuhn, and Richard Rorty today represent a strong nonfoundational response to traditional epistemological questions. Instead of a model of knowledge as an entity resting on fixed and immutable foundations, they offer a picture of human knowledge as an evolving social phenomenon within a web of beliefs. Belief systems are here discovered within a contextual matrix that is itself groundless. Justification becomes a matter of accommodating those beliefs that are being questioned to another body of accepted beliefs. Whatever theories we might have about anything that might be "given" in religious or scientific experience, epistemic justification will not have an unproblematic, uninterpreted "given" at its foundation. With this in mind it becomes clear not only that in theology all forms of foundationalism and fideism go hand in hand, but also that nonfoundationalism will present a very special challenge to the Christian concept of revelation.

Neither theology nor science, then, is based on incontrovertible grounds of knowledge. Each demands a commitment to a corrigible point of view and to the fact that an element of the unexplained will always remain.[26] Both theology and science, furthermore, have to speak of entities that are not directly observable and both must therefore be prepared to use models and metaphors as heuristic devices. This is also the context within which John Polkinghorne can state that mathematics is the natural language of physical science, while symbol and metaphor can be seen as the natural language for theology.[27]

The epistemological move beyond foundationalism in science points to the biggest revolution in physics since the days of Newton: the discovery of the elusive and fitful subatomic world of quantum theory. Here our world has been proved to be strange beyond our powers of anticipation. If this is true for physics, it undoubtedly can be true for theology as well. The quantum world exhibits a counterintuitive non-

25. See Garrett Green, *Imagining God: Theology and the Religious Imagination* (San Francisco: Harper and Row, 1989), 34.

26. See Robert J. Russell, "Cosmology, Creation, and Contingency," in Ted Peters, ed., *Cosmos and Creation* (Nashville: Abingdon Press, 1989), 201.

27. Polkinghorne, 2.

locality, a togetherness-in-separation that provides a powerful image of holistic solidarity that may even be a suggestive consonant image for the field of theology. Quantum theory has indeed taught us to be open to the totally unexpected, even to the initially apparently unintelligible.[28]

To reject foundationalism in theology, however, is not to embrace nonfoundationalism or antifoundationalism per se — in any case not a type of antifoundationalism that claims that one can engage in theological reflection without attention to the explanatory nature and epistemic status of theological truth-claims. In fact, it could be convincingly shown that the whole debate between foundationalism and antifoundationalism is based on the false dichotomy of an outdated epistemological dilemma.[29] Moreover, a postfoundationalist shift to a fallibilist epistemology, which honestly embraces the role of traditioned experience, personal commitment, interpretation, and the provisional nature of all of our knowledge-claims, avoids the alleged necessity of opting for either foundationalism or antifoundationalism.

Leaving behind the dichotomy that framed the older faith/reason debate now opens the way to a postmodern holist epistemology that may have a major influence on theological methodology: it is no longer necessary to hold that the traditional project of theological prologomena is always ancillary to theology, functioning (as in fundamental theology) as a foundation to be dealt with prior to theological reflection and then always assumed in what follows. In a postfoundationalist theology the epistemological link between theology and the other sciences can be left open because the project of theological methodology and "prologomena" now becomes part of theological reflection as such, that is, as part of an ongoing interdisciplinary inquiry within the practice of theology itself.

The Shaping of Rationality in Theology and Science

What will be needed in this interdisciplinary theology-and-science discussion is a methodological approach that not only recognizes theology

28. See Polkinghorne, 3ff.
29. See Philip Clayton, *Explanation from Physics to Theology: An Essay in Rationality and Religion* (New Haven: Yale University Press, 1989), 152.

as an explanatory discipline, but also takes seriously the epistemological problem of the shaping of rationality in theology and science, the hermeneutical problem relating context and meaning, the explanatory role of religious experience and beliefs, and the fallibilist and provisional nature of both theological and scientific truth-claims. To this end the discussion of the problem of rationality in contemporary philosophy of science has recently more and more proved to be an important guide to theology, and perhaps the most fruitful theology-and-science link to date. This discussion not only opens up definitions of rationality and indicates the sort of criteria needed to govern theological assertions, it also highlights the centrality of experiential factors in rational explanation and therefore in rationality in general.

The problem of the shaping of rationality in theology to a great extent centers on the possible role of explanatory justification in theological thought and will therefore eventually force us to address the difficult epistemological issues of degrees of truth and the objectivity (if any!) of our statements. Generally speaking, the nature of rationality consists of the intelligent pursuit of certain epistemic values, of which intelligibility is the most important. Theology obviously shares the quest for intelligibility with all other sciences, whatever the differences or similarities between theology and the other sciences might be.

Now, if rationality is a means to the goals of science[30] and as such primarily consists of pursuing intelligibility, intelligibility itself can be seen as a quest for understanding at the deepest possible level. In theology, as in the other sciences, this will be attained by inferring — through evaluation and argument — to the best possible explanations. Rationality is thus primarily shaped by the quest for intelligibility, and in theology this intelligibility is attained through the explanatory role of religious experience and beliefs in our theological reflection. In both theology and science we therefore should be aware of an overly narrow and rationalistic conception of rationality. Rationality as such is complex, many-sided, extensive, and as wide-ranging as the domain of intelligence itself.

Following the lead of Nicholas Rescher we can now identify at least three contexts of rationality that are highly relevant not only for the-

---

30. See E. McMullin, *Construction and Constraint: The Shaping of Scientific Rationality* (Notre Dame: University of Notre Dame Press, 1988), 25.

ology, but also for the social, human, and natural sciences: the *cognitive* context, the *evaluative* context, and the *pragmatic* context. What this means for theological reflection is that also in theology we have good reasons for hanging on to certain beliefs, good reasons for making certain choices, and good reasons for acting in certain ways. Within a holist epistemology these three contexts go together as a seamless whole and also can be regarded as the three resources for rationality in theology: they merge in the common task of uniting the best reasons for belief, evaluation, and action. We therefore act rationally in matters of belief, action, and evaluation when our reasons "hang together," that is, are cogent. In theology, rationality implies the capacity to "give account," to provide a rationale for the way one thinks, chooses, acts, and believes.

In both theology and science, rationality therefore pivots on the deployment of good reasons: believing, doing, choosing the right thing for the right reasons. Being rational is therefore not just a matter of having some reasons for what one believes in and argues for, but having the best or strongest reasons to support the rationality of one's beliefs within a concrete context. Rationality in theology and science, as we saw earlier, is shaped primarily by the quest for intelligibility. And this understanding at the deepest possible level is attained by inferring to the best possible explanations. In this sense rationality and explanation go together very closely.

The hazy intersection between the diverse fields of theology and the other sciences is therefore not in the first place to be determined by exploring methodological parallels or degrees of consonance between theology and the sciences. What should be explored first is the epistemological question of the nature and status of explanations and explanatory claims in theology and the other sciences, since theological doctrines and constructs, as well as scientific theories, aim at giving the best possible explanations in their respective fields. In this reflection we should be wary of dangerous epistemological shortcuts: rationality should never be reduced to scientific rationality, and scientific rationality should never be reduced to natural scientific rationality.

Explanations in Theology and Science

In theological explanations religious beliefs play a central role. Religious beliefs of course have important functions for the believer. They describe the rites and practices of believing communities, express in the language of faith psychological and sociological needs, and also answer philosophical questions in religious terms. In short, religious beliefs help to explain the world and the place of believers in it. In doing this, religious beliefs reflect a general sense of meaningfulness on the part of the believer, a meaningfulness that extends from an existential level to the level of particular theories and dogmas.[31] But of central importance among the various functions of religious beliefs is that of *explanation*.

The question that now arises is whether there is a unitary theory of explanation that would allow us to speak of explanation in the singular when referring to the broader spectrum of academic disciplines. Eventually it will become clear that there are important parallels between explanation in the sciences and in theology. However significant these parallels might be, religious and theological explanations do have unique aspects as well: they are normally all-encompassing and deeply personal, they often arise from vague and elusive questions concerning the meaning of life, and as religious answers they provide ultimate meaning in life. Religious — and eventually theological — explanations thus provide a context of security for the believer and also involve a faith commitment to God. This implies that both the scope and content of theological explanations may set them apart from explanations in other areas. In assessing the explanatory role of religious experience and beliefs we therefore should assess the continuities as well as the discontinuities between theological and other types of explanations. Scientific explanations, of course, are never completely impersonal, but they are capable of achieving a high degree of interpersonal agreement. Art and ethics are much more personal than science and as such may not represent areas in which universal agreement is attainable; even more personal is the realm of religious experience, where also the refracting influence of culture is powerfully present.[32]

The central goal of natural scientific theories is to explain the

31. See Clayton, 1f.
32. See Polkinghorne, 54.

empirical world. Theories of explanation, however, have been directly influenced by important shifts in the problem of natural scientific rationality, especially since the advent of Thomas S. Kuhn's revolutionary paradigm theory.[33] This contextualist shift in the philosophy of the natural sciences clearly indicates a very specific hermeneutical awareness as well as the realization that criteria for explanation function only within a particular paradigm. Seen in the light of this contextualist shift, explanations in science are relativized and become an element within the broader hermeneutical task of science.[34]

In the social and human sciences a long and learned tradition has opposed explanation to emphatic understanding. Explanation in the social sciences, however, does not need to be downplayed in the light of the broader hermeneutical purpose of the social and human sciences. It also would be incorrect to claim that, because of their subject matter, the social and human sciences are more subjective than the natural sciences: the role of subjective factors in the formulation of natural as well as social scientific explanations is today widely accepted. Eventually we shall see that not only in theology, but also in the social, human and natural sciences, the subjectivity of interpreting belongs right in the heart of the explanatory task. On another level the explanatory task in the social sciences is closer to explanations in theology than to explanations in the natural sciences. Both in the social and human sciences and in theology the object of research is itself already symbolically structured, mainly as a result of a long and ongoing history of interpretation. Therefore, if all science then is hermeneutical, in the human and social sciences, and especially in the history of theological ideas, we encounter what some scholars have called a "double hermeneutic" of having to interpret again the already preinterpreted world of our experience.[35]

From this we may conclude that explanation — whether in the natural, social, or human sciences or in theology — is always a form of rational reconstruction, that rational thought is never purely objective, that context greatly influences the interpretative theoretical process, and that any research program and its explanations can be

---

33. Wentzel van Huyssteen, *Theology and the Justification of Faith: The Construction of Theories in Systematic Theology* (Grand Rapids: Wm. B. Eerdmans, 1989), 47-70.

34. See Clayton, 39.

35. See Clayton, 88.

only partially evaluated at any given time. And in our quest for intelligibility, coherence — although a necessary criterion for rational thought — can by itself never be a sufficient condition for the stories in which we articulate our hope and symbolically unify our fragmented experience.[36]

Our quest for some form of epistemological consonance between theology and science thus brings us to philosophical explanations. Philosophical explanations, like other explanations, aim to address and coherently answer some specific question. They are philosophical in that they are not limited in scope to any particular discipline or aspect of experience.[37] In trying to understand the explanatory role of religious experiences and the beliefs that constitute them, it is important to note that religious explanations share some very significant features with philosophical explanations. The most important of these are their greater generality or depth and an emphasis on systematic coherence and meaningfulness.

For philosophical and religious (and eventually also theological) explanations, both the context principle of rationality and the coherence theory of meaning are of prime importance: from the perspective of a coherence theory of meaning, a philosophical or a religious explanation is not all that different from other explanations. When therefore we reflect on a portion of our experience, it is possible to put this reflection on a problem within an ever-broadening horizon of contexts until we reach a context that reaches out to the whole of human experience. At this level one is involved in making sense of total experience, and this broadest context could be labeled "metaphysical" or "religious." Within this broader context of religious experience, Philip Clayton has recently identified at least three types or forms of explanation:

1. Private explanations: these explanations are warranted solely by the fact that they make sense of experience for the individual believer. Private explanations can be quite comprehensive in scope and can account for broad areas of human experience, but the justification of these explanations is rooted in personal value alone.

36. See Lash, 277.
37. See Clayton, 104.

2. Communal explanations: here the standards of adequate explanations are set by the particular believing and practicing community.

3. Intersubjective or transcommunal explanations: this category of explanation supposes that religious beliefs can be justified in a way that transcends the boundaries of the individual religious community. Within the Christian community apologetics and natural theology fit this notion of transcommunal justification. Christian beliefs are held as a rational and best available explanation that the believer takes to have more than merely communal validity.[38]

The importance of these distinctions for theology is apparent: any comparison between theology and science would be meaningful only if a form of transcommunal explanation is at least one viable form of epistemic justification in theological reflection.

As far as specifically theological explanations go, theologians should first and foremost beware of the fideist miscontrual where faith is seen as evidence for the truth of religious or theological propositions. Faith — as the "heart" of religion — implies a total commitment to the object of one's belief. In the context of rational argumentation, however, faith does not make the object of faith more probable and thus should not be seen as an epistemic virtue, nor of course, as an epistemic vice.[39] It now becomes clear that the believer's efforts to understand and come to terms with her or his faith display a structure quite similar to scientific rationality. Seen against this background, theological explanations attempt to establish a link between the inherited beliefs and practices of a specific religious tradition and the contemporary experience of its adherents.[40] These explanations arise out of traditioned experience and can be phrased in terms of traditional doctrines, the practices (liturgies and rites) of a religious community, its norms or codes of behavior, or they can be constructed in terms of the broader intellectual, social, and ethical intersubjective life experience of believers.

As such, theological explanations function to continually ensure a

---

38. Clayton, 5, 113ff.
39. See Clayton, 143.
40. See van Huyssteen, "Theology and Justification of Faith," 200ff.

tradition's relevance to the challenges posed by contemporary contextual questions. Clayton is therefore right when he states that theology is not primarily a descriptive (first-order) but an explanatory (second-order) endeavor. There are indeed good reasons for theology to pursue explanatory adequacy and academic excellence.[41] All theological explanations should therefore be open to intersubjective examination and criticism, which means that theological statements should at all times be construed as hypotheses.[42] And since all attempts to clarify Christian beliefs necessarily involve dependence on categories not drawn from the Christian tradition, as well as the use of general notions such as truth, meaning, coherence, and reference, Christian theology will always find itself in necessary discourse with other theologies, and with the science and philosophy of its times.

In conclusion I would therefore like to claim that the quest for intelligibility and explanatory progress in theology is dependent on the evolving nature of the epistemic values that shape theological rationality in history. This implies that the realist assumptions and commitments of experienced Christian faith are relevant epistemological issues to be dealt with seriously in the theology and science discussion. By doing this, theology could move away from the absolutism of foundationalism as well as from the relativism of antifoundationalism. This can further be achieved by showing that because theology is an activity of a community of inquirers, there can be no way to prescribe a rationality for that activity without considering its actual practice.

The theology-and-science discussion in a very specific way reveals how the explanatory role of interpreted experience in theology can be adequately explained only in terms of an experiential epistemology. This not only means that religious experience is better explained theologically, but that in explaining the role of experience, the philosophical theologian will have to move from the question of rationality to intelligibility, from intelligibility to the question of personal understanding, and from personal understanding to personal experience. This is something the scientist need never do. Dealing with personal commitment in this way may show that the rationality of theology is often shaped by epistemic values different from that of science. The dependence of

41. Clayton, 149.
42. See van Huyssteen, "Theology and Justification of Faith," 143ff.

theology on experiential adequacy for determining and maintaining its explanatory adequacy, could, however, never again mean that theology is less rational or less contextual than science.

The complex nature of the ongoing discussion between theology and science should help us to realize that, in spite of a promising and emerging new field of study, the complex relationship between scientific and religious epistemology is more challenging than ever. This becomes all the more clear not only when we keep in mind deconstruction and discovery of the limitations of the natural sciences in the post-Kuhnian era, but also when we focus carefully on the nature of the natural sciences. The sciences are eminently competent when it comes to theory construction and to experimental and pragmatic enterprises, but they are incompetent when it comes to finding answers to our deepest religious questions.

The fundamental differences between theology and science should therefore be respected, as should the difference between different forms of explanations not only in the different sciences, but also between theology and the other sciences. In spite of important differences and sometimes radically different levels of explanation, theology and science do share a common ground of rationality. A theology and a science that come to discover this mutual quest for intelligibility in spite of important differences will also be freed to discover that nothing that is part of, or the result of, natural scientific explanation need ever be logically incompatible with theological reflection. Stephen Hawking's disturbing question, What place would there be for a creator in a universe without a beginning in time?[43] could then be answered with: every place. Whether the universe had a beginning in time or not does not affect our reading of the Genesis story in its depiction of the complete dependence of the universe on God. God is not a God of the edges[44]; God is the Christian theologian's answer to why there is something rather than nothing. Science can tell us little or nothing about our experience of subjectivity, about the astonishing emergence of personhood, and about why we have an intelligible universe. God is the name that we give to the best available explanation of all-that-is.[45]

43. Hawking, 140f.
44. See Polkinghorne, 81.
45. See Peacocke, *Theology for Scientific Age*, 134.

In focusing on the importance of the natural sciences, we should then have an openness to that which reaches beyond the world of the natural sciences, that is, to the world on which the social sciences, history, philosophy, and theology focus. In this wider context we could discover that theology and science share not only a mutually enriching quest for intelligibility, but also the importance of tradition and of the explanatory role of interpreted experience. An honest analysis of the differences between the sciences and between theological and scientific explanations might just yield more intelligibility in the apologetic attempt to understand our postmodern world as truly God's own world.

Chapter Twelve

The Shaping of Rationality
in Science and Religion

A NYONE WHO TAKES TIME TODAY TO REFLECT ON THE ENDURING BUT troubled "science and religion" dialogue will inevitably find the intellectual and spiritual mood of our contemporary Western culture at the heart of this complex debate. This mood is radically pluralist and postmodern, and as such would resist any attempt to catch it in one name or one overarching description. Yet, I do believe that we have good reasons for calling our culture at least, or also, a decidedly empirical culture: a culture determined by a tradition where the sciences — especially the natural sciences — not only dominate the way we live our lives but ultimately function as the paradigm and apex of human rationality.

That religion and religious faith are often and in many ways intellectually marginalized in this situation is by now a fact of life and as such taken more or less for granted. Many theologians, and also scientists who are believers, have of course taken on the ongoing conflict between science and religion as a special challenge to identify possible models for creative dialogue and even consonance or harmony between theology and science.[1] In many ways this reflects an enduring attempt to identify religious faith as an autonomous moment in human experience, which as such can never be completely reduced to science, or even to metaphysics or morality. On this view religion has its own

---

1. See Ian Barbour, *Religion in an Age of Science* (San Francisco: Harper and Row, 1990), 1-30.

238

integrity, with both religious belief, reflection, and practice viewed as valid expressions of the religious dimension of life.[2]

Strong pleas for the autonomy of religious faith and experience will of course always fuel the ongoing "religion and science" dialogue, but it also reinforces some important — and confusing — stereotypes that have kept alive some of the typical or "classical" problems of this debate. The most important of these problems reveal strong contradictions and even conflict between scientific thought and religious faith, and can be stated as follows:[3]

scientific statements are hypothetical, fallible, and tentative, while statements of religious faith are dogmatic, ideological, and fideistic;

scientific thought is always open to critical evaluation, justification, or falsification, while religious faith goes against the facts and often defies empirical evidence;

scientific thought delights in critical dissent and constructive criticism, while faith more often than not depends on massive consensus and uncritical commitment;

scientists therefore seem to base their beliefs on evidence and argument, while religious beliefs appear to be founded on "faith" only.

It comes as no surprise that, on this view, science emerges as the great alternative to religious faith.[4] Many of us, in fact, did grow up learning an account of our intellectual history as the story of the steady triumph of science over superstition and ignorance.[5] Almost all of these stereotyped contrasts between science and religion, however, assume far too simple a picture of what both science and religion are about. When, therefore, we dig deeper into this complex issue, much more is revealed

2. See Wayne Proudfoot, *Religious Experience* (Berkeley: University of California Press, 1985), xiiif.

3. See G. Theissen, *Biblical Faith: An Evolutionary Approach* (London: SCM, 1984), 4ff.

4. See Mary Midgley, *Science as Salvation: A Modern Myth and Its Meaning* (London: Routledge, 1992), 139.

5. See William C. Placher, *Unapologetic Theology: A Christian Voice in a Pluralist Conversation* (Louisville: Westminster/John Knox, 1989), 14.

about the philosophical and epistemological complexities of trying to contrast religion and science in this way. What emerges — often surprisingly — is a shared epistemological pattern: a foundationalist notion of empiricist science is, after all, philosophically not all that different from an equally foundationalist conception of biblical literalism or religious fideism. Though scientific materialism seems often to be at the opposite end of the spectrum from biblical literalism or theologies that claim self-authenticating notions of divine revelation, their foundationalist approaches may share several characteristics:

> both believe that there are serious conflicts between contemporary science and religious beliefs;
> both seek knowledge with a secure and incontrovertible foundation, and find this either in logic and sense data (science), or in an infallible scripture or self-authenticating revelation (theology);
> both claim that science and theology make rival claims about the same domain and that one has to choose between them.

Ian Barbour has convincingly shown that both these approaches not only prolong a stereotyped conflict-model, but also represent a misuse of what science and religion are about.[6] The fact that religion and science may in actuality share foundationalist views while at the same time claiming to be in conflict also reveals why genuine conflicts between religion and science are exceedingly difficult to detect and specify accurately: in retrospect many of the serious clashes between religion and science turn out to be not so much clashes between religion and science as clashes between incompatible, even incommensurable, worldviews or philosophies.[7] I hope to show in this paper that the current dialogue between religion and science at the very least implies a fall from epistemological innocence as far as this complex and fascinating issue goes.

6. Barbour, 1ff.
7. See Nicholas Lash, "Production and Prospect: Reflections on Christian Hope and Original Sin," in E. McMullin, ed., *Evolution and Creation* (Notre Dame: University of Notre Dame Press, 1985), 277.

I

This epistemological challenge becomes even more fascinating when we take note of remarkable shifts in the minds of scientists who seem to come up against the limits of scientific rationality in their own work. In his important book *God and the New Physics*, Paul Davies still worked from a fairly simplistic but strong contrast between science and religion.[8] The implied conflict between these two explains his reductionist use of scientific explanations to assess religious claims, his startling claim that science offers a surer path to God than religion,[9] and his choice for a "natural God" who would be wholly within the universe, constrained by physical laws and accessible — at least in principle — to scientific investigation.[10] Because of the theory of relativity and quantum theory, the "new physics" not only demands a radical reformulation of the most important aspects of reality, but is as such uniquely placed to provide answers to even ultimate questions formerly reserved for religion only. Now in his latest work, *The Mind of God*, Davies seems to make some important shifts: where previously he came up against a "natural God" by pushing the logic of scientific rationality as far back as it would go in search of ultimate answers, Davies now acknowledges the "mystery" at the end of the universe.[11] He eventually seems to be arguing for alternative modes of knowledge — even mystical knowledge — as valid ways of understanding the existence and properties of the universe, in categories that may lie outside the categories of regular scientific thought.

In a similar vein Bernard D'Espagnat states that scientific rationality has its own inherent limitations, and then argues for a "window" within scientific rationality that seems to point to a "more" beyond this kind of rationality: if someone would want to move beyond the limitations of empirical observation and experimentation, that is, the domain of the natural sciences, in a focused concern for the whole of reality, such a project could therefore not in advance be judged to be incoherent, illegit-

---

8. Paul Davies, *God and the New Physics* (New York: Simon and Schuster, 1983).

9. Davies, *God and New Physics*, ix.

10. Davies, *God and New Physics*, 209.

11. Paul Davies, *The Mind of God: The Scientific Basis for a Rational World* (New York: Simon and Schuster, 1992), 223ff.

imate, or irrational.[12] This window, even if epistemically very small, is an opening made by rational means on the basis of the experienced limitations of scientific rationality, and as such suggests a richer notion of rationality that transcends the purely cognitive dimension of our human knowing. Along the same lines much of modern physics is understood to have done away with the essentially classical ideal of an objective world existing securely out there, waiting for us to measure and analyze it. Instead, quantum mechanics and relativity challenge the possibilities and limits of empirical knowledge and expose us as inalienable — but also limiting — participants in the world we are trying to understand.[13]

Nuanced views of the limits of scientific rationality such as these become a special challenge to theologians and also scientists who want to move away from the false certainties provided by overblown foundationalist epistemologies. Moving away from the narrow focus on a strictly scientific rationality to broader and alternative ways of understanding may, however, turn out not to be enough, and serious issues remain that need to be addressed. Special attention needs to be given, for instance, not only to differences and apparent contrasts between science and religion, but also to the important distinction between religion and theology. For instance, it will not be enough to allow only for crucial differences between, say, mysticism and scientific rationality when theological reflection also presents itself as a form of knowledge — and then as a form of rational reflection that not only may differ from mysticism in important ways, but may in fact even overlap significantly with scientific rationality. Theology, in this reflective mode, may turn out to share more with scientific reflection than with mystical experience. Paul Davies may want to take human reasoning as far as it will go and eventually not opt for mysticism and revelation, even if these — in transcending human reason — may indeed turn out to be valid alternative routes to a more comprehensive form of human knowledge.[14] In a nuanced notion of theological rationality we may, however, for good reasons choose to see theology (as a reflection on religion and religious experience) not as bypassing human

---

12. Bernard D'Espagnat, *Reality and the Physicist* (Cambridge: Cambridge University Press, 1989), 205.

13. See David Lindley, *The End of Physics: The Myth of a Unified Theory* (New York: Basic Books, 1993), 54.

14. See Davies, *Mind of God,* 24ff.

reason at all, and therefore not as an *alternative* to scientific rationality. It may still transcend and be different from a strictly scientific rationality, but it may at the same time in very important ways turn out to overlap with scientific rationality, and as such share in the human quest for intelligibility and ultimate meaning, a quest that has always been crucial for defining scientific rationality.

At the heart of the contemporary "religion and science" problem, therefore, lies the deeper problem of how the epistemic values that shape the rationality of religion and of theological reflection will be different from or similar to those that shape the rationality of science. The challenge of postmodernist pluralism, of course, makes it virtually impossible even to speak so generally about "rationality," "science," "religion," or "God." And yet, even if we should acknowledge the possibility of radically different forms of rationality, the crucial question still remains whether the rationality of science is in any significant way superior to other forms of rationality.

Mainly as a result of the pervasive influence of the classical model of rationality in our culture, the natural sciences — especially the physical sciences — are indeed still regarded by many as the paradigm for rationality today. Postmodern philosophy of science has recently, however, severely challenged this special status of the natural sciences.[15] Postmodern philosophy of science understandably rejects epistemological foundationalism as well as all metanarratives that would claim to legitimate scientific knowledge, practices, and results. In its extremist form this leads to the dismissal of philosophy of science itself as our traditional means of gaining an understanding of science.[16] On this view traditional philosophy of science is replaced by a postmodern reconstruction of the local activity of scientists, where scientific claims, explanations, procedures, and experiments are seen as part of a series of activities situated within the narrative field of science. On this view, then, all global legitimation of the epistemic status and ontological standing of science through philosophical argument is seen as typically modern, and challenged as such.

15. See J. Rouse, "The Politics of Postmodern Philosophy of Science," *Philosophy of Science* 58 (1991): 607-27.

16. H. P. P. Lötter, "A Postmodern Philosophy of Science?" *South African Journal of Philosophy* 13, no. 3 (1994): 153ff.

Postmodernism, however, has proved to be as protean and multi-interpretable as it is challenging. Not only in philosophy of science, but also in the theology-and-science dialogue, alternative interpretations of postmodern themes, as well as constructive appropriations of some of these, have become viable options. In his seminal work on the nature of rationality, Harold Brown too rejects all epistemological foundation-alism and argues persuasively that an adequate model of rationality should indeed be exemplified by those disciplines that we, with good reasons, take to be paradigm cases of rational endeavor.[17] This ultimately brings us face to face with the important question, Is there a special sense in which science, in spite of the pervasive influence of the positivist or classical model of rationality and the challenge of postmodernism in contemporary philosophy of science, still provides us with a crucial test case in our quest for the nature of rationality, since it currently still seems to stand as our clearest example of a rational enterprise?

Today, in a postpositivist and post-Kuhnian age, we know about the interpreted character of all knowledge and the rediscovery of the hermeneutical dimension of scientific knowledge, and we know that the rules according to which scientific decisions are made change as science itself develops.[18] And the fact that the rules change shows that they do not meet the conditions of universality and necessity imposed by the classical model of rationality. The historicist turn in philosophy of science initiated by Thomas S. Kuhn has thoroughly replaced the foundationalism of the classical model and has opened the way to various attempts at nonfoundationalist or antifoundationalist models of rationality in philosophy of science. In his most recent work *Rationality and Science*, Roger Trigg alerts us to the dangers of complete relativism that may follow the necessary move away from objectivist notions of truth and verification.[19] In a strong reaction against a modernist notion of rationality that stresses universality and necessity, nonfoundationalism can indeed easily align itself with a relativist mode of postmodern

17. Harold Brown, *Rationality* (London/New York: Routledge, 1990), 79ff.

18. Richard J. Bernstein, *Beyond Objectivism and Relativism* (Oxford: Basil Blackwell, 1983), 30ff.; William Dean, *History Making History: The New Historicism in American Religious Thought* (New York: SUNY, 1988).

19. Roger Trigg, *Rationality and Science: Can Science Explain Everything?* (Oxford: Basil Blackwell, 1993).

thinking and as such can highlight the fact that every group and every context has its own rationality.

If this nonfoundationalist view were true, then any social or human activity could in principle function as a test case for rationality. This notion would leave us with an extreme relativism of rationalities: a relativism that not only forms the opposite of the classical model's objectivism, but also would be devastating for any intersubjective truth-claims in both scientific and theological reflection. Proponents of the relativism of this "many rationalities" view hold that the rules that govern science are internal to science in the same way that other human activities (e.g., religion, business, magic, etc.) are also governed by rules internal to them. In the relativism that flows from this nonfoundationalism it is therefore maintained that each area of human activity has criteria internal to a specific culture or social group. Since each area can therefore claim its own criteria of rationality, there can be no independent framework for deciding whether one framework is more rational than another.[20] On this view science, along with religion, is seen as just one more feature of postmodern Western society, where all cultures or societies create cognitive structures that explain the world around them. On this view it is also obviously denied that the body of beliefs developed by science could be in any way cognitively superior to other beliefs.

Over against the objectivism of foundationalism and the extreme relativism of most forms of nonfoundationalism, some of us want to develop a postfoundationalist model of rationality that is thoroughly contextual, but that at the same time will attempt to reach beyond the limits of its own group or culture in interdisciplinary discussion. This view of rationality aims to capture those features of science that indeed make it a paradigmatically rational enterprise without falling back onto the foundationalism of the classical view of rationality. It is only within a postfoundationalist view of rationality very similar to this that Harold Brown can persuasively argue that, while science did indeed develop in the Western world, there are still powerful grounds for maintaining that science has a significance that indeed transcends the particular culture in which it first appeared.[21]

Whatever else a postfoundationalist model of rationality might

20. See Brown, 113.
21. Brown, 114.

mean, it certainly means at least the following: while we always operate in terms of concepts and criteria that appear within a particular culture, we are nonetheless able to transcend our specific contexts and reach out to more intersubjective levels of discussion. Over against a nonfoundationalist "many rationalities" view then, a postfoundationalist model of rationality wants to show that science can indeed be a potential and reliable source of knowledge that not only transcends the cultures in which the various sciences first appeared, but also can epistemically relate to broader and different notions of rationality.

This relates closely to the fact that post-Kuhnian philosophy of science has shown us that there can be no sharp line of demarcation between scientific rationality and other forms of rationality.[22] In fact, scientific rationality relates to a preanalytic reasonableness of a more basic kind of human rationality that informs all goal-directed action. Within this broader context Christian theology too should seek as secure a knowledge as it can possibly achieve, a form of knowledge that will allow an optimal understanding of that to which Christian believers are committing themselves in faith. In the end this epistemic goal of theological reflection, more than anything — and in spite of important differences between a theological and a strictly scientific rationality — will determine the shaping of the rationality of theological reflection. And if in both theology and science we strive to explain better in order to understand better, then surely the epistemological problem of the nature of rationality should be one of the most important foci of our attempts to meaningfully relate religion and science to one another today.

II

As a first step towards a broader and richer notion of rationality, we can now follow the lead of Nicholas Rescher and identify at least three sources of rationality that are highly relevant not only for the natural, the social, and the human sciences, but also for theology as a reflection

22. See J. W. van Huyssteen, *Theology and the Justification of Faith: The Construction of Theories in Systematic Theology* (Grand Rapids: Wm. B. Eerdmans, 1989), 63ff.

on religious experience: the cognitive context, the evaluative context, and the pragmatic context.[23] None of these resources of rationality has priority over any of the others, even if cognitive rationality, or the cognitive dimension of rationality, is often dominant in intellectual issues. In both science and theology we are therefore challenged to sound, rational judgment in our quest for intelligibility: good reasons for hanging on to certain beliefs, good reasons for making certain moral choices, and good reasons for acting in certain ways. Within a holist epistemology these three go together as a seamless whole and merge in the common task of uniting the best reasons for belief, evaluation, and action.

In his move to an alternative, postclassical model of rationality, Harold Brown links on to the evaluative resources of rationality by highlighting the role of judgment in human cognition. Judgment in this broader epistemic sense is the ability to evaluate a situation, to assess evidence, and then to come to a reasonable decision without following rules.[24] In Brown's concept of rationality, judgment plays a crucial epistemic role, and its focus on the particular and the contingent — instead of the general and the necessary — is a very definite step beyond the classical model of rationality's foundationalism. Brown argues persuasively that we cannot understand human knowledge fully without recognizing the role that judgment plays at key epistemic junctures. Judgments must be made by individuals who are in command of an appropriate body of information that is relevant to the judgment in question. Brown therefore develops the idea of rational judgment and intersubjective criticism as epistemic skills that should be performed by experts.[25] Brown's notion of the role of judgment in rational decision making is exciting because in the end it frees us from the idea that only infallibility or perfectibility counts in epistemic matters. When at any point in time we make a decision for something in the light of the best reasons available to us, there need be no incompatibility between ac-

23. Nicholas Rescher, *Rationality* (Oxford: Clarendon Press, 1988); *A System of Pragmatic Idealism,* vol. 1 (Princeton: Princeton University Press, 1992).

24. Brown, 137; see also A. A. van Niekerk, "To Follow a Rule or to Rule What Should Follow? Rationality and Judgment in the Human Sciences," in Johann Mouton and Dian Joubert, eds., *Knowledge and Method in the Human Sciences* (Pretoria: HSRC Publishers, 1990), 180.

25. Brown, 137.

cepting a set of fallible claims for a substantial period of time and being prepared to reconsider them when we have good reasons for doing so. On this view the development of cognitive skills is closely analogous to the development of physical skills, and the conscious, explicit rule following that has long been taken as the paradigm of intelligent mental life indeed captures only a small portion of our cognitive resources.[26]

Earlier we saw that perhaps the most central idea in our preanalytic concept of rationality is that we normally have good reasons for our rational beliefs. And precisely because our rational beliefs are based on good reasons, we also regard them as more rational than nonrational or irrational beliefs. Next to rational beliefs, however, we also need to identify rational persons, that is, persons who can exercise good sense and good judgment in difficult and complex circumstances. We expect a rational person to be open to new ideas, and — as Harold Brown puts it — to function well in the context of discovery.[27] Brown therefore wants to retrieve neglected features of the classical concept as a possible basis for an alternative model of rationality. He does this in three steps:

1. In the first place the notion of a rational agent is taken as fundamental, and notions like "rational belief" are seen as derivative in the sense that a rational belief will be one that is arrived at by a rational agent. Moreover, the classical notion of rationality stresses the idea that a belief's rationality is connected with the way we arrive at that belief, that is, by way of a body of appropriate evidence, which then makes it a rational belief. This aspect of the classical model of rationality is now included by Brown in his own model, but it is developed very differently. In the classical model the central emphasis is placed on the logical relations between the evidence and the belief, while the role of the agent is minimized. In the new, alternative model the agent is taken to be basic, and the way that an agent deals with evidence in arriving at a belief will be determinative of the rationality of that belief for him or her.[28]

2. The ability to make judgments in those situations in which we

26. Brown, 177.
27. Brown, 183.
28. Brown, 185.

lack sufficient rules to determine our decisions is seen as a characteristic feature of a rational agent. As in Rescher's model, the evaluative dimension and the accompanying notion of judgment here become central to this model of rationality. It furthermore also entails that our ability to act as rational agents is limited by our expertise.[29] This does not mean that only experts can be rational, but it does mean that in cases where I may lack expertise, there may be only one rational decision open to me: to seek expert advice.

3. The third step required for Brown's alternative model is the introduction of a social element: rational decision making is a socially mediated rather than a rule-governed process.[30] For a belief based on judgment to be a rational one, it must be submitted to the community of those who share the relevant expertise. This demand, that rational beliefs be subject to evaluation and criticism, is in conformity with our normal understanding of rationality. Brown now correctly argues that this idea can be developed without its foundationalist implications, precisely by taking rationality to be a social phenomenon. Judgment therefore becomes necessary exactly when no general rules are available, and rationality thus always requires other people. And not just any people, but people with the skills needed to exercise judgment on a particular issue within a specific context.

Brown here differs significantly from Thomas Kuhn and his consensus model of rationality. For Kuhn the social aspect replaces positivist rules as the basis for scientific research and decision making, rational decisions are those made by the scientific community, and in normal science these become embodied in communally approved and transmitted practices.[31] Kuhn thus holds to the position that when the majority of a relevant scientific community reaches agreement, we have a rational decision. Brown, however, differs from Kuhn precisely at this point: agreement of the majority does not automatically make a belief rational. Brown's model requires only that individuals submit their judgments for evaluation by

29. See Brown, 185.
30. Brown, 187; see also van Niekerk, 184.
31. See Brown, 191.

their peers, and that they take this evaluation seriously. This is also much closer to real-life situations where, as academics and even as Christian theologians, we often hardly agree at all. Brown's model thus does not require that each member of the community agrees with the majority, since agreement with the majority view is neither necessary nor sufficient for rationality.[32] Scientific practice clearly demonstrates that rational disagreement is a pervasive feature of science. Brown's model therefore allows for and accepts the fact that human judgment is always fallible and that our best chance of eliminating error is by exposing our judgments and decisions to the critical scrutiny of other people.

In a postfoundationalist notion of rationality, therefore, the predicate "rational" characterizes an individual's decisions. It does not — in the first place at least — characterize beliefs, propositions, or communities. Even if a community of experts is necessary for an individual to arrive at a rational belief, it still is the individual's belief that is rational, and not the community.[33] Brown's alternative model of rationality makes the human agent who exercises judgment central to rational procedures, and it is the fallibility of this judgment that leads to the requirement of critical evaluation. And because of the way judgment is exercised here, our interpreted and traditioned experience enters the process that leads to rational judgment, even if we cannot always capture the experience in propositions.

At this point, however, we are faced with an important question: How does Brown's alternative model of rationality get him beyond the social relativism of nonfoundationalism? If rationality involves nothing more than judgment and critical evaluation by the members of an appropriate community, then we may find rational belief and decision making in communities that may even be characterized as irrational. For Brown, theologians are a case in point: "Various groups of theologians who belong to different religions may all be engaged in a fully rational endeavor, and the same may hold for, say, Azande witch doctors."[34] Brown is fully aware of the fact that this possibility follows from his model of rationality, and therefore argues along the following lines: (1) to claim that a belief is rational is not the same as to claim that a belief is true; (2) while rational acceptance of a claim indeed depends on the assessing of evidence, some

32. Brown, 192.
33. See Brown, 193.
34. Brown, 194.

forms of evidence provide a stronger warrant for belief than other forms of evidence. In his own words: "Thus while questions of denominational theology may be capable of a rational solution, it does not follow that we have no basis at all for choosing between, say, a scientific and a theological world-view at those points at which the two views conflict."[35] Although on this view theological rationality still seems to come a distant second to scientific rationality, Brown's argument for a richer notion of rationality does show that rationality in the classical sense is not at all enough when it comes to the cognitive assessment of knowledge-claims. A postfoundationalist notion of rationality therefore does not return us to the relativist position according to which every group or language game is automatically rational in terms of its own internal rules. This model indeed involves tighter constraints, and therefore moves beyond just agreed-upon rules to submitting results for critical evaluation by experts in the field. On this view not rationality, but rational beliefs are always situated contextually. The thesis that what is rational to believe or do is relative to a particular situation should therefore not be confused with the thesis that rationality itself is relative.

The relation between rationality and context invariably raises the question of the relation between rationality and truth. It does seem that the notion of truth is so deeply embedded in our thinking about cognitive matters that we can barely get along without it.[36] On the classical notion of rationality there is a close tie between rationality and truth, and for this reason false propositions could never be rationally accepted. Contemporary antifoundationalist and postmodern thought, on the other hand, emphasizes that people from different societies can accept radically different sets of claims as true, and that it is impossible to determine which of these claims are really true. Both Kuhn and Laudan have also shown that human beings have managed to function very successfully on the basis of beliefs that they later reject as false.[37] It is, however, extremely difficult to dispel the notion of truth completely.[38]

---

35. Brown, 195.
36. See Brown, 198.
37. T. S. Kuhn, *The Structure of Scientific Revolutions* (Chicago: University of Chicago Press, 1970); L. Laudan, *Progress and its Problems: Towards a Theory of Scientific Growth* (London: Routledge and Kegan Paul, 1977).
38. See Brown, 197.

Whatever we say or claim about truth or true premises does us little good unless we have reasons for believing that they are indeed true. This, according to Brown, is where rationality enters the picture, since rationality is concerned with assessing reasons for believing one claim or another.[39] This of course makes the great attraction of the classical model and the search for foundations so understandable. The epistemic failure of foundationalism, however, has left us without any strong truth-claims; the only reasons we now have for hanging on to our cognitive claims are that we judge them as the best ones available to us.

Brown's point is that the notions of truth and rationality are distinct in the sense that achieving one of them in no way entails that the other has also been achieved.[40] There is, however, a weaker but vital tie between rationality and truth: we proceed rationally in attempting to "discover" truth, and we take those conclusions that are rationally acceptable, in terms of our own judgments, as our best estimates of the truth. Brown thus argues persuasively that the search for truth is a long-term process and that we need coherent procedures to carry out this pursuit for optimal intelligibility, which for Brown is the ultimate function of rationality.[41] Brown's argument for a weak tie between truth and rationality indeed turns out to be very persuasive for any attempt to arrive at a plausible postfoundationalist notion of progress in science. Even if we are committed to the view that later theories are better theories, it does not have to imply a closer-to-the-truth position. In his argument against such a theory of verisimilitude, Nicholas Rescher too warns against the temptation to think of improvement in warrant (having better reasons) in terms of improvement in approximation (moving closer to the truth).[42] In fact, since we now accept that science often progresses through revolutions and radical shifts, there is no way that we can still think of science as developing by way of convergence or accumulation.

What is achieved in scientific inquiry is therefore not an approximation of truth but an estimation of it: scientists form, as best as they can, a reasoned judgment of where the truth of the matter lies. In this

39. Brown, 201.
40. Brown, 202.
41. Brown, 202.
42. Rescher, 48.

way we too do not manage to get nearer to "the truth," but we do present our best estimates of what we believe the truth within a specific context might be. On the level of scientific theorizing, our present world picture thus represents a better estimate than our past attempts only in the sense that it has accommodated, comparatively speaking, a wider range of data. This fallibilism is also strengthened by Rescher's consistent and helpful distinction between a *better estimate* (one that has fewer deficits and may be based on fuller information) and a *closer estimate* (one that claims to be closer to the "real truth"): in scientific theorizing we must settle for a qualitative "better" because there is obviously just no way of monitoring the issue of a measurable "closer."[43] The fact that scientific knowledge also moves through radical changes and discontinuities thus invalidates any talk of successive approximation. Our accepted truths — in both science and theology — should therefore be viewed as nothing more than the best estimates that we are able to make in the present moment. For pragmatic reasons, however, it might still make sense to talk about "pursuing truth."[44]

A postfoundationalist model of rationality thus preserves the idea of progress, and also the idea that rational beliefs are based on good evidence, although there now are different sources of evidence for different claims. This becomes even clearer when we take a closer look at the concept of objectivity. Obviously we first need to disassociate ourselves from the view that objectivity requires that we approach our subject without any preconceptions. What Brown argues for is that objectivity means at least this: that the evidence or good arguments supporting an objective belief must derive from a source that is independent of that belief.[45] The example that Brown uses to illustrate this is taken from physics: A physicist, working within a certain historical and social context, might claim that all matter is constructed of electrons, neutrons, and protons. What is normally claimed here is that these are actually features of the physical world. Of course these claims, like all intellectual or specifically scientific claims, are made from a certain historical and social context. Brown correctly argues, however, that such claims are nevertheless not solely claims about that context,

43. Rescher, 53.
44. See Rescher, 56.
45. Brown, 203.

culture, or language. One of the things that language permits us to do is precisely to make claims about items that exist apart from us and our language.[46]

So, once we have acknowledged the cultural, linguistic, or social context of a claim, the point remains that many claims make assertions about some state of affairs that is independent of those claims. For Brown these are paradigm examples of the pursuit of objectivity,[47] and as such come very close to what Nicholas Rescher has called the pursuit of truth. It is, of course, important to remember that not all matters can be studied objectively: some subjects may not have what Brown has called a "required ontological status."[48] We have, for example, no objective basis for evaluating ethical claims. This, however, does not by itself block the exercise of rationality in these fields, for there may be other considerations that can provide the basis for rational evaluation. One may, for example, have good reasons for believing that an ethical system ought to have a certain degree of coherence, and that this should provide grounds for rational analysis.

This argument for a weak notion of objectivity is certainly not meant to function as a basis or "foundation" for a strong metaphysical realism. What is argued for is that we normally study items or issues that are relatively independent of the claims we make about them. Even more crucial, however, is always to carefully distinguish between rationality and objectivity: rationality is indeed possible even in the absence of regular scientific objectivity. Still, objectivity remains epistemically important because it provides us with an especially powerful body of evidence to be used in the rational assessment of our claims.

III

This discussion of the role and characteristics of truth, progress, and objectivity in science brings us to the problem of the status of science, and to how much we can hope to achieve through scientific knowledge

46. Brown, 203.
47. Brown, 204.
48. Brown, 205.

vis-à-vis theological knowledge. The key question here is, How far can the scientific enterprise advance toward achieving complete intelligibility or a definite understanding of nature? The fallibilism implied in a postfoundationalist notion of scientific rationality necessarily leads to what has been called the imperfectibility of science.[49] A fallibilist epistemology necessarily implies that our knowledge — even our scientific knowledge — can never be complete or perfect. For Nicholas Rescher this *fait accompli* invites a description of the cognitive situation of the natural sciences in theological terms: expelled from the Garden of Eden, we are deprived of access to the God's-eye point of view. We yearn for absolutes but have to settle for plausibilities; we desire what is definitely correct but have to settle for conjectures and estimates.[50] The ideal of a perfected science, though unattainable, is nevertheless epistemically highly useful. Rescher calls this idea of a perfected science a *focus imaginarius,* whose pursuit canalizes and thereby structures our scientific inquiry: "As such it represents the ultimate telos of inquiry, the idealized destination of an incompletable journey, a grail of sorts that we can pursue but not possess."[51]

With this we have again returned to one of our most important initial questions: If scientific knowledge itself is so imperfect and essentially fallibilist, why does it provide such an important test case for our reflection on rationality and for our attempts to discern a meaningful epistemological consonance between science and theology? Having moved beyond the foundationalism of the classical model of rationality and its restrictive notions of verification and empirical evidence, we may now claim the following: rationality, specifically a postfoundationalist notion of rationality, still requires serious assessment of evidence, and we should therefore find our best examples of rationality in an area or field where the most reliable evidence is systematically gathered and deployed. Objective procedures still provide the richest and most reliable evidence, and one of the most important features of science is precisely its systematic pursuit of objective evidence.[52]

With this, I think, the selection of science, as possibly our best

49. See Rescher, 77f.
50. See Rescher, 85.
51. Rescher, 94.
52. See Brown, 207.

example of the cognitive dimension of rationality at work, is indeed still justified. This special position of science, which now, in a much more qualified sense, is still the paradigm of rationality at work, is ultimately also the reason why contemporary philosophy of science still forms the most important epistemological link in the current religion-and-science debate. What is not justified, however, is any claim that uncritically extends the nature of a strictly scientific rationality to the rationality of religious or theological reflection. Because of the nature and the comprehensive resources of human rationality, the rationality of science and the rationality of religious reflection do seem to overlap at some very crucial junctures. The theologian shares with the scientist the crucial role of being a rational agent, of making the best possible rational judgments within a specific context and for a specific community. The theologian also shares with the scientist the fallibilism implied by the contextuality of rational decision making, and thus the experiential and interpretative dimension of all our knowledge. Precisely the experiential and interpretative roots of religious knowing, however, are much more complex than the mostly empirical roots of scientific knowledge. Rationality in religion and in theological reflection is therefore indeed a broader and more complex affair than what emerges as a strictly scientific rationality.[53] The lingering imperialism of scientific rationality should, however, not close our eyes to the remarkable epistemic consonance between scientific and theological ways of thinking. At the same time some scientists and philosophers of science, as we saw before, are acknowledging the limitations of scientific rationality too,[54] and are thereby also opening the way to the acknowledgment of broader notions of rationality.

The close ties between science and rationality of course present the religion-and-science debate with yet another challenging question: Why is natural science possible at all? What happens so that the lawful order of nature becomes intelligible to us in the conceptual terms that we have devised? Philosophers such as Nicholas Rescher and scientists such as Paul Davies have persuasively argued that the problem of the intelligibility of nature is eminently expressed in the question of the cognitive

53. See G. Moore, "A Scene with Cranes: Engagement and Truth in Religion," *Philosophical Investigations* 17 (1994): 1-13.

54. See D'Espagnat; Davies, *Mind of God*.

accessibility of nature to mathematicizing intelligence.[55] In fact, the belief that the underlying order of the world can be expressed in mathematical form lies at the very heart of science, and as such is rarely questioned.[56]

Rescher's answer to this crucial question not only reveals a post-foundationalist move to an interactionist or relational model of rationality that enables him to transcend the rigid realism/antirealism debate, but also gets him to a position that is very close to what Jerome Stone has called transactional realism.[57] The answer to the question of the cognitive accessibility of nature to mathematizing intelligence can be found only in a somewhat complex, two-sided story in which both sides, intelligence and nature, must be expected to have a part.[58] This of course is consonant with the most basic thrust of a modest form of critical realism: it is precisely the interaction between our thoughts and the world that conditions our sense of order, beauty, regularity, symmetry, and elegance. Evolutionary pressure thus coordinates the mind with its environment. For Nicholas Rescher this leads to a crucial epistemological insight: the mathematical mechanisms we employ for understanding our world reflect the structure of our (interpreted) experience. In this sense it is no more a miracle that the human mind can understand the world through its intellectual resources than that the human eye can see it through its physiological resources.[59]

A model of rationality that in this interactionist way allows us to acknowledge that we devise our mathematics and science to fit nature through the mediation of experience reveals an unexpected epistemological consonance between theology and science: I have argued before that all religious (and certainly all theological) language reflects the structure of our interpreted experience.[60] In science our concepts and theories can therefore be seen as products of an interaction in which

55. Rescher, 99.

56. See Davies, *Mind of God,* 140.

57. Jerome Stone, *The Minimalist Vision of Transcendence: A Naturalist Philosophy of Religion* (New York: State University of New York Press, 1992).

58. Rescher, 99.

59. Rescher, 100.

60. J. W. van Huyssteen, "Critical Realism and God: Can There Be Faith after Foundationalism?" in A. van Niekerk, W. Esterhuyse, and J. Hattingh, eds., *Intellektueel in Konteks* (Pretoria: HSRC Publishers, 1993), 253-65.

both nature and ourselves play a formative role. To talk abstractly about the intelligibility of nature, about the regularities of nature and the laws that express them, indeed remains incomplete until we answer the more basic question: intelligible for whom? This frees us to realize that science, like all intellectual endeavors, is, in Rescher's words, *our* science. This implies that reality can never be described or presupposed in any absolute way, but is known through investigator-relative results that will differ with different modes of interactions between our world and us.[61]

What is at stake in this postfoundationalist model of rationality is therefore not so much the ontological question as to the existence or not of the "real world" (mind-independent or not, as in the realism/antirealism debate), but rather the status of our knowledge of reality as presupposed in the epistemic process. Rescher also convincingly argues, in his own way, that regardless of the extent to which reality may be "mind-independent," our knowledge of this reality represents information grounded only in an interpretation of our experience.[62] What is relevant and important for us therefore depends on how we go about experiencing our world and how we interact with what we see as reality. For the religion-and-science discussion, a plausible epistemological consonance emerges only on this level: as we have seen, the resources of rationality are indeed broader than just cognitivity. But epistemological fallibilism and rational accountability become viable options only when we realize that our exclusive cognitive access to reality is via the construction of a "world picture" or models in which our own intellectual resources play a crucially conditioning and shaping role.

Obviously the issue of objectivity (in the sense of mind-independence) is pivotal for any form of realism. Rescher argues that realism in this broad sense has two inseparable and indispensable constituents — the one existential and ontological, the other cognitive and epistemic.[63] The former maintains that there is indeed a real world, a realm of mind-independent, physical reality. The latter maintains that we can to some extent secure information about this mind-independent realm. What is crucial about Rescher's position on realism — vis-à-vis strong forms of scientific realism (that argue for realism on the basis of

61. Rescher, 111.
62. Rescher, 119.
63. Rescher, 256.

the success of science), and also some forms of critical realism that attempt to ground reference to reality in a correspondence view of truth — is that the ontological component of this philosophical realism is not a matter of discovery or the result of argument, but rather a functional or pragmatic presupposition for our inquiries.[64] Without this presupposed conception of reality it would be hard to maintain a fallibilist epistemology. The justification of this fundamental presupposition of objectivity is not evidential, and therefore not foundationalist: it is, rather, a functional one.

This account of the pragmatic basis of a weak form of realism thus results in a truly postfoundationalist move: on this view realism is a position to which we are constrained not by the push of evidence, but by the pull of purpose.[65] Realism in this mode does not represent a discovered fact or a justified position, but rather the methodological presupposition of our praxis of inquiry. Traditional realists see the basis for realism in the success and progress of science.[66] Because of its necessary fallibilism, however, a pragmatic form of critical realism implies an epistemic humility that pivots on the inevitable provisional character of all our knowledge and on the idea that — whether in theology or in science — there is more to reality than we can actually know. A postfoundationalist notion of rationality, shared as a rich and mutual source by both science and religion, thus reveals an epistemic consonance that transcends the important differences between scientific and religious reflection. In so doing it honors the provisional, contextual, and fallibilist nature of all human knowledge while at the same time enabling us to retain our ideals of truth, objectivity, rationality, and progress.

Thus, once again, a broader and richer notion of human rationality is revealed with its distinct cognitive, evaluative, and pragmatic dimensions. Whether in religion or in science, in each of these fields we have good reasons for hanging on to certain beliefs, good reasons for making certain judgments and moral choices, and good reasons for acting in certain ways. In theology, as a critical reflection on religion and religious

---

64. Rescher, 257.
65. See Rescher, 270.
66. See J. Leplin, *Scientific Realism* (Berkeley: University of California Press, 1984), 1-8.

experience, rationality implies the ability to give an account, to provide a rationale for the way one thinks, chooses, acts, and believes. Here too theory-acceptance has a distinct cognitive dimension. When we ask, however, what besides belief is involved in theory-acceptance, the pragmatic and evaluative dimensions of theory-acceptance are revealed.[67] Here the rationality of science and of theology very much overlap, in that both exhibit what intellectual practice would be like for those who adopt a specific model of thought. From this it does not follow that the natural sciences are "just like" theology at all. Furthermore, what sets science apart is not at all that decisions between scientific theories are made by some objective procedure, a procedure forever unavailable to theological decision making.[68]

In both theology and science, then, rationality pivots on the deployment of good reasons: an act of judgment in which we, through believing, doing, choosing the right thing for the right reasons, become rational persons. Being rational is therefore not just a matter of having some reasons for what one believes in and argues for, but having the strongest and best available reasons to support the rationality of one's beliefs within a concrete context. The hazy intersection between the diverse fields of theology and the other sciences is therefore not in the first place to be determined by exploring possible methodological parallels or degrees of consonance between theology and science. What should be explored first is a common and shared resource found in a richer notion of human rationality, even if these important epistemological overlaps sometimes are overwhelmed by equally important differences between religion and science. Thus too are revealed the unacceptable epistemological shortcuts that come into play when the rationality of science is contrasted with the so-called irrationality or nonrationality of religion, or even when the rationality of religion, and of theological reflection, is proclaimed to be radically different in every possible respect from scientific rationality. We now know that rationality cannot be narrowed down to a strictly scientific rationality, and scientific rationality cannot be reduced to natural scientific rationality.

I would therefore like to claim that the quest for intelligibility and

67. See van Fraassen, *The Scientific Image* (Oxford: Clarendon Press, 1989), 3ff.
68. See Placher, 50.

ultimate meaning in theology is also dependent on broader resources than just the purely cognitive, that is, on the evolving nature of the epistemic values that have shaped theological rationality in history. But what does this imply concretely for theology? At the very least it implies that the realist assumptions and faith commitments of experienced Christian faith are relevant epistemological issues to be dealt with seriously in the theology-and-science discussion. By doing this, theology could move away from the absolutism of foundationalism as well as from the relativism of nonfoundationalism. This can further be achieved by showing that because theology is an activity of a community of inquirers, there can be no way to prescribe a rationality for that activity without considering its actual practice, along with the way this reflective practice grows out of the way Christian believers live a daily life of faith.

The science-and-religion discussion in a very specific way therefore reveals how the explanatory role of interpreted experience in theology can be adequately appreciated only in terms of an experiential epistemology. This means not only that religious experience is better explained theologically, but that in explaining the role of experience, the philosophical theologian will have to move from the question of rationality to intelligibility, from intelligibility to the question of personal understanding, and from personal understanding to personal experience. This is something the scientist need never do when doing science. Dealing with personal commitment in this way may show that the rationality of religion, and therefore of theology, is often shaped by epistemic values different from those of science. The dependence of theology on this kind of experiential adequacy for determining and maintaining its explanatory adequacy need, however, never again mean that theology is less rational, or less contextual, for that matter, than science.

The nature of the ongoing discussion between theology and science should help us to realize that, in spite of a promising and emerging new field of study, the complex relationship between scientific and religious epistemology is more challenging than ever. This becomes all the more clear not only when we keep in mind the deconstruction and discovery of the limitations of the natural sciences in the post-Kuhnian era, but also when we focus carefully on the nature of the natural sciences. The sciences are eminently competent when it comes to theory construction and to experimental and pragmatic enterprises, but they are unqualified when it comes to finding answers to our deepest religious questions. In religion, and in theological reflection, we go beyond strictly scientific reflection when we focus on the role of story and ritual, and on the often noncognitive functions of religious models in evoking attitudes and encouraging personal transformation.[69]

The fundamental differences between religion and science should therefore be respected, as should the differences between different forms of explanations not only in the different sciences, but also between theology and the other sciences. However, in spite of important differences and sometimes radically different levels of explanation, theology and science do share common resources of rationality. A theology and a science that come to discover this mutual quest for intelligibility in spite of some very important differences will also be freed to discover that nothing that is part of, or the result of, natural scientific explanation need ever be logically incompatible with theological reflection. Science can tell us little or nothing about our experience of subjectivity, about the astonishing emergence of human consciousness and personhood, and about why we have an intelligible universe. God is the name that Christian believers give to the best available explanation of all that is.[70]

In focusing on the importance of the natural sciences, we should then have an openness for that which reaches beyond the world of the natural sciences, that is, to the world on which the social sciences, history, philosophy, and theology focus. In this wider context we could discover that theology and science not only share a mutually enriching quest for intelligibility, but also share the importance of tradition and of the explanatory role of interpreted experience. An honest analysis of the differences between the sciences and between theological and scientific explanations might then yield more intelligibility in the apologetic attempt to understand our postmodern world as truly God's own world.

69. See Barbour, 66ff.
70. See Peacocke, 134.

IV

In conclusion: in this paper I have tried to address three important questions:

1. Are there good reasons for still seeing the natural sciences as our best available example of rationality at work?
2. If so, does the rationality of religion and of religious reflection have anything in common with scientific rationality, and what would the significance of these epistemological overlaps be?
3. Even if there are large and impressive overlaps between these two modes of rationality, how would the rationality of science and the rationality of religious reflection be different?

My conclusion has been that science can still, but in a qualified sense, be seen as the best available example we have of human rationality at work. This does not mean that science or scientific rationality is in any way superior to other modes of rationality. On the contrary, a postfoundationalist notion of rationality reveals rich and complex resources for human rationality that are shared by scientific and religious reflection. With this it also has been possible to reject a nonfoundationalist "many rationalities" view, in which science and religion represent radically different and often incommensurable forms of life. Today, in our postmodern culture, not only religion, but also science turns out to be a surprisingly pluralist affair.[71] With the demise of positivism and the classical model of rationality, the claim that the problems of pluralism and relativism in science can be solved by appealing to universality and objectivity on the basis of scientific method is long gone. Different modes of rationality should therefore today be judged not in terms of a superior scientific rationality, but by the way in which they share in the common cognitive, evaluative, and pragmatic resources of human rationality.

It would therefore not be justified to extend the nature of a strictly scientific rationality to the rationality of religion or theological reflection. The theologian, in her or his reflection on the meaning of religious experience, does, however, share with the scientist the following:

71. See Placher, 14f.

1. the crucial role of being a rational agent, and of having to make the best possible judgments within a specific context, and within and for a specific community;
2. the epistemological fallibilism implied by contextual decision making;
3. the experiential and interpretative dimension of all our knowledge;
4. the fact, therefore, that neither science nor theology can ever have demonstrably certain foundations.

The methods of science, as our best example of cognitive rationality at work, are therefore unique: but not unique in the sense of providing a uniquely rational or uniquely objective way of discovering truth. Science is unique only because of its history of success in coping with the problems of empirical reality.

Beyond the fact that religion and science share the rich resources of human rationality, it always remains important to take note of the equally important differences between scientific and theological rationality. William Stoeger has recently and successfully argued that we should move away from simplistic contrasts between religion and science, which often try to pinpoint the difference between the two in terms of their very different objects.[72] The difference between these two claimants to human rationality is not, for instance, based only on the difference between "empirical problems" and "religious mysteries." The difference between the two is a much more refined one, and is found rather in significant differences in *focus, experiential grounds,* and *heuristic structures.* Stoeger, therefore, is right: in the religion-and-science discussion, as in any interdisciplinary discussion, what is important is more than differences in object, language, and method. What is important is the often radical differences in epistemological focus and evidential grounds.[73]

A postfoundationalist notion of rationality should therefore be able to open our epistemological eyes to broader and more complex notions

---

72. W. R. Stoeger, "Contemporary Cosmology and its Implications for the Science-Religion Dialogue," in Robert J. Russell, William R. Stoeger, SJ, and George Koyne, SJ, eds., *Physics, Philosophy and Theology: A Common Quest for Understanding* (Rome: Vatican Observatory, 1988), 232f.

73. Stoeger, 233.

of rationality, where scientific rationality — even if still our best example of rationality at work — cannot and should not be taken as normative for religious faith. And although theology, as the reflection on this religious faith, shares with science the contextual, experiential, and interpretative dimension of all human knowledge, the experiential and interpretative roots of religious knowing are always much more complex than the experiential and interpretative roots of empirical, scientific knowledge. Religious beliefs can therefore not be too easily likened to empirical hypotheses, because they grow out of much more complex situations. Religion and religious faith (and theological reflection, in spite of important epistemological overlaps with scientific reflection) are therefore in many ways not like science at all: for the adherents of many religious traditions, faith involves not just a way of looking at the world, but also a personal trust in God. An ultimate faith commitment to God is, in this respect, more like trust in a friend or a spouse than like belief in a scientific theory.[74] On this very personal level religion and science indeed seem to be very different kinds of activities, each with their own rules in their own domains, but neither one necessarily less rational than the other.

74. See Placher, 141.

Chapter Thirteen

Is There a Postmodern Challenge in Theology and Science?

DESPITE THE CURRENT FLOOD OF PHILOSOPHICAL TEXTS ON POST-modernism, relatively few attempts have been made to measure the importance of postmodern ideas for the philosophy of science. Of course, Lyotard's influential *The Postmodern Condition* focused on science and knowledge and reads like a philosophy of science text most of the time.[1] Lyotard distinguished between narrative and scientific knowledge as two distinct species of discourse that can both fulfill legitimate functions.[2] He does, however, claim that narratives provide a certain kind of knowledge that cannot be had in any other way. This narrative knowledge can also function as a legitimation for scientific knowledge instead of the grand narratives that previously legitimated science in the modern world.[3] Without this kind of narrative legitimation science would just presuppose its own epistemic validity, and proceed on prejudice.[4]

Most of us would agree today that the typically modernist view of science found its apex in the positivistic view of science: here objective, true scientific knowledge is grounded in empirical facts that are unin-

1. J. F. Lyotard, *The Postmodern Condition: A Report on Knowledge* (Manchester: Manchester University Press, 1984); see also H. P. P. Lötter, "A Postmodern Philosophy of Science?" *South African Journal of Philosophy* 13, no. 3 (1994): 154.

2. Lyotard, 29f.

3. Lyotard, 18ff.

4. Lyotard, 29.

terpreted, indubitable, and fixed in meaning; theories are derived from these facts by induction or deduction and are accepted or rejected solely on their ability to survive objective experimentation; finally, science progresses by the gradual accumulation of facts.[5] *Postmodern science,*[6] however, finds its best expression in postpositivist, historicist, and even post-Kuhnian philosophy of science and has revealed the theory-ladenness of all data, the underdetermination of scientific theories by facts, and the shaping role of epistemic and nonepistemic value-judgments in the scientific process. Postmodern philosophy of science also reveals the hermeneutical dimension of science to us by acknowledging that science itself is a truly cultural and social phenomenon.[7] This results not only in the cross-disciplinary breakdown of traditional boundaries between scientific rationality and other forms of rational inquiry, but also in the inevitable movement from being objective spectators to being participants or agents in the very activities that were initially thought to be observed objectively. Stephen Toulmin puts it succinctly: *All postmodern science must start by reinserting humanity into nature, and then integrate our understanding of humanity and nature with practice in view.*[8] Epistemologically this is ultimately recognized as *the turn from foundationalism to holism,* but also as the move away from a modernist notion of individualism to the indispensable role of the community in postmodern thought. In Nancey Murphy's terms: it is the community of scientists that decides when to take anomalous facts seriously; it is the community — and not merely a tyrannical majority — that must decide when to make changes in the accepted web of beliefs.[9]

5. See Wentzel van Huyssteen, *Theology and the Justification of Faith: Constructing Theories in Systematic Theology* (Grand Rapids: Wm. B. Eerdmans, 1989), 3ff.; Stanton Jones, "A Constructive Relationship for Religion with Science and Profession of Psychology: Perhaps the Boldest Model Yet," *American Psychologist* 49, no. 3 (1994): 3.

6. According to Stephen Toulmin, the phrase "postmodern science" was coined by Frederick Ferré. Stephen Toulmin, *The Return to Cosmology: Postmodern Science and the Theology of Nature* (Berkeley: University of California Press, 1985), 210.

7. See Richard J. Bernstein, *Beyond Objectivism and Relativism* (Oxford: Basil Blackwell, 1983), 30ff.

8. Toulmin, 210, 237f., 257.

9. Nancey Murphy, *Theology in an Age of Scientific Reasoning* (Ithaca: Cornell University Press, 1989), 201, 205.

A Rejection of "Superior" Metanarratives

Theologians who are engaged in serious dialogue with the sciences will find the postmodernist rejection of grand, legitimizing metanarratives and the seemingly complete acceptance of pluralism a formidable challenge for both theology and science. A crucial and increasingly controversial theme throughout the development of twentieth-century philosophy of science has been precisely the justification for interpreting the history of science in terms of a modernist story of progress or rational development.[10] Postmodern philosophy of science now challenges this ubiquitous notion of progress by its combination of respect for the local context of inquiry with a resistance to any global interpretation of science that could constrain local inquiry. As such it refuses any overall pictures or grand narratives that would want to explain science as a unified endeavor with an underlying essence, and makes sense of everyday science by seeing it as a set of narrative enterprises.[11] At the same time, of course, it also raises serious political issues by sharply focusing on the autonomy and cultural authority of the sciences. The concern to uphold the political autonomy and cultural authority of successful scientific practice is part of the modernist legacy of logical positivism, which had always claimed the epistemic and cultural primacy of mathematical physics by asserting that mathematics exemplifies the very structure of rational thought, and that our sense experience can be the only basis for knowledge of the world.[12] Postmodern philosophy of science, on the other hand, realizes that science must be understood as a historically dynamic process in which there are conflicting and competing paradigm theories, research programs, and research traditions.[13] This important fact reveals that the reasons, arguments, and value-judgments employed by the community of scientists are fundamentally related to, or "grounded" in, social practices. The very criteria and norms that guide scientific activity thus become open and vulnerable to criticism, as does in fact the idea of philosophy of science

10. See Joseph Rouse, "The Politics of Postmodern Philosophy of Science," *Philosophy of Science* 58 (1991): 610.

11. See Lötter, "Postmodern Philosophy of Science," 160.

12. See van Huyssteen, 3-10; also Rouse, "Politics of Postmodern Philosophy of Science," 613.

13. See Bernstein, 171ff.

itself. Postmodern philosophy of science in this mode therefore rejects any attempts at legitimating science by means of grand narratives, and urges scientists to resolve philosophical issues pertinent to their work themselves, or at most in interdisciplinary dialogue with knowledgeable philosophers of science.

The emergence of postmodernism in the domains of science and philosophy of science may of course be said simply to reflect intellectual currents in the larger society, but even so it presents a sharp rejection of the uncritical confidence in much of modern science, and especially the smugness about objective knowledge and progress. Postmodernists indeed sharply critique the uncritical acceptance of foundationalism, the Enlightenment heritage, and the methodological suppositions of modern science.[14] Although it is extremely difficult to try to fit postmodern ideas into some coherent conceptual scheme, it is helpful to take note of an important distinction that has surfaced in at least some of the recent literature on postmodernism. When Calvin O. Schrag referred to "antireason postmodernists," it already seemed to imply that some postmodernists, at least, may not be so eager to jettison rationality and epistemology.[15] Zuzana Parusnikova similarly distinguishes deconstructive postmodernists from other postmodernists,[16] an idea that is very clearly developed by Pauline Marie Rosenau when she tentatively distinguishes two broad strands within the current postmodern debate: *affirmative* and *skeptical* postmodernism. Skeptical postmodernism is the dark side of postmodernism,[17] and offers a pessimistic, negative, gloomy assessment by arguing that the postmodern age, in its complete break with modernity, is an age of only fragmentation, disintegration, and meaninglessness, with a vagueness or even absence of moral parameters, a postmodernism of despair.[18] Affirmative postmodernists, on the

14. See P. M. Rosenau, *Postmodernism and Social Science* (Princeton: Princeton University Press, 1992), 9.

15. Calvin Schrag, "Rationality between Modernity and Postmodernity," in Stephen K. White, ed., *LifeWorld and Politics: Between Modernity and Postmodernity* (Notre Dame: University of Notre Dame Press, 1989), 86.

16. Zuzana Parusnikova, "Is a Postmodern Philosophy of Science Possible?" *Studies in History and Philosophy of Science* 23, no. 1 (1992): 36.

17. See also H. P. P. Lötter, "Postmodernism and Our Understanding of Science," in G. J. Rossouw, ed., *Life in a Postmodern Culture* (Pretoria: HSRC Press, 1995), 55.

18. See Rosenau, 15.

other hand, although they agree with skeptical postmodernists in their critique of modernity, have a more hopeful and optimistic view of the postmodern age. This kind of postmodernism is open to positive political action and the making of responsible normative choices, and seeks an intellectual practice that is nondogmatic, nonideological, and tentative.

The postmodern challenge is furthermore complicated by the fact that not all postmodernists agree on whether a postmodern philosophy of science is even possible at all. This obviously would have serious implications for the shaping of scientific rationality, and thus for any attempt to bring theological reflection into a meaningful interdisciplinary discussion with contemporary notions of scientific rationality. In a careful and intriguing analysis, Zuzana Parusnikova focuses on the difficult issue of trying to bring together an enigmatic phenomenon such as postmodernism with something as positive and concrete as science.[19] Parusnikova's question, "Is a postmodern philosophy of science possible?" is eventually answered with a tentative no,[20] and she reaches this negative conclusion by analyzing how a philosophy of science would look if developed along the lines of the two most important postmodern tendencies of our time. The first tendency is directly related to Lyotard's idea that our world is fragmented into a plurality of worlds constituted by local discourses that cannot be unified by any grand metanarrative. Parusnikova engagingly relates how scientists that she talked to would respond quite positively to a popularized version of Lyotardian postmodernism: scientists often turn out to appreciate the antiauthoritarian and antidogmatic component inherent in postmodernism, identifying it with a rejection of any methodological normativism, of any constraints imposed by the rules and goals of their research. Postmodernism in this interpretation allows for unconventional approaches in doing science and for greater flexibility in various organizational and administrative arrangements concerning scientific life.[21]

Parusnikova is right in claiming that these views reflect some highly relevant features of postmodernism, namely the focus on imagination

19. Parusnikova, 21-37.
20. Parusnikova, 36.
21. Parusnikova, 22.

and the rejection of any higher authority for the legitimation of the rules and goals of science. This antiauthoritarianism especially implies a rejection of any possibility of defending the universal validity of scientific discourse itself, and with that its alleged supremacy over other kinds of discourse. In a postmodern world, however, which has been fragmented into a collage of many isolated worlds that cannot be unified by any "grand" metanarrative, what is to become of science, philosophy, and any possible philosophy of science? From a postmodern attitude science and philosophy of science are just two specific discourses among many others. Furthermore, from a postmodern view "science" as such does not exist anymore: instead there now exists a plurality of sciences playing their own games and generating their own, local rules for what they do.[22] In this postmodern space where science displays its own diversity and plurality, there seems to be little room for the philosopher of science to initiate a metadiscourse for elucidating what is going on in science, or what the rationality of science should be about. In this postmodern pluralism of local discourses, postmodern philosophy of science can either attempt to develop as an ironical conversation about science or become superfluous because a philosophy of science that appears to be merely parasitic on science might in any case best be carried out by the experts, namely the scientists themselves.[23]

The second postmodern tendency that Parusnikova considers as relevant for science is the deconstructionist one, the poststructuralist idea of meaning as fundamentally elusive, slippery, and ungraspable, normally associated with Derrida and other French theorists such as Barthes, Lacan, Kristeva, Deleuze, and Foucault.[24] The Lyotardian version of postmodernism tried to remove the problem of meaning from a universal to a local dimension. In a deconstructive postmodernism, however, it is already fundamentally impossible to make meaning present, regardless of the scope within which meaning is situated and analyzed. Deconstructive postmodernism thus turns out to be even more damaging to philosophy of science, since it could lead only to a literary deconstruction of scientific texts in which any authority of meaning would be destabilized.[25]

22. Parusnikova, 23.
23. Parusnikova, 37.
24. Parusnikova, 31f.
25. Parusnikova, 37.

Parusnikova thus presents us with a rather bleak vision for a postmodernism reflection on scientific rationality: in both its Lyotardian and its deconstructionist versions, postmodern philosophy of science would therefore dissolve into other activities performed by academics better equipped than philosophers.[26] Philosophers would here no longer provide any unique philosophical insight relevant to science.

Postmodernism and Science

A more positive appreciation for the possibility of a postmodern philosophy of science is found in the recent work of Joseph Rouse.[27] Rouse classifies most twentieth-century philosophers of science as being truly modernist and as such concerned mainly with some form of broad or global legitimation of science.[28] Because a truly postmodernist philosophy of science would — for Rouse at least — have to break away completely from all modernist notions, even Kuhnian and post-Kuhnian philosophy of science are still seen here as exemplifying the "persistent narratives of modernity."[29] In developing his position, Rouse takes up some of the most important themes of Lyotardian postmodernism. Crucial for this philosophy of science, is, of course, the complete rejection of any grand narrative legitimation of the history of science as a history of rationality, of progress, or of the search for truth. Rouse also warns, however, against the debunking of science in some of the more extreme reactions against modernist science, and then claims that the legitimation of scientific practices and beliefs always has to be partial, within specific contexts, and for specific purposes.[30] The idea that there is a "natural world" for natural science to be about, entirely distinct from the ways human beings as knowers and agents interact with it,

26. See Lötter, "Postmodern Philosophy of Science," 154.

27. Joseph Rouse, *Knowledge and Power: Toward a Political Philosophy of Science* (Ithaca: Cornell University Press, 1987); "The Narrative Reconstruction of Science," *Inquiry* 33, no. 2 (1990); "Politics of Postmodern Philosophy of Science."

28. Joseph Rouse, "Philosophy of Science and the Persistent Narratives of Modernity," *Studies in History and the Philosophy of Science* 22, no. 1 (1991): 141f.

29. Rouse, "Persistent Narratives," 161.

30. Rouse, "Persistent Narratives," 161.

must similarly be abandoned. On this view scientists are recognized as situated and participatory agents with inescapably partial positions, and instead of thinking of the sciences as in some sense being "representations" of the world, we should look at the actions they involve, and the way they transform the situation for further action.[31]

This nonfoundationalist move beyond any appeal to grand metanarratives should help philosophy of science to finally move beyond "modernity." That does not mean, however, that it gets us beyond the telling of stories, in which science still plays an important role. There is indeed no possibility of occupying a meta-standpoint from which to interpret science: all our interpretations of science imply a move within the contested terrain within which scientists themselves operate, a terrain in which science names both the outcome and the shape of the contested terrain. Rouse thus argues for a narrative reconstruction of science by taking up another Lyotardian idea, namely the importance of narratives in everyday life.[32] In an important article, "The Narrative Reconstruction of Science," Rouse develops this further by arguing for the epistemic significance of narrative and by explaining why narrative is important in natural scientific knowledge.[33] To fully grasp this, we must understand narrative here not as a literary form in which knowledge is written, but as the temporal organization of the understanding of practical activity. Scientific research is a social practice through which researchers structure the narrative context in which past work is interpreted and significant possibilities for future work are projected.

Rouse's understanding of science is therefore thoroughly postmodern: this narrative reconstruction of science as action does not need the modernist global legitimation, since scientists do not need philosophical explications of the epistemic and ontological standing of scientific research. The reason for this is found in the fact that scientists have a developing sense of what counts as an adequate explanation, of when a claim is well confirmed, even if interpretations of these concepts are local rather than general.[34] In this narrative reconstruction of science Rouse thus shows that any attempt to impose a grand narrative scheme

31. Rouse, "Persistent Narratives," 162.
32. See Lötter, "Postmodern Philosophy of Science," 157.
33. Rouse, "Narrative Reconstruction."
34. Rouse, "Narrative Reconstruction," 193.

on science should be rejected, since even in science we all live within various ongoing stories. Rouse strengthens his position on a postmodern philosophy of science by also endorsing what Arthur Fine has called the "natural ontological attitude."[35] This proposal by Fine is another example of a development of Lyotardian postmodernism, although Fine does not present his views as being explicitly postmodern.[36] In this postrealist proposal Fine too wants to develop a philosophy of science without any grand metanarratives, and he does this by arguing for what he calls a natural ontological attitude as a "commonsense epistemology."[37] What a natural ontological attitude would imply for philosophy of science is a move beyond all realist and instrumentalist attempts to make sense of science in a global or totalizing way. This does not mean that science has no meaning or aim, but rather that such questions can be asked only locally, that is, what meaning or goals a specific investigation or research program may have.

In Fine's — and Rouse's — model for a philosophy of science, "truth" will therefore function only in a pragmatic way, and in a local scientific context where scientists themselves negotiate their meaning for use in their specific context. This pragmatic trust in the local activity of science thus rejects the need for any "added" unified philosophical interpretation of science (the problem, for Fine, with both realist and antirealist interpretations of science). The "naturalness" of the natural ontological attitude is precisely the fact that we would do better to take scientific claims *on their own terms*, with no felt need for further interpretations, no further additives — a naturalness which Rouse, following Fine, has wittily, and possibly aptly, called "California naturalism," which implies a "what you see is what you get" attitude.[38] Underlying Fine's California naturalism is the claim that science can do for itself what the various philosophical additives were supposed to do for it, namely, situate science within an interpretative context. So, Fine's natural ontological attitude is part of a generally trusting attitude toward local contexts of practice, and what the natural ontological attitude is asking us

---

35. Arthur Fine, "The Natural Ontological Attitude," in J. Leplin, ed., *Scientific Realism* (Berkeley: University of California Press, 1984).

36. See Lötter, "Postmodern Philosophy of Science," 156.

37. Fine, 98.

38. Rouse, "Politics of Postmodern Philosophy of Science," 611.

to trust are scientific *traditions,* where these are understood not as a consensus of authority, but rather as a field of concerns within which both consensus and dissent acquire a local intelligibility.[39]

At this point it may be useful to evaluate some of the outlines of Rouse's postmodern philosophy of science in order to eventually bring it into the broader discussion of the shaping of rationality in theology and science. Rouse certainly manages to move beyond Parusnikova's negative assessment of the possibility for a postmodern philosophy of science. His use of the idea of narratives for providing a deeper understanding of science is clearly a success: it provides us with insight into the way scientists judge the significance of any new scientific work while reevaluating previous work. It also deepens our understanding of the fierce competition among scientists for getting their results accepted.[40] Rouse's endorsement of Fine's philosophy of science also helps him to describe science as having no overall aim, no typical or exclusive rationality, and no general theory of truth. Scientists are furthermore urged to answer their own conceptual questions, while philosophers are cautioned to resist interpreting science through their own philosophical categories or theories.

Rouse's assumption about postmodernism itself does, however, shine through all his work and eventually creates problems for scientific rationality as such. He assumes, most importantly, a complete break between modernity and postmodernity, and ends up with a too rigid definition of postmodernity as something that indeed has to overcome and help us move beyond modernity.[41] Lötter correctly finds that at this stage of the debate, with so much controversy on the characteristics of postmodernism, Rouse would do better to recognize various kinds of both modern and postmodern characteristics, see postmodernism as a critical reflection on the nature, potential, and shortcomings of modernity, and therefore place different philosophies of science on a continuum somewhere between being completely modern and, alternatively, completely postmodern.[42] To this I would add that without this kind of corrective critical suggestion even an affir-

---

39. Rouse, "Politics of Postmodern Philosophy of Science," 614.
40. See Lötter, "Postmodernism and Understanding of Science," 63.
41. Rouse, "Persistent Narratives."
42. Lötter, "Postmodernism and Understanding of Science," 64.

mative postmodern philosophy of science would have a hard time taking the typical cross-disciplinary character of postmodernism seriously, because the narrative reconstruction of science could easily slide into the incommensurability of Wittgensteinian language games and a relativism of local disciplinary rationalities. The dominance of a culturally superior natural scientific rationality may thus be averted, but at the cost of losing forever any interdisciplinary reflection that could reveal the values that shape the rationality of different interacting modes of human knowledge.

Postmodernism and Theology

Along with the typical traits of a postmodern philosophy of science, postmodernism's general embracing of pluralism, and the resulting rejection of grand metanarratives that universally legitimize the cultural dominance of scientific thought, now indeed seems to have serious implications for the interdisciplinary location of theology, and thus also for the theology-and-science discussion. The fundamental question, Is postmodern religious dialogue possible today?[43] now translates into an even more complex question: Is any meaningful dialogue between postmodern philosophy of science and postmodern theology possible, or does the pluralism and localization of postmodern discourse throw theologians, philosophers, and scientists who share some common quest for human understanding into near-complete epistemological incommensurability? Disturbingly enough, some postmodern theologians seem to accept just this in their enthusiastic embracing of a postmodernism of reaction[44] that calls for a "postliberal" return to orthodox or neo-orthodox epistemic values and confessional traditions. This should again alert us to the fact that postmodernism is a complex phenomenon, and that no position in either theology or philosophy of science — just because it claims to be postmodern — should be accepted uncritically.

43. See Gary L. Comstock, "Is Postmodern Religious Dialogue Possible?" *Faith and Philosophy* 6, no. 2 (1989): 189ff.

44. See Peter C. Hodgson, *God in History: Shapes of Freedom* (Nashville: Abingdon Press, 1989), 29.

Postmodern thought challenges theologians to account for the "fact" of Christianity[45] and to rediscover the explanatory function of religious experience in postfoundationalist theology. In this sense the postmodern theological project can actually be seen as an attempt to reaffirm and re-vision faith in God without abandoning the powers of reason.[46] Obviously, this will imply a careful re-visioning of what "the powers of reason" and rational reflection might mean today. Also, the postmodern challenge to the theology-and-science dialogue invites a serious countercritique: if postmodernism's anti-metanarrative stance should be uncritically equated with a bias towards the broader epistemological problem of the shaping of rationality in religious reflection, a few epistemological eyebrows would have to be raised. Even a postmodern attitude or position is capable of masking a repressive and intolerant neopositivist epistemology.

For Christian theology the ultimate postmodern challenge to its rationality and its credibility as a belief system can be stated as follows: Do we still have good enough reasons to stay convinced that the Christian message does indeed provide the most adequate interpretation and explanation of one's experience of God, and of our world as understood by contemporary science? Put differently: Does it still make sense within a postmodern context to be committed to the fact that the universe, as we have come to know it through science, ultimately makes sense only in the light of Sinai and Calvary?[47] One of the most crucial challenges for theology and science today can therefore be stated as follows: Can we successfully deal with the problem of the shaping of rationality, and thereby also identify the epistemic and nonepistemic values that shape religious and scientific reflection within a postmodern context? With this in mind, a statement like the following gains special epistemological significance: Many Christians today, whether "postmoderns" or not, have trouble both with the biblical injunctions and with the rules supplied by modern theology.[48] We are indeed uncomfortable with the idea, whether it is loosely derived from the Bible or more strictly taken from

45. See P. G. R. De Villiers, "The End of Hermeneutics? On New Testament Studies and Postmodernism," *Neotestamentica* 25, no. 1 (1991): 155.

46. See David Harvey, *The Condition of Postmodernity: An Enquiry into the Origins of Cultural Change* (Oxford: Basil Blackwell, 1989), 41.

47. Peter L. Berger, *The Heretical Imperative* (New York: Anchor Books, 1979), 165.

48. See Comstock, 190.

reason, that the same universal principles undergird every particular conversation. This skepticism, I think, is well-founded since too many of our conversations have in the past been decided in advance by our patriarchal, sexist, classist, or racist metanarratives. For "pre-postmodernists" it apparently seems less complicated to strive for truth, to distinguish between right and wrong interpretations of the biblical text and true and false propositions, and to maintain some form of objective moral truth. In a postmodern world, however, we worry about efforts to plan and build one world, one conversation for humankind, one story of humanity.[49] For the dialogue between theology and the sciences this has serious implications: *If our trusted metanarratives cannot be trusted anymore to provide the basis for interdisciplinary conversation, how can they ever provide a basis for the dialogue between theology and the sciences?*

But should we even be asking these questions? To ask this is to ask whether our postmodern skepticism will allow us to continue trusting in the ability of language to somehow "hook up" with the world. It is also to ask whether postmodern religion can still provide us with a certainty of faith that will "weigh us down," or whether we are doomed to "the unbearable lightness of being postmodern."[50] I am convinced that, for the theology-and-science dialogue to have a purpose and to be carried out meaningfully, we seriously need to try to find answers to these questions. A first step in the right direction will be to rule out one of the most important and influential misconceptions about postmodern thought, that is, the assumption that it is radically opposed to modern thought. Rather, it is important to view it as an ongoing and relentless critical return to the questions raised by modernity. From this more affirmative and constructive perspective, postmodern thought is undoubtedly part of the modern, and not only modern thought coming to its end. Seen in this way, the modern and the postmodern are also unthinkable apart from one another, because the postmodern shows itself best in the to-and-fro movement between the modern and the postmodern,[51] that is, in the relentless interrogation of our foundation-

---

49. See Comstock, 191.

50. Gary J. Percesepe, "The Unbearable Lightness of Being Postmodern," *Christian Scholar's Review* 20 (1991): 118ff.

51. See Calvin O. Schrag, *The Resources of Rationality: A Response to the Postmodern Challenge* (Bloomington: Indiana University Press, 1992), 7.

alist assumptions. Following Lyotard it therefore becomes possible to acknowledge the postmodern as part of the modern.[52] Or in Calvin O. Schrag's words: "It is thus that the discourse of modernity remains within the web of the discourse of postmodernity."[53] It therefore is possible to appropriate postmodern thought in a constructive way by interpreting it as a reflection on the potential, nature, shortcomings, and darker sides of modernity.[54]

The shift to postmodern thought will immediately mean that the central theological terms like religious experience, revelation, tradition, and divine action can no longer be discussed within the generalized terminology of a metanarrative that ignores the socio-historical location of the theologian as an interpreter of experience and an appropriator of tradition. Within the context of a postmodern, holist epistemology it will eventually also prove to be epistemologically impossible for theologians to continue seeing religious experience and tradition (which includes theological interpretations of revelation) as two opposing poles that somehow have to be related to one another.[55] Trying to think through the troubled relationship between theology and science, as well as the complex sets of epistemic and nonepistemic values that shape the rationality of each, we may begin to realize that rediscovering the rational resources shared by theology and science may provide us with an important interdisciplinary link in the face of the challenge of postmodernism. We may then also begin to realize that postmodern religion need not be so heavy and serious, and that we can indeed readjust our thinking to resist the excessive "weight" of any form of foundationalism, religious conflict, and intellectual terrorism. This kind of epistemological fallibilism may finally get us to the point where we can celebrate the truth behind truth, the God behind God, and the religious behind religion.[56]

52. Lyotard, 79.

53. Schrag, *Resources of Rationality*, 17.

54. See Lötter, "Postmodern Philosophy of Science," 159.

55. See William Dean, *History Making History: The New Historicism in American Religious Thought* (New York: SUNY, 1988).

56. See Percesepe, 134.

Index

280